LATINO MIGRANTS IN THE JEWISH STATE

LATINO MIGRANTS

IN THE JEWISH STATE

UNDOCUMENTED LIVES IN ISRAEL

BARAK KALIR

Indiana University Press

Bloomington and Indianapolis

This book is a publication of

Indiana University Press
601 North Morton Street
Bloomington, Indiana 47404-3797 USA

www.iupress.indiana.edu

Telephone orders 800-842-6796
Fax orders 812-855-7931
Orders by e-mail iuporder@indiana.edu

♾ The paper used in this publication meets
the minimum requirements of the American
National Standard for Information Sciences—
Permanence of Paper for Printed Library
Materials, ANSI Z39.48-1992.

Manufactured in the United States of America

Library of Congress Cataloging-in-Publication
Data
Kalir, Barak.
Latino migrants in the Jewish state : undocumented
lives in Israel / Barak Kalir.
p. cm.
Includes bibliographical references and index.
ISBN 978-0-253-35507-2 (cloth : alk. paper)
ISBN 978-0-253-22221-3 (pbk. : alk. paper)
1. Immigrants—Israel. 2. Migrant workers—Israel.
3. Latin Americans—Israel—Ethnic identity.
4. Latin Americans—Israel—Government relations.
5. Latin Americans—Cultural assimilation—Israel.
6. Deportation—Israel—Government policy. 7.
Assimilation (Sociology)—Israel. 8. Israel—
Emigration and immigration.
9. Israel—Ethnic relations. 10. Israel—Politics and
government. I. Title.
JV8749.I8K35 2010
323.1168′05694—dc22
2009053822

1 2 3 4 5 15 14 13 12 11 10

For Margo, Tim, and Daan

Living with the other, with the foreigner, confronts us with the possibility or not of *being an other*. It is not simply—humanistically—a matter of our being able to accept the other, but of *being in his place*, and this means to imagine and make oneself other for oneself. [. . .] Being alienated from myself, as painful as that may be, provides me with that exquisite distance within which perverse pleasure begins, as well as the possibility of my imagining and thinking, the impetus of my culture.

—JULIA KRISTEVA, *Strangers to Ourselves*

CONTENTS

ACKNOWLEDGMENTS

More than anyone else who has helped me along the way in writing this book, I would like to thank all of my informants for letting me into their lives. This was, for them, not just a matter of finding the time. Sharing their experiences and insights meant taking real risks—for themselves and, in many cases, for their families. I deeply appreciate the trust they had in me, as well as their hospitality and friendship. From the bottom of my heart I say *gracias* to: Naxania, Ernesto, Sergio, Blanca, Vicente, Lupe, Rosa, Cristina, Fernanda, Rodrigo, Negro, Jason, Héctor, Ángel, Pepe, Mireya, Washington, Alejandro, Raúl, Sara, Ramón, Antonio, Gabriela, Félix, Hernán, Andrea, Livia, Enrique, Fernando, Javier, Carlos, Luis, Esther, and Martha.

Doing fieldwork in Israel on the lives of non-Jewish undocumented migrants has been at times a confronting experience for me as an Israeli. I would like to say *toda* to some of my closest friends in Israel, for their support, advice, and pleasant distractions: Ori, Sharona, Boaz, Ophir, Nitzan, Lior, Ofer, and Inon. Also in Israel, I would like to thank Sigal Rozen, Emi Saar, and all the people working and volunteering in the Hotline for Migrant Workers. A special thanks goes to the ActiveVision group for allowing me to include in the book several photos from the "Identity Document" project for which they had the children of undocumented migrants taking photos of life in Israel from their viewpoint.

Turning to academia, more than anyone else at the University of Amsterdam—my academic home in recent years—it is Gerd Baumann to whom I am indebted. Gerd read and commented on most parts of this book. I benefited greatly from his unreserved dedication to my project, sharpness of mind, and great humor. For the numerous ways in which he has inspired me to become a better scholar, I am eternally grateful.

Alex Strating has been my partner for the occasional round of beers after a day of work. His talent for making my difficulties and struggles during the writing phase seem simple and solvable, as well as his stimulation and friendship, made a great difference. Salut, Amigo!

I'd like to thank many more of my colleagues at the University of Amsterdam who directly commented on my work and, more generally, who created an enjoyable and stimulating environment: Irfan Ahmad, Miriyam Aouragh, Christian Bröer, Kamenko Bulic, Alex Fernandez-Jilberto, Enrique Gomezllata, Rob Hagendijk, Peter van Rooden, Peter van der Veer, and Willem van Schendel. The regular lunch-at-the-street-corner with my colleague and friend Bowen Paulle became a solid occasion to try out my more theoretical ideas on a critical mind. Shifra Kisch was my best-bet-in-town for sharing painful critique over my country of origin, and making sure I mean what I say.

A few scholars whom I met in conferences and workshops provided me with especially valuable insights (although I doubt they recall the occasion). These include Saskia Sassen, Karin Fog Olwig, Akhil Gupta, Bram de Swaan, Philippe Bourgois, and Moshe Shokeid. I will never forget the night out in Amsterdam with the late Eduardo Archetti, whose enthusiasm about my work reassured me.

On the home front, my parents, Menachem and Ziva, cultivated in me, each in their own special way and both with much patience and love, the desire to explore, and the courage to think independently and critically about what I discover. Their unconditional support provided a solid basis for my adventures. My Oma, Margot Bayer, at the age of 102 is still an inspiration for me. Having survived the Holocaust, and after being forced to trade in her bohemian life in Berlin for a Spartan existence on an Israeli kibbutz, she taught me with few words and many deeds about the significance of keeping one's Self while continuously changing.

My final and dearest gratitude goes to my family. Margo Hintzen, my wife and soul mate, is a contributor to this book in more ways than I can express. Apart from wholeheartedly supporting me, she also, while busy with her own job, read and improved every chapter I wrote. In the period that I produced this book she produced our sons, Tim and Daan. They provided me with many sleepless nights, some computer failures, and the greatest happiness of all. This book is dedicated to my family.

Latino Migrants in the Jewish State

Chapter One

Introduction

An ambiguity, then, is not satisfying in itself,
nor is it . . . a thing to be attempted; it must in
each case arise from, and be justified by, the
peculiar requirements of the situation.

—*William Empson*

In 2004, after a decade in Israel, Daniel was arrested when the Immigration Police raided the aluminum workshop in which he had worked for more than seven years. Eldad, the Israeli owner of the small workshop in south Tel Aviv, pleaded with the police officers to release Daniel, telling them what a loyal and well-behaved worker Daniel was. As the determined police officers handcuffed Daniel and pushed him into their patrol car, Eldad resentfully lashed at them: "What harm would it do to anyone if you let him stay? He's a better person than most Israelis I know." Two days later Daniel was deported from Israel. Three weeks later Daniel's wife, Esther, and their two boys, Yuval and Nadav, left Israel to join him in Ecuador. On the way to the airport, with their lives in Israel packed into four giant suitcases, Esther fixed her eyes on a distant point outside the window of the taxi, trying to hide from her children an unstoppable stream of tears. Yuval, who turned seven just before his father was deported, held his mother's hand and gently but desperately asked, what he already knew by then to be a hopeless question: "But Mami, why do we have to leave? Why can't Papi come back to us here?"

Daniel and Esther were non-Jewish undocumented migrants in Israel. As such, they were part of a larger group of an estimated twelve thousand undocumented migrants who reached Israel from different countries in Latin America and settled there in the mid 1990s. The couple's children, Yuval and Nadav,[1] were both born in

Israel. They were now on their way to Ecuador, a country that they did not know but had heard much about.

   This ethnographic study describes and analyzes the immigration and lives of Latinos in Israel.[2] Based on extensive fieldwork among Latinos in Israel, as well as among returnees, deportees, and potential migrants in Ecuador, the book traces the full circle of this migration flow, beginning with how the idea of emigrating to Israel first emerged in the minds of many non-Jewish people across Latin America. What life strategies did Latinos develop in order to mitigate their precarious undocumented status in Israel? What were their relations with other Latinos and with Israeli employers, ordinary citizens, and officials? This ethnography focuses on the lived realities of Latinos as they found accommodation and jobs, made friends, developed a rich recreational scene, formed families, raised children, attempted political mobilization, and developed a deep sense of belonging to Israeli society.

   In its capacity as a Jewish state, Israel represents an extreme case in which the dominant Jewish national group has managed formally to imprint its own ethnoreligious identity onto the very logic of the state. Israel adheres to the principle of *ius sanguinis* (literally, law of the blood), qualifying the incorporation of immigrants by an ethnic belonging to what Zionism has redefined as the Jewish nation. With a declared purpose to serve as a home for all Jews, and driven by a Zionist ideology that called for the "Ingathering of the Diaspora" (*Kibutz Galuyot*), Israel actively encouraged and financially facilitated the immigration of Jews worldwide. At the same time, Israel utterly rejected non-Jewish immigration, not least in order to prevent the return of thousands of Palestinians who fled the country when the Independence War broke out in 1948. The notion of national belonging in Israel is being challenged regularly by Palestinian citizens of Israel and the wider Arab-Israeli conflict in the Middle East.

   In this book I offer a different take by considering the strategies and impact of Latinos, and non-Jewish undocumented migrants in general, on the construction of national belonging in Israel. Why, for the first time in the country's history, did approximately one hundred thousand undocumented migrants enter Israel in the mid-1990s and settle down? How did the Israeli public, and Israeli civil society actors in particular, react to the settlement of undocumented non-Jewish migrants? What eventually led Israel in 2003 to deport the majority of undocumented migrants, and then in 2005 to legalize the status of a few hundreds of them?

   The influx of Latino migrants from the other side of the globe into a country that is fraught with territorial and national conflicts offers a vivid illustration of the uneven process of globalization. This migratory trajectory becomes even more interesting when we consider that there are no historic connections—colonial, economic, or cultural—between Israel and Latin American countries of the kind that could readily stimulate or assist the development of migration flows. While Latinos in Israel developed social and religious networks that span various parts of Latin America, their condition in Israel represented a case of what I call "constrained transnationalism." Given the cost of traveling back and forth between Israel and Latin America, and even more the fact that it was very difficult for exiting undocumented migrants to re-enter Israel, most Latinos never went back to visit their countries of origin. The experiences of undocumented migrants under this variant of "constrained transnationalism" have not received much attention in the literature on transnational migrants.

Officially, the state of Israel categorized non-Jewish undocumented migrants as deportable trespassers. In 1996, when the Israeli government first decided to address the phenomenon, it launched a campaign to deport undocumented migrants, whose presence in Israel was called a "social ticking time bomb" by some politicians. While deportation was repeatedly championed as the sole solution for confronting the "problem," the earnestness of Israel's deportation policy varied in the years thereafter. In fact, it can be argued that in practice, until the year 2002, Israel largely turned a blind eye to the presence of non-Jewish undocumented migrants. Yet in September 2002, the government moved vigorously to implement a decision to deport tens of thousands of undocumented migrants. A mighty and heavily funded Immigration Police was established, and its agents managed to arrest and deport thousands of undocumented migrants as well as to create a ripple effect of intimidation that induced tens of thousands more undocumented migrants to exit the country. As part of this move toward a much more aggressive line of action against undocumented migrants, Eli Yishai, Israel's interior minister, reiterated his view on the "problem":

> I want everybody who is not Jewish out of this country. Non-Jewish migrants come here and build churches! They should stay in their own countries. We must negate all migrants who are not Jewish according to the *Halacha* [the Jewish law]. . . . There are families in Israel with Christmas trees, something we never knew here before. They cause acculturation and deterioration of the values of the Jewish state. We want to build here in the Jewish state synagogues and not churches. (*Maariv* 25.11.2002)

In his capacity as a democratically elected MP and an appointed interior minister, Eli Yishai's statement clearly represented the broader uncompromising inclination of the state of Israel to preserve its Jewish character and prevent the settlement of non-Jewish migrants in it.

A few days after the interior minister's combative statement was aired, I was walking in one of Tel Aviv's busiest streets with Antonio, a non-Jewish undocumented immigrant from Ecuador. At one point and for no apparent reason, Antonio spontaneously told me:

> It is amazing but there is no racism in Israel. Nobody treats you badly here because of who you are. I know that Eli Yishai and some other bad

politicians want us out, but they do not represent the people here. Israelis are warm and open. It is a blessed country and I am proud to be here. If I could, I would stay here forever. We feel at home here. We work and we live here, and we get along with everyone. My children go to Israeli schools, and if I were only allowed to, I would join the Israeli army tomorrow and defend this land with my life.

Antonio's statement was pronounced not so much in a conversational mode that necessitated my response, but rather as a counter-statement directed straight at the Israeli interior minister in a virtual debate taking place in front of an Israeli-Jewish public. Antonio, like many other Latinos, had been living in Israel for more than eight years, ample time to experience and understand life as an undocumented Latino migrant. Antonio's statement represented the larger ability of many Latinos to establish their economic and family life in Israel, and to develop a strong sense of belonging to the country and its people.

De Facto Integration into Society versus Official Rejection by the State

Latinos were part of a larger flow of undocumented migrants who reached Israel from four continents and more than ninety countries. Although estimates of undocumented migrants' numbers in Israel have been disputed and politicized, most statistics indicate that in the late 1990s around one hundred thousand undocumented migrants resided in Israel (Ministry of Labor 2000). Like most undocumented migrants, Latinos resided initially in the poor neighborhoods of south Tel Aviv, Israel's economic capital and most secular city. They worked mostly as domestic servants and office cleaners in the affluent northern parts of the city and its middle-class suburbs. Latinos earned what they perceived to be highly attractive salaries of around US$1,000 per month. Many Latino families were reunited in Israel after the initial immigration of one of the spouses, while numerous new households were formed when single Latino migrants met and got married in Israel.

Although their immigration was often emotionally taxing, and the process of settlement always involved hardship, most Latinos adapted well to their new lives. Despite their undocumented status as migrants, Latinos were able to enjoy much improved livelihood, rich family and social life, and a vibrant recreational scene. It was not uncommon to hear them casting positive judgments on their lives in Israel and their interactions with Israelis. It was especially interesting to hear the perceived cultural similarities that many Latinos claimed to share with Israelis. This perceived cultural closeness was neatly captured by Guirremo, a 29-year-old undocumented migrant from Colombia, who once at a social gathering cheerfully proclaimed that "Israelis are the Latinos of the Middle East."

For their part, Israelis often expressed positive images of Latinos, singling them out for being "more like us." Israelis tended to associate Latinos with favorable contributions to Israeli culture, referring to Latinos' passion for football, music, food, and "lively and open lifestyle." Israelis have experienced multiple exposures to Latino culture in recent years, from the popularity of Latino music on the radio to the widespread broadcasting of Latino soap operas (*telenovelas*) on television, and from massive support among Israelis for South American football to the attractiveness of various countries in Latin America as a travel destination for tens of thousands of young Israelis after their release from obligatory military service.

When a social demographer asked seventy Israeli residents in south Tel Aviv about their views of the four major groups of "foreigners"—Africans, Romanians, Filipinos, and Latinos—he discovered that while on average only 20 percent of Israelis held a positive image of "foreigners," 66 percent held a favorable image with respect to Latinos. In accounting for this marked positive Israeli perception of Latinos, it was argued that "[t]he presence of Latinos is less striking in public spaces [and] they more openly engage in their way of life with Israeli society" (Schnell 1999: 50–51).

I am not trying to draw here an overly harmonious picture of the lived realities of Latinos in Israel. Let there be no doubt about the exploitation experienced by some Latinos from greedy and callous Israeli employers, or the ruthless treatment that hapless Latinos, like many other undocumented migrants, received when they were pulled out of their beds by the Israeli Immigration Police who raided their apartments in the middle of the night. On the contrary, it is precisely because such incidents were not uncommon for undocumented migrants in Israel that I find it particularly interesting to focus on and explicate the positive interactions between Latinos and Israeli citizens.

One important factor that distinguished Latinos from other undocumented migrants in Israel was the fact that Latinos' phenotypical resemblance to Israelis did not cause them to stick out in an Israeli crowd. The hair color, complexion, and general appearance of most Latinos allowed them to "pass as" Israelis, to use Goffman's term (1963). As Willen (2007: 15) asserts,

> Although there exists considerable cultural and ethnic heterogeneity within Israeli society, most citizens—whether Jewish or Palestinian Arab—are, and phenotypically appear to be, of either European or Middle Eastern decent. Until the 1990s, this relative homogeneity meant that many Israelis had never seen a person from Africa, Southeast Asia, or other distant world regions in the flesh.

It was through their possession of a bodily capital that was effective in the Israeli setting that many Latinos, rather than black sub-Saharan African or Asian undocumented migrants, became sensitive to the possibilities of a specific path toward assimilation.

In order to foster their phenotypical invisibility in Israel, many Latinos conformed their haircut, ornaments, and dress code to what they perceived to be the prevailing

Israeli style. Realizing the benefits of semblance to their chances of survival in Israel, some Latinos invested in a more comprehensive cultural assimilation, paying increasing attention to cultural aspects of living in Israel. For example, many Latinos did their utmost to learn the Hebrew language; some of them regularly practiced it at work with their Israeli employers, while others invested their time and money in taking Hebrew courses. In public spaces, Latinos often chose to speak Hebrew, and at home they sometimes blended Hebrew words into their mother tongue. Some Latinos also practiced Israeli manners and typical gestures at home to embody, and achieve mastery in, what they perceived to be a distinctive Israeli cultural code of behavior and a display of bodily conduct. It became common among some Latinos to use the phrase "This is not how the Jews do it" in order to correct each other's behavior whenever it markedly deviated, according to their judgment, from the customary Israeli way. Latinos corrected one another, for example, about the "proper" Israeli way of making and serving coffee, carrying and offering cigarettes, or cracking and eating salted sunflower seeds. Although this corrective remark was always made in a joking manner, it was indicative of the importance that Latinos attributed to developing such mastery of Israeli cultural practices.

The settlement of Latinos, and other undocumented migrants, was facilitated by several dynamics in Israel. Firstly, consecutive Israeli governments unofficially adopted a blind-eye policy with respect to undocumented migrants. This was the case not least because these new sub-proletarians provided the Israeli economy with cheap, flexible, and disenfranchised labor. Moreover, policymakers who feared a permanent settlement of non-Jewish temporary migrant workers assumed that deportable undocumented migrants were less likely than ever to be able to claim formal recognition from the state. Secondly, an "implementation deficit" was evident in the execution of Israel's policies toward undocumented migrants. A number of officials and professionals who worked in semi-state- and state-sponsored institutions neither shared nor conformed to the objectives that were set forward by the official national policy. This was most obvious in the approaches and actions of physicians and head teachers, who had direct contact with undocumented migrants and whose professional ethics, based on universalistic and humanist values, prevailed over the measures that were stipulated in official policies. Thirdly, the selective democratic characteristics of Israel permitted civil society actors to contest and partly subvert repressive state policies against non-Jewish migrants. A number of Israeli nongovernmental organizations (NGOs), as well as some journalists and academics, supported undocumented migrants and offered them practical and legal assistance.

Finally, widespread interactions between ordinary Israeli citizens and undocumented migrants undermined attempts by the state to prevent the de facto integration of undocumented migrants. For Israeli citizens, these interactions were based on a mixture of everything from economic motivations to friendly openness to plain indifference. Most obviously, in admittedly self-serving defiance of the law, hundreds of thousands of Israelis employed undocumented migrants. Employers included not only private businesses but also many ordinary citizens who sought domestic workers. Yet such economic-based interactions with undocumented migrants did not remain confined to the economic sphere. Many Israelis unreservedly interacted with undocumented migrants in recreational sites, residential neighborhoods, and public spaces. In some cases, these interactions led to the development of friendly ties and matrimonial relations between migrants and Israelis.

Notwithstanding the success of Latinos' efforts to settle down and assimilate culturally, their undocumented status was still often obvious in more substantial interactions with Israelis. Most clearly, Israeli employers who hired Latinos knew about their status from the outset, as this was often the very reason why they employed them. In these settings, Latinos showed much sensitivity to the powerful role that Jewish identity played in the manufacturing of national belonging in Israel. Accordingly, Latinos regularly voiced their supportive views of Israel, and their political orientation to Israeli matters tended toward the right-wing, "patriotic" end. Probably thinking it earned them credibility with Jewish Israelis, many Latinos publicly expressed their will to serve in the Israeli army, and adopted militant views regarding Palestinians. By achieving increased cultural assimilation, Latinos improved their position in the host society. They experienced more positive interactions with Israeli employers as well as ordinary members of the dominant Jewish Israeli group.

Yet cultural similarities and enhanced assimilation to Israeli society was not a silver bullet for Latinos' predicaments as undocumented migrants. The evident settlement of non-Jewish migrants since the late 1990s rendered it unsustainable for governments in Israel to continue practicing a blind-eye policy. In the early 2000s, the Israeli government came under increasing political fire for allowing the situation to "get out of hand." Ruling coalitions were blamed for not safeguarding the sovereignty and the Jewish character of the state. Consequently the powerful Immigration Police was established, and according to its spokesperson, by the end of 2005 after three year of operations, the number of undocumented migrants that were displaced from Israel stood at 150,752 (*Haaretz* 13.01.2006). Among the deportees were many Latinos whose apartments in south Tel Aviv were raided, or who were ambushed by the police in working places, on football pitches, in salsa clubs, and outside the footsteps of evangelical churches.

The Israeli massive deportation campaign was challenged by several NGOs, human rights activists, journalists, and left-wing politicians. These counter-hegemonic actors mounted consistent pressure on the state of Israel to consider alternative lines of action in dealing with the situation, including the legalization of status for non-Jewish migrants according to agreed criteria. Activists filed numerous appeals to the Israeli High Court of Justice against the government's immigration policies, and they drummed up public opinion for the cause of undocumented migrants, in part by comparing the prosecution of Jews throughout history to the treatment of non-Jewish migrants in the Jewish state.

Legal appeals by NGOs often put on the spot Israel's increased accountability to an emerging global regime of human rights that has been anchored in international conventions to which Israel is a signatory. Interestingly, Israel has ignored UN resolutions and violated international conventions whenever they seemed to interfere with what Israel perceived to be its national responsibility. Israel's immigration regime is closely tied to its aspiration to maintain a Jewish state, and it is therefore definitively considered an internal affair by the state. Despite much pressure from the international community, Israel refused for decades to allow the return of the Palestinian inhabitants of Israel who fled the country in 1948. Nevertheless, or possibly because of its already damaged international reputation in this respect, Israel found it particularly difficult to ignore the rights of undocumented non-Palestinian migrants.

In 2005, this concerted pressure partly succeeded, and the Israeli government passed a resolution that granted permanent legal status leading to full citizenship to undocumented migrants' children over the age of ten who were born in Israel and "became part of Israeli society and its culture [and] whose deportation from Israel would constitute a cultural expulsion to a state with which they have no cultural affinity" (Government Resolution 26.06.2005). Although it was declared by the government to be "a unique amendment not to be repeated in the future," it was described by one of Israel's most popular daily newspapers as nothing less than a "revolution" that marked a break with the exclusionary ethno-religious logic that historically underlined Israel's immigration policies (*Maariv* 26.06.2005).

Ariel Sharon, Israel's prime minister at that time and leader of the right-wing Likud party, explained somewhat emotionally his support of the government resolution: "I was deeply touched by a television program about the children of undocumented migrants who grew up here and became members in the *Tzophim*. I reached a conclusion that there are many more similar cases and that we must make an effort so that they can remain in Israel" (*Maariv* 26.06.2005). The *Tzophim* is a Zionist youth movement (affiliated with the International Boy and Girl Scouts) that is based on the values of mutual help and equality. Not without irony, the *Tzophim* movement urges its members to settle across Israel, in line with the Zionist ideal of populating the country (*Yeshuv Ha'aretz*).

Although the government resolution for legalization of undocumented migrants' status essentially applied to children, it also stipulated the granting of permanent residence to children's parents and siblings who were not born in Israel. It was for this reason that the most crucial element in the legalization of status for undocumented migrants was their cultural assimilation and de facto integration into Israeli society. The enhanced assimilation of Latinos, later recognized by the state, increased their chances to do well in the labor market, prolong their settlement, form families, become embedded in Israeli social networks, endure deportation campaigns, and deal with the related mental stress.

Unpacking Citizenship: National Belonging versus State Membership

Substantively, this book is about undocumented belonging, undocumented in two senses. In the first sense, the book is about the belonging of undocumented Latino migrants in Israel. The second sense pertains to the fact that Latinos' belonging to Israeli society, like that of many other undocumented migrants, was left for many long years undocumented in Israeli immigration policies and the wider public debate. It seemed that a recurring reference to the fact that Israel is a Jewish state explained away the need to deal with the developing situation in an integrative and humane way. This book does not pretend to "give voice" to undocumented migrants in Israel; there have been many concerned Israeli journalists, filmmakers, and other social activists who did much more for this cause than I can aspire to do here.[3] My major concern is with the powerful workings of the notion of belonging in the context of the nation-state.

The notion of belonging is a powerful yet irredeemably ambiguous one, for individuals as well as nations, because it charges with emotions our ideas about identity, membership, and place. To understand the role that national belonging plays in modern states we need to remind ourselves that at the root of the contemporary debate on migrants' incorporation into host societies lies the historic link between national membership and corresponding entitlements of rights and duties. Formally, the concept of citizenship is supposed to guarantee individual equality to all members in the state. The logic that guided this liberal republicanism, first in France and later in most liberal nation-states around the world, was simple: if one belongs to the nation, then one is a member in the political organization of the nation, namely, the modern state. As a member in the state, as a citizen, one is entitled to all the rights and duties that flow from this status. Of course, with this logic of equality as a constituent of the modern state, the crucial question then became: who belongs to the nation?

The definition of citizenship, however, has never been a universal one; instead, each sovereign nation-state has used its authority to set its own criteria for membership. Every logic of inclusion entails, albeit less explicitly, a complementary logic of exclusion. Given that both such logics are based on discretion, they naturally lend themselves to contestation, mainly by those individuals and groups who are placed outside the boundaries of inclusion. A historic account of the institution of citizenship in different countries testifies to the concomitant emergence of contention everywhere, and the fact that the notion of citizenship has been in flux from the very beginning (e.g., Marx 1996, Wallerstein 2003).

One iconic answer to the question of who belongs was provided in 1882 by the French philosopher Ernest Renan. In his famous lecture "What is a Nation?" Renan articulated his understanding of the nation as "a soul, a spiritual principle" that is based on the legacy of the past, and more importantly, on the present solidarity among people who are bounded by their "clearly expressed desire to continue a common life." Yet at the end of the nineteenth century, to ensure this "common life," ruling elites across Europe engaged in what Benedict Anderson (1983) calls "official nationalism" that aimed to homogenize the nation in a top–bottom move toward the standardization of language, education, and value system. Notwithstanding the limitations of this homogenizing move to eradicate vast cultural differences among citizens, the idea that the nation was unified under a normative project was consolidated and cherished.

The twentieth-century assimilative "melting pot" model for integrating immigrants into host societies is the most obvious residual of this organic conception of the nation. Under this conception, belonging to the nation was widely considered a prerequisite for inclusion in the definition of citizenship (Soysal 1996). Nevertheless, since the 1950s, global restructuring in the postwar era has carried some significant implications for the ever-changing definition of citizenship in Western liberal states (Castles and Miller 1998, Freeman 1986). In Europe, thriving economies allowed for an expansion in citizens' social rights on the one hand, and favored the importation of *gastarbeiter* (guest workers) on the other. Although states moved to enhance closure in their definition of citizenship, the temporariness and restrictiveness that initially characterized the employment of guest workers gradually gave way to workers' long-term and even permanent settlement (Layton-Henry 1990, Teitelbaum and Weiner 1995, Sassen 1996, Shafir 1998).

Beginning in the late 1970s, many Western nation-states deserted the melting pot model and moved toward a multiculturalist model of integration, which championed a liberal-communitarian notion of citizenship (Kymlicka 1995). While multiculturalism has been variously institutionalized in different states, ideally it looks to ensure all members' equality of rights and participation in the political process, while recognizing and considering legitimate the maintenance of cultural and religious distinctiveness of migrant groups (but also indigenous ones) that differ from the dominant national group. Nation-states thus sought to create more room for the particularities of ethnicity and "culture" to exist within the supposedly universal governing system of the state.[4] As Hage (1998) argues in the Australian case, this move toward multiculturalism was to large extent dictated by events on the ground:

It happened because Australia's demographic and socio-cultural reality changed such that assimilation could no longer work. Despite the presence of an overwhelming policy of promoting assimilation, there were too many inevitable social and cultural processes happening outside the monocultural Australian mould that no assimilation program could prevent. (236)

Yet, the incorporation of migrant workers into Western states met significant resentment; while many voiced concerns for the sustainability of the welfare state, resentment has not been confined to economics (Cornelius, Martin, and Hollifield 1994, Miller 1995). Instead, it has largely been articulated in a cultural idiom. A confluence of "culture" and citizenship has been increasingly featured in political debates, and it appears that "as guest workers are increasingly incorporated into the membership schemes of European host polities, the debate over how well they 'adjust' intensifies, and their cultural otherness is accentuated" (Soysal 1994: 134).

On their part, migrant groups have often been claiming the right to "keep their culture." Employing "identity politics" as a platform for contesting the hegemonic definition of citizenship (Taylor 1994, Rosaldo and Flores 1993), some migrant groups demanded "cultural rights" as the fourth, missing pillar in the classic definition of citizenship, which includes social, civic, and political rights. "Cultural citizenship" was thus proclaimed in order to safeguard "the right to be different (in terms of race, ethnicity or native language) with respect to the norms of the dominant national community, without compromising one's right to belong" (Rosaldo 1984: 57).

Minority groups' insistence on cultural rights has proven to be a double-edged sword when the emphasis on and endorsement of cultural particularities has compounded the cultural resurgence among many members in the dominant national group. Some right-wing politicians then insisted on immutable cultural differences between "native" citizens and members in migrant communities. Such insistence was meant, not least, to promote exclusionary and often hidden racist ideologies (Balibar 1991, Soysal 1994, Stolcke 1995).

Criticism of multiculturalism has been mounted from the right as well as the left end of the political spectrum. Progressive critics often charged multiculturalism with covering up a lack of effort and/or will from the hegemonic majority group to take on the painstaking task of incorporation of Others (Goldberg 1994). "Splintered" multiculturalism, as Wieviorka (2001) has called it, simply provides recognition to groups' cultural identity without taking measures to combat related social inequalities. Certain forms of multiculturalism are actually being blamed for stimulating the production and reification of ethnic and religious groups (Turner 1993, Baumann 1998). As cultural differences provide state recognition and legitimate access to resources, groups become increasingly preoccupied with the maintenance of their reified boundaries, and they often hinder dynamic changes and interactions across groups.

Conservative critics have focused on the normative project that the very notion of a nation-state typifies, and the substantive rather than the instrumental meaning that the notion of citizenship carries. They thus have called for the preservation of national heritages through education, language, and customs. As it is perhaps most vividly expressed in debates over the process of naturalization, and in particular the issue of dual citizenship, conservatives have often stressed that national membership must tightly correspond to a sense of national belonging, that is, an emotional investment in, and commitment and loyalty to, the nation-state (Schuck 1998, Koslowski 2000, Gustafson 2005). Identification and conformity with the nation's (allegedly) distinctive norms and values is also expected (Jones-Correa 1998, Faist 2004).

Notwithstanding such critiques of multiculturalism as a political model, it appears that the very liberal-communitarian attempt to divorce "culture" from the definition of membership encounters considerable limits in practice. While states have formally moved to decouple the link between identity and rights, the cultural "ghost in the machine" has never been completely exorcised in the new logic. Actualizing many of the rights that are stipulated in the definition of citizenship requires the bureaucratic and interactional mediation of officials in state institutions. These mediators frequently employ informal exclusionary and discriminatory practices at their discretion, which is either intentionally or unconsciously tainted with a cultural bias. There is ample evidence from different nation-states to suggest that migrants who hold full citizenship often suffer institutional and social discrimination that prevents them, in practice, from actualizing what are in theory their equal rights (Schuck 1987, Soysal 1994, Ong 1995, 1996, Dorr and Faist 1997, Fuglerud 2004). Such modes of discrimination hamper the social, civic, and economic integration of migrants. In mid-1990s America, Ong (1996: 738) still found it useful to consider the existence of a "white-black continuum" along which recent Asian migrants "[w]ho seem obviously non-white" are placed by "discriminatory modes of perception, reception, and treatment."

Thus, rather than symbolically branding the end of migrants' incorporation process, the attainment of citizenship has actually often marked its de facto beginning (Kymlicka 2003). This is the case because, as many scholars have pointed out, the concept of citizenship should be understood not only as being an egalitarian juridical category but also as having intricate links to a national identity that is socially constructed, embodied, and performed (Gilroy 1987, Hall 1991, Bhabha 1994, Ong 1996, Spivak 1996). A focus on the importance of the embodiment of "culture" has been widely influenced by Bourdieu's (1984, 2001) elaboration of the ways in which symbolic capital reproduces the established social order and conceals relations of domination.

Ghassen Hage (1998) draws a subtle distinction between "official citizenship" and "practical nationality." While the former clearly refers to a state's formal recognition of membership, the term "practical nationality' is defined as

> [t]he sum of accumulated nationally sanctioned and valued social and cultural styles and dispositions (national culture) adopted by individuals and groups, as well as valued characteristics (national types and national character) within a national field: looks, accent, demeanour, taste, nationally valued social and cultural preferences and behaviour, etc. (53)

"Practical nationality" thus points toward the kind of cultural assimilation of migrants that promotes a daily socio-emotional acceptance by members of the dominant national community. Echoing Hage, Carruthers (2002) stresses that the implicit "either/or" logic of formal citizenship should be contrasted with the notion of "practical national belonging" that is characterized by a cumulative logic. The notion of practical national belonging is thus conceptualized as a form of symbolic capital that is recognized as legitimate and legitimating by the dominant national community. Accumulating and embodying this symbolic (national) capital matters because "[i]n the daily life of the nation there are nationals who, on the basis of their class or gender or ethnicity, for example, practically feel and are made to feel to be more or less nationals than others" (Hage 1998: 52).

The significance of acquiring practical national belonging as symbolic capital has been illustrated by Aihwa Ong's "flexible citizens" (1999). These affluent Hong Kong Chinese immigrants to the United States attempt to convert their economic capital into the symbolic and cultural capital that is necessary for maximizing the potential benefits that their transnational position in America bestows on them. Ong's description of one such young "flexible citizen" is illuminative:

> Like many teenage émigrés, she was actively taking lessons—piano, tennis, singing, and dancing—to be able to participate in the social activities of upper class life. But she surprised me by confessing that she and her Chinese American classmates . . . had also signed up for modeling classes. They were not really interested in becoming models, for that would lower their social value, but they were intent on learning how to dress, walk, and generally comport themselves in ways that would make them "more acceptable to the Americans." (Ong 1999: 88)

The accumulation of national belonging has meaning only within a specific field where the assimilation into a particular national "culture" is at stake. Ong's "flexible citizens" seek to approximate what they perceive to be an ideal American identity. In the Australian context, Hage conceptualizes the accumulation of national belonging as taking place within the field of "Whiteness," which is dominated by the image of a white Anglo-Saxon Australian. "Whiteness" includes all sorts of characteristics such as: speaking English with a distinctive Australian accent, being a Christian, and enjoying "distinctive" Australian recreational activities (barbequing, surfing, watching and/or playing Australian rugby, etc.). Although "Whiteness" also includes skin, eye, and hair color, it should be understood "not as a biological essence, but as an agglomeration of nationally valued physical and cultural styles" (Carruthers 2002: 430).

Realizing that the ability of citizens to actualize their equal rights, and feel themselves at "home," depends partly on their ability to embody and perform a dominant national "culture" moves us away from vague debates about the culturalization of citizenship, and closer to an understanding of the power relations and stakes involved in this cultural dynamic. Every field of national "culture" constitutes a social field of struggle that is being shaped in an ongoing process of interactions between contesting groups. Members of the dominant national group exercise most power in the construction and maintenance of a particular national "culture" that is likely to reflect and reproduce what they perceive to be their own salient characteristics. Members of minority groups can follow two basic strategies in accommodating their position in the field of national "culture." On the one hand, they can strive to approximate the dominant national identity in order to enjoy an enhanced sense of belonging to, and acceptance by, the dominant national group. On the other hand, members of minority groups can choose to challenge the construction of the hegemonic national "culture," by withering down its cultural essence or by reshaping it to resemble more what they perceive to be their own typical characteristics. These two strategies are not mutually exclusive. For example, Chicanos in the United States might do their utmost to speak English with no detectable accent, and at the same time insist that Spanish should become the second formal language in America.

Two major factors are central in an analysis of the strategies that migrants adopt in the field of national "culture." First, migrants' position within society, which can be accounted for by the different forms and amounts of capital that they possess (financial, cultural, social, linguistic, legal, etc.); and second, migrants' dispositions, or "socialized subjectivity" to use Bourdieu's term, that lead them to perceive certain strategies as suitable for advancing their interests in a particular field.

The modern nation-state, with its symbolism and formal authority, becomes a primary arena for coding, communicating, and at times enforcing the parameters for the construction of a particular national "culture." Ong (1996) reminds us that identity-making is a dialectically determined process involving both the state and its subjects. Criticizing Rosaldo's notion of "cultural citizenship," Ong claims that "[i]t gives the erroneous impression that cultural citizenship can be unilaterally constructed and that immigrant or minority groups can escape the cultural inscription of state power and other forms of regulation that define the different modalities of belonging" (1996: 738). Therefore, irrespective of their hope for legalization of status in the long term, Latinos in Israel not only chose but were also forced into the pursuit of cultural assimilation as a prime strategy for achieving a de facto socialization into the dominant Jewish Israeli group.

The Accumulation of National Belonging among Latinos

The accumulation of practical national belonging has been so far studied mainly as a process leading to, or standing in the way of, the full civic inclusion of documented migrants. Hage (1998) has developed the concept of practical nationality in order to criticize the perturbing deficiencies in Australia's alleged multicultural incorporation of "Third-World-looking" migrants with legal status. Other scholars have used the same analytical framework in order to elucidate the practices of transnational migrants or returnees in their relation with members in the dominant national group (see Ong 1999, Carruthers 2002). The case of undocumented migrants has been mostly ignored in an analysis that stresses the notion of national belonging. It is my contention that the scholarly treatment of undocumented migrants as a fundamentally different case is a prime example of "methodological nationalism," whereby social scientists uncritically accept and reproduce the categories and understandings of the state in their own analytical schemes. In my view, settled albeit undocumented migrants become, and should be seen by scholars as, part and parcel of the society in which they live.

Having said that, I do not somewhat naively ignore the somber fact that migrants' physical and social presence is markedly contravened by their formal negation as "illegals" (Coutin 1993, 2000). I also share with De Genova (2002: 427) an understanding that "the social space of 'illegality' is an erasure of personhood—a space of forced invisibility, exclusion, subjugation, and repression." However, in this book I choose to highlight undocumented migrants' creativity and agency in trying to escape such impositions. My main argument is that Latinos by and large managed to circumvent the Israeli state's attempts at their social and cultural Othering, and they thwarted the government's push for an hermetic categorization of Latinos, like all other undocumented migrants, as non-belonging-cum-deportable "illegal foreign workers."

By ethnographically describing the practices and experiences of Latinos in Israel, I demonstrate the relevance, applicability, and usefulness of a framework that considers the accumulation of practical national belonging among undocumented migrants. In fact, since undocumented migrants are condemned to an illegal status by states' immigration policies, they often strive more intensely than legal migrants (especially those who follow a communitarian tendency) to accumulate practical nationality. They accumulate national belonging *because* of their illegal status (to diminish their public "visibility") and *despite* their illegal status and attempts by the state to prevent them from doing so.

Reducing migrants like Daniel and Esther to categories such as "illegals," and seeing them merely as the pawns of macro-structural forces, reveals as much about the observer as it does about the observed. While such reduction has been widely criticized in the literature, it has mainly been done in a programmatic rather than an empiric way. An overview of the treatment of "illegality" by academics reveals that "[r]emarkably, little of this vast scholarship deploys ethnographic methods . . . to elicit the perspectives and experiences of undocumented migrants themselves" (De Genova 2002: 421). The challenge, in other words, is to get a lived sense of undocumented migrants' creativity and constraints by depicting and bringing into the analysis direct observations of everyday life.

Leo Chavez (1992) focused on the ability of some undocumented Mexican migrants who spent years in the United States to "accumulate links" in the host society. He concluded that their incorporation was "blocked because of their undocumented status and the larger society's view of them as 'illegal aliens'" (1992: 4). In a twist to Chavez's focus on the need of undocumented Mexican migrants to learn to live as "illegal aliens" in the United States, I illustrate how Latinos in Israel learned to live as native Jewish Israelis. While Chavez essentializes "society's view" of undocumented migrants, I demonstrate that this "view" is not only non-monolithic but also susceptible to manipulation and alteration by undocumented migrants' own actions.

Up to now, I have been discussing Latinos as if they formed one homogenous group. This makes sense within a comparative effort to distinguish their primary life strategy from that of other undocumented migrant groups in Israel, such as Africans and Asians. Yet bundling all Latinos into one group is clearly unavailing for the pursuit of a more nuanced analysis of the ways in which different Latinos were disposed to act differently in Israel. A distinction among migrants according to their countries of origin most readily suggests itself, not least because of its domination in migration studies. Yet even if I were to find differences in Israel between the behavior and attitudes of, for example, Ecuadorians and Colombians, or Chileans and Peruvians, I would still have to account for these differences analytically rather than attribute them simply to migrants' nationality. My participant-observation among Latinos revealed some discernable differences in their attitudes. However, these differences cut across migrants' nationality, pointing instead toward the decision-making processes and motivational structures that induced Latinos to reach Israel in the first place. I was sensitized to these distinctions as I tried to answer a more basic question regarding the decision of people in Latin America to emigrate to Israel.

From the migration stories that I collected in Israel, as well as from my fieldwork in Ecuador, I could discern three major groups of migrants. "Economic migrants" based their decision to go to Israel principally on cost-benefit calculations. After the migration of a few people, most economic migrants relied for the operationalization of their immigration on a family member or a close friend who had settled in Israel and was ready to facilitate the immigration of others. "Religious migrants" were driven by a pious fervor regarding the Holy Land. These migrants first conceived of the idea to emigrate to Israel in the evangelical churches that they attended in their countries of origin. Pastors in these evangelical churches encouraged congregants to consider emigration to Israel, and they often facilitated the immigration and initial settlement of these migrants as part of an organized tour to the holy sites of Israel. Some Latino pastors remained in Israel as undocumented migrants, and they established clandestine evangelical churches in south Tel Aviv as part of an emerging transnational religious network.

The third group can be described as "spontaneous migrants." They did not fit either of the former two groups, nor was their decision-making process and emigration to Israel compatible with existing migration theories. "Spontaneous migrants" based their decision on very little knowledge about Israel, and they decided to emigrate in a rather impulsive way, without first consulting their spouse or other family members. Moreover, while the emigration of most Latinos to Israel was facilitated by transnational social and religious networks, "spontaneous migrants" conducted their migration in an individual and isolated fashion with no solid ties to such networks. The case of "spontaneous migrants" led me to develop the concept of a "migratory disposition" (Kalir 2005) in order to account for people's life-long immersion in an emigration environment and the ways in which these people make sense of their position in it. The formation of a particular habitus among groups of people living in traditional sending areas can elucidate decisions to emigrate that otherwise appear spontaneous, isolated, and irrational. The notion of a "migratory disposition" more generally incorporates an understanding of migration as an affective decision, and it accounts for the emotions involved around the determination of certain people to leave.

Stressing that I distinguish migrants' decision-making processes rather than types of migrants, the data I collected nonetheless allowed me the shorthand of "economic," "religious," and "spontaneous" migrants. The shorthand of ideal-types offered itself especially in that migrants with different decision-making histories tended also to adopt different ways to accumulate, embody, and perform practical national belonging in Israel.

Economic migrants tended to focus on the workplace as the locus of assimilation. They sought to make friends with Israeli employers and co-workers, and learned Hebrew as well as Israeli customs from them. Economic migrants widely imitated what they perceived to be the secular Israeli lifestyle, which often meant a consumerist lifestyle that needed to be reconciled with their original goal to save as much money as possible. Religious migrants found their participation in evangelical churches to be a rich avenue for approximating Israeli expectations and attempting cultural assimilation. The general theological flexibility of evangelicalism, and in particular the allur-ing interpretations of Christian Zionism by Latino pastors in Israel, enabled and facilitated for Latinos the construction of both spiritual and practical inroads into Israeli society. Finally, spontaneous migrants often accumulated practical national belonging in the recreational scene. These migrants greatly appreciated the oppor-tunity to interact socially with Israelis in settings far removed from their workplaces, which tightly defined the hierarchy and quality of such interactions. In the emerging Israeli salsa dance scene, which contributed richly to Tel Aviv's nightlife at the late 1990s, or on football pitches across the city, Latinos could display other, non-labor-related, skills and desires that were recognized and appreciated by many Israelis. Interactions in the recreational scene often led to the integration of Latinos into Israeli social networks, and sometimes to the development of romantic relations.

Chances and Pitfalls: Studying Undocumented Migrants

My choice to focus on Latinos in Israel largely stemmed from the fact that while I was born and raised in Israel, I had lived and studied for more than three years of my adult life in Latin America. More specifically, I was driven by some practical method-ological considerations, such as my fluency in Spanish and my partial familiarity with the reality Latino migrants came from. Although not without difficulties, as I shall detail in this section, I eventually conducted a multi-sited ethnography in Israel, Ecuador, and Spain, from October 2001 to September 2005.[5]

Given that police efforts to arrest undocumented migrants included deploying undercover agents and using snitches from among migrant groups, Latinos, like most other undocumented migrants, were very suspicious. I realized from the outset that doing fieldwork among Latinos as an Israeli would be a delicate task. Trust became a key element in the lives of undocumented migrants, not only as a resource essential for mutual assistance and community building, but as a precondition for avoiding an abrupt deportation that so often translated into economic and social devastation for migrants and their families.

Latinos were extremely vigilant about sharing even basic information like their residential addresses, let alone the more "juicy" stuff an anthropologist wants to know (e.g., their informal practices, life strategies, emotional experiences, and transnational network building). Conducting semi-structured interviews, tape-recording formal and informal conversations, taking photos, and being able to participate in regular as well as special events were all dependent on my ability to generate trust and establish meaningful relationships with informants.

I considered joining an Israeli NGO that assisted undocumented migrants in Israel, but feared that it would significantly determine Latinos' view of me as a part of the Israeli establishment. I was well aware of my need to negotiate carefully my position as a researcher. I preferred an unmediated contact and thus valued what I considered to be my distance from the field, namely, the ability to stress my independent position as a researcher at a university in the Netherlands.[6] I therefore rented an apartment in an area where many Latino migrants lived, hoping to establish unmediated contact with some of them. I hung out in places that Latinos often visited, such as calling centers and street corners. But in all these sites I was markedly out of place, and the Latinos I approached were very suspicious of me. A chance to get someone to sit with me for an interview about his or her immigration to Israel seemed remote. I considered paying migrants for interviews but was afraid that it would lead to a mechanical mode of engagement and compromise my ability to form more sociable relationships with informants. I knew that such relationships were crucial in facilitating a meaningful participant observation that was essential for the kind of ethnographic work I was after.

I ended up trying another method; I called on Israeli employers to ask their Latino workers if they would be willing to meet me for an interview as part of an academic research project. For example, I called on some Israeli families with whom I had friendly relations, and thus knew that they were employing Latinos as domestic cleaners. Whenever migrants gave their consent I got their telephone number and called them to set up a meeting. In those meetings, I did my utmost to communicate the fact that I was neither a member of any Israeli institution nor a potential employer. I regularly explained the essence of my research project, and stressed that it was conducted for a Dutch university. I quickly learned to omit from my lexicon words such as "research" or "investigation" as they immediately alerted and deterred Latinos. I further told interviewees about the years I spent in Latin America, hoping to create openings for informal conversation and in addition to insinuate that my commitment was not to the Israeli side. Despite my best efforts, most Latinos remained puzzled and suspicious about the academic interest in their lives. I usually managed to interview them but was very dissatisfied, as their answers seemed to be of the most evasive kind. It seemed as if Latinos agreed to be interviewed only because they feared to disappoint their employer.

My appeals for cooperation and my self-presentation as a trustworthy anthropologist were not about to clear the thick cloud of suspicion created by the context of my field site. I became frustrated as I failed to develop any deep and steady engagement with migrants. Notwithstanding my irritation, I could identify with their reluctance to collaborate with me. I consoled myself by thinking that if I were in their place I would probably not have acted differently.

My biggest breakthrough came with a touch of luck. I received the telephone number of Antonio, a 28-year-old Ecuadorian migrant, from his Israeli employer. I called up Antonio, and he warily agreed to meet, indicating as our meeting place a shabby bar in south Tel Aviv. As we sat down Antonio nervously asked what it was that I wanted to know. In an attempt to break the tension, I first told him about my visits to Ecuador, and we found out that I had been to Loja, his hometown. As it seemed that Antonio was becoming less edgy, I then explained the motivation behind my research and empathetically asked Antonio about the reasons that drove him to leave Ecuador and come to Israel. We had been talking for an hour when, all of a sudden, two policemen came into the bar ordering everyone to present their identity cards. I could clearly see Antonio was petrified, and I was horrified by the tragedy of his inevitable arrest.

When the policemen approached our table I quickly waved my Israeli identity card while Antonio worryingly produced an outdated Ecuadorian certificate. Asked by the agitated police agents about his uncommon document and status in Israel, Antonio, in the Hebrew he had picked up, told them he had already been living and working in Israel for three years and that for safety reasons he preferred to keep his passport at home. The unconvinced policemen then turned to me and inquired about my connection with Antonio. Almost without thinking, I assured them that Antonio was a legal guest worker and had been a good friend of mine for over two years. Satisfied by my familiarity with Antonio, to my surprise, they handed back our identity cards and moved on to the next table. Later that evening I learned that a Palestinian suicide bomber had set off an explosion in another café in south Tel Aviv and the police were frantically searching for a second bomber who was believed to be still at large.

The implications of this incident for my fieldwork prospects were fundamental: instead of leading to Antonio's deportation, to suspicion of me as an undercover policeman and a warning to relatives and friends about the "academic cop," the incident confirmed my loyalty to Antonio. We eventually developed a close friendship, and Antonio became a vital gatekeeper who opened many doors for me. Nevertheless, however helpful Antonio was in facilitating access, Latinos I met through him often remained suspicious. A sign of the overriding atmosphere of mistrust was that many Latinos, as I learned much later from some of them, initially suspected that Antonio had become a snitch for an Israeli undercover policeman (me). It took another unplanned incident for me to break that stubborn cycle of suspicion.

At a social gathering to which Antonio had invited me, one migrant from the Dominican Republic, Daniela, was clearly in distress, constantly crying as people around tried to comfort her. Antonio explained to me that Daniela's husband had been arrested the week before and was to be deported that night, and Daniela was afraid to go to the airport with her infant daughter to see him, thinking the police would arrest and deport her on the spot. Moved by the agony Daniela was going through, and believing that the chances the police would arrest anyone at the departure hall were slim, I more or less instinctively offered to accompany Daniela. I suggested that while in the airport, I would ask the police if I could meet her husband, and then only if it was safe would I signal her to join us. After some hesitation, and no doubt driven by desperation, Daniela agreed.

As it was already late and we had to leave for the airport at four o'clock in the morning, Daniela suggested that I sleep the few remaining hours at her apartment, which she shared with two other Dominican families. An old couch in the living room was made up for me, and after a few hours of sleep Daniela woke me with a cup of hot coffee. Her roommates also woke up and accompanied us downstairs to wait out in the street for the taxi I had called to pick us up. The plan succeeded; Daniela safely met her husband, who enjoyed a last goodbye with his wife and daughter, whom he would not see for some time as Daniela was to remain in Israel to work for the family.

Daniela was extremely grateful for my help, and on our way back she invited me to dinner with her brother and other Latino friends. In front of the others she stressed that I could ask all the questions I wanted. My relationship with Daniela exposed me to her living conditions, life strategies, and personal network. I had finally reached the position I was hoping for, and in the months thereafter I built on the trust I gained and expanded my relations with many more Latinos. With the formation of friendship, over time, Latinos increasingly accepted me into their social networks.

It was, however, clear that a viable modus operandi for a meaningful interaction between migrants and myself had to be based on recognizable reciprocity and genuine commitment. This could not simply be stated but had to be actively demonstrated. In order to increase my social capital among Latinos, I deployed my cultural, symbolic, and social capital among Israelis that accrued to me as an educated, middle-class Israeli who had lived in Latin America.[7] I was thus able to assist some of my informants with getting medical attention, bank services, and so on. In terms of Marcel Mauss's "gifting process," I entered into a binding relation with Latinos, where their way to reciprocate my help mainly took on a social form, leading to my participation in migrants' parties, national festivities, and religious ceremonies. I regularly visited my informants in their apartments and workplaces, and also spent much of their free time with them. As trust was further established I was even invited to some more clandestine activities such as going out to "home bars" (apartments of Latinos that on weekends were converted into bars for a close circle of friends).

My participant observation has been invaluable for my ethnography. It allowed me exposure and access to some of the most intimate and confidential aspects of migrants' closely guarded emotions and experiences. I was able to converse with Latinos about their views on all kinds of issues, such as adjustment to Israeli society, (failed) family reunification, strategies of investment and remittances, and so on. I could also ask many informants to sit down with me for more formal and lengthy recorded interviews. I thus surveyed the motivational structure and migration stories of sixty-five Latinos, and more carefully documented the life histories of six migrants.

Gaining my informants' trust was never a once-and-for-all accomplishment; instead, it was something I needed continuously to cultivate. It also consequently compounded my proximity to Latinos in two major ways. First, physical proximity, which was enhanced already by sharing many activities and occasions, became a sign of commitment in itself. Whenever I was not around for more than a day or two, migrants became "worried" about me, and later always inquired about my whereabouts. Even a partial detachment often proved to be very disruptive as it raised, in some cases, the old suspicion about my "real" intentions. On an even more personal level, being an Israeli rendered me an attractive "catch" for Latina women, who often sought to marry an Israeli man, not least because this was a way to legalize their status in Israel. Stressing that I was married, but that my wife could not accompany me to Israel, did not always convince everyone. I was thus forced to manage delicately interactions with some female informants in a way that made my personal situation clear without offending them and rendering them reluctant to cooperate with me.

Concomitantly, moral proximity was also increasingly demanded from me. With time, Latinos' requests for assistance grew bolder, putting the legality of my own actions on the line, as I was asked to help in issues such as trying to bring over more relatives to Israel and buying falsified documents. Although migrants always asked kindly for my help, any hesitation on my side met with evident bitterness and strained my relations with the requesting migrant. Furthermore, stories about how some Latinos cheated their Israeli employers were sometimes told in my presence, as my loyalty to migrants was apparently taken to be nothing less than absolute. I was thus faced with an ethical predicament in my relations with some Israeli employers with whom I had friendly relations, and who had initially assisted me with getting access to migrants.

Under these conditions of sustained proximity, it was difficult for me to act consistently in a calculated way, or project consciously the type of persona I thought would be constructive in my interactions with informants. I mostly acted spontaneously and intuitively as new situations presented themselves. Consequently, my personal politics, emotional dispositions, and general worldview became crucial in managing my fieldwork. I thus had to turn necessity into a methodological virtue; I was clearly biased in favor of Latinos in the confrontation with what I often perceived to be an unfairly exclusionary host state. My empathy for migrants, together with my desire to conduct fieldwork, significantly shaped my sense of morality in the field, and thus allowed me to overcome some ethical predicaments.

In comparison to the difficulties I faced in establishing rapport with Latinos in Israel, doing fieldwork among returnees and deportees in Ecuador and Spain was an easy and pleasant undertaking. By then my work was cut out for me. I enjoyed a steady friendship with my key informants, who all kindly invited me to stay with them in their homes. In most cases I accepted the invitation, which then provided me with the opportunity to spend intensive time with informants and get exposed firsthand to their daily routine, economic conditions, social position, lifestyle, and so on. As I could clearly note, some of my informants in Ecuador valued my visit to their home not only because it was a final confirmation for my role as an anthropologist (and not an undercover agent), but also because my presence there earned them much status. They often proudly presented me to their extended families, friends, and neighbors.

PART ONE

Chapter Two

Unsettling Setting

Thou shalt neither vex a stranger, nor oppress him:
for ye were strangers in the land of Egypt.

—*Exodus 22:21*

I want everybody who is not Jewish out of this
country.

—*Eli Yishai, Israel's interior minister and chairman
of the religious orthodox political party Shas*

There are two apparent paradoxes regarding immigration to Israel in the 1990s. The first is that while receiving approximately one million Jewish immigrants in the period between 1990 and 2000, Israel still found it necessary to import, since 1993, around one hundred thousand non-Jewish guest workers. The second paradox is that Israel also received in the 1990s around one hundred thousand undocumented migrants, whose lives and working conditions on the whole were better than those of non-Jewish guest workers. What has rendered illegality a resource for the life strategies of Latinos and other non-Jewish migrants in Israel?

To understand the first paradox we need to consider, in addition to economic factors, the cultural dynamics that shaped the structure of the Israeli labor market historically. The jobs in which Palestinian workers have been employed in Israel for decades have been rendered unfitting for Jewish Israelis. These jobs were tagged "Arab jobs" (*Avoda Aravit*) by Jewish Israelis, indicating unskilled and defectively executed jobs. Recent Jewish immigrants to Israel were very conscious of this cultural logic. Thus, in the 1990s, after the first intifada saw a reduction in the number of Palestinian workers in the Israeli economy, Jewish immigrants, aspiring to the best position within the dominant Jewish national group, became reluctant to take on "Arab jobs." Eventually, and under pressure from the political lobbies of organized Israeli employers in the agricultural and construction sectors, Israel opted, for the first time in its history, for the importation of non-Jewish guest workers.

The Israeli government was determined to rectify its commitment to the Jewish character of the state by denying guest workers the possibility of settling down in the country. Israel thus installed a highly restrictive scheme to regulate the importation of guest workers. This restrictive scheme severely disadvantaged guest workers in their relation with Israeli employers. As employers took advantage of their power, and engaged in a systematic exploitation of guest workers, the latter received very little protection of their rights from Israeli law enforcement authorities and the relevant officials in the government. To better comprehend the systematic exploitation of guest workers in Israel, we must recognize that they inherited almost in its entirety the underclass and largely dehumanized status of their Palestinian precursors in the Israeli labor market, and in the field of national belonging more generally.

For almost three decades, Palestinians in the Israeli labor market were subjected to systematic and durable exploitation by private employers, lacked protection of their rights from trade unions, and suffered from intentionally lagging regulation and enforcement of their rights in Israel (Semyonov and Lewin-Epstein 1987). This patterned exploitation was not centrally orchestrated by the state, but emerged at different organizational levels out of a general condescending view of Palestinians that led to their cultural and social marginalization, and was essentially constructed against the backdrop of the larger Arab-Israeli conflict. Accordingly, it was not perceived as wrongdoing to exploit Palestinians, and the enforcement of their (limited) rights also became something of an unworthy task for Israeli law enforcement. The institutionalized exploitation and the dehumanized status of those who occupy these positions in the Israeli labor market and society were not readily altered when guest workers replaced Palestinians in the Israeli workforce.

The importation of non-Jewish guest workers was politically an unsustainable policy, as the government was accused by political parties of betraying Zionist ideals, while unemployment among the Israeli workforce reached beyond 10 percent. Since 1996, the government has curbed the number of guest workers reaching Israel, leaving many Israeli employers wanting. The demand for cheap low-skilled labor was thus gradually filled by undocumented migrants who entered Israel as tourists. In addition, the internal Israeli dynamics that permitted the systematic exploitation of guest workers pushed thousands of them to forfeit their legal status and look for alternative employment as an undocumented worker.

Yet if guest workers have suffered from severe exploitation and lack of protection from the Israeli authorities, we could have expected undocumented migrants to receive at least the same treatment, if not a worse one. After all, on top of being non-Jewish workers, undocumented migrants were strictly defined by Israel as illegal trespassers who undermine its sovereignty. Nevertheless, undocumented migrants in general and Latinos in particular enjoyed better salaries and working conditions, and enhanced social contacts with Israeli employers and ordinary citizens.

An effort to elucidate this apparent incongruity calls for a more nuanced understanding of the construction of the field of national belonging, and the role of the state in this construction process. While Max Weber foregrounded the monopoly of the modern state over the use of physical violence, it was Pierre Bourdieu who drew our attention to a complementary monopoly of the state over symbolic power. Symbolic power, according to Bourdieu, is the power to define the categories and concepts with which members in society perceive and make sense of their realities. The census, especially in its use in the colonies by colonial states, is a classic example of how the state dictates the categories through which institutions and people learn to make sense of populations (Anderson 1983). It is therefore important to realize that "the state is not only 'out there' in the form of bureaucracies, authorities, and ceremonies. It is also 'in here,' ineffaceably engraved within us, lodged in the intimacy of our being in the shared manners in which we feel, think, and judge" (Wacquant 1996: xviii).

Yet just as the monopoly of the state over the use of violence is an ideal type, so is its apparent monopoly of symbolic power. In practice, individuals and groups might be swayed, to different degrees, by the power of the state. They might also, of course, resist and challenge it. At any rate, the monopoly of the state over symbolic power is always imperfect. It is within this imperfection that undocumented migrants in Israel have maneuvered to achieve a better position as informal members in society. More particularly, in the case of Latinos it was the cracks in the exclusionary shield of the Jewish state that they used in their efforts to accumulate practical nationality.

I discern three main dynamics that have created such cracks in Israel. The first concerns a degree of ambivalence in the policies of the state. While on the level of official rhetoric Israel fiercely objected to the presence of undocumented migrants in the country, unofficially Israel tolerated for almost a decade the entrance and work of tens of thousands of undocumented migrants because of the benefits that such cheap, flexible, and disenfranchised labor provided its national economy. The second dynamic is based on an "implementation deficit"; that is, even when Israel adopted repressive policies toward undocumented migrants, there was usually an observable gap in their actual implementation (cf. Cornelius, Martin, and Hollifield 1994, Joppke 1998, Van der Leun 2003). Inconsistencies in the case of undocumented migrants emanated from varying, and possibly conflicting, views of Israeli officials. For example, the professional ethics of physicians and head teachers often led them to address the needs of undocumented migrants and their children in defiance of the official state policy. The third dynamic builds on the attitudes of the local population and civil society. NGOs, academics, and journalists often publicly contested official Israeli policies and helped to mobilize resources and support (often related to a global discourse of human rights) for undocumented migrants. Ordinary citizens also sometimes facilitated the de facto settlement of undocumented migrants in various ways, for example, by providing them with employment in their houses.

Undocumented migrants were freed from all kinds of restrictions that applied for guest workers. For example, guest workers were habitually kept close to their working site and separate from larger Israeli society; construction workers were often lodged at the sites on which they were working, agricultural workers were accommodated in caravans placed at the perimeters of the fields they cultivated, and caregivers resided in the home of the person receiving care. Guest workers' social isolation and physical proximity to their working environment not only had an alienating effect, but also rendered workers "ready-on-demand" for their employers. Guest workers were under constant supervision and could enjoy recreational activities only when employers permitted it. In contrast, undocumented workers could decide whether to take on jobs that entailed isolating living conditions or to rent their own apartment and commute to their jobs daily. If they chose the latter option, they usually resided in Tel Aviv or another big city, sharing an apartment with other migrants. They then enjoyed the company and support of friends (and not only of co-workers), had daily access to recreational activities after working hours, and lived away from the monitoring eye of their employer. Furthermore, as they grew more embedded in Israeli society they began to interact with other Israelis apart from their employers. Such contacts induced the expansion of social networks that improved the social as well as economic position of undocumented workers. It occasionally led to friendship and even marriage with Israelis. Finally, guest workers in Israel could not be joined by their families. Fearing that it would promote their settlement, the state of Israel strictly prohibited the partners, and particularly the children, of guest workers from joining them. This prohibition was explicitly mentioned in guest workers' contracts and firmly monitored by state officials. The Interior Ministry categorically rejected all allocations of work permits for married couples, and it was made clear to guest workers that if they were to form matrimonial or even romantic relationships while in Israel, they would be dismissed and sent back home.[1]

Apparently, an unintended outcome of this development was that legality in the case of guest workers, while stipulating enormous restrictions, provided little protection of limited rights, and therefore paradoxically rendered the conditions of guest workers inferior to those of undocumented migrants.

Reconfiguring the Paradox: The Replacement of Palestinian Labor by Overseas Guest Workers

After five years in Israel, Orlando, an undocumented migrant from Bolivia, was still a bit confused about the status of Palestinians in the country. One late afternoon, as we were sitting on a bench in the seafront of Tel Aviv, watching the surfers and drinking beer from a can that we bought on our way there, Orlando tried to see if he got it right. "Some of them are Israelis, they have an Israeli ID and all, but they are Muslims, right?" he paused and searched in my face for a sign of confirmation. I nodded my head as if to say "go on," and Orlando continued, "So what I don't get is, if they are not happy here, because this is a Jewish state, why don't they go to other Arab countries? I mean, there are many Arab counties all around Israel. Why don't they go live there?" Just as I was about to clarify this complex situation and place it in a historic context for Orlando, he put things conclusively in the context that was most relevant for him: "If Israel gives me here an Israeli citizenship, I would be happy and grateful. I would be an honored and loyal citizen for this country. I don't get why these Arabs are always having to make problems here."

Many Latinos were trying to figure out the exact place of Palestinians in Israel. Probably sensing that they, like Palestinians, might also belong to the Other for Jewish Israelis, Latinos found it important to distinguish themselves from Palestinians in a very clear way. To them, the contrast with Palestinians was obvious. While "they" hate Israel and look to make problems, "we" love Israel and would be loyal citizens if we were only given the chance. While "they" don't get along with Israelis, "we" manage to build friendly relationships with most people. Latinos' views of Palestinians were influenced by their religious beliefs (with evangelicals tending to have more extreme opinions against Palestinians), by a sense of competition in the labor market, and by a desire for self-presentation that they believed would appeal to Jewish Israelis. Some Latinos who were first sympathetic to the suffering and cause of Palestinians have drifted while in Israel toward a negative standpoint. A negative view of Palestinians developed among many Latinos, who believed that due to competition in the Israeli labor market, Palestinian suicide bombers who blew themselves up in crowded areas in south Tel Aviv deliberately aimed to kill undocumented migrants.

Indeed, Latinos and other non-Jewish workers replaced Palestinians in the Israeli labor market. But before explication of this transition and its implications for all sides, it is useful to examine the place that Palestinians occupied in Israel, and especially to map their position within the field of national belonging.

National belonging in Israel is dominated by an ethno-religious criterion. The historic Israeli Declaration of Independence, dating from May 14, 1948, unambiguously states:

> On the 29th November, 1947, the United Nations General Assembly passed a resolution calling for the establishment of a Jewish State in the land of Israel. . . . This recognition by the United Nations of the right of the Jewish people to establish their State is irrevocable. This right is the natural right of the Jewish people to be masters of their own fate, like all other nations, in their own sovereign State. [By] virtue of our historic right . . . [we] hereby declare the establishment of a Jewish State in the Land of Israel to be known as the state of Israel.

While Israel is defined as a Jewish state, due to the historical circumstances that led to its establishment in Palestine, around 20 percent of Israel's citizens are members of the indigenous Arab population (Muslim and Christian). Israel is thus a de facto multi-ethnic and multireligious society. Accordingly, and notwithstanding its definition as a Jewish state, in the same Declaration of Independence, Israel vowed to "ensure complete equality of social and political rights to all its inhabitants irrespective of religion, race, or sex; it [the state of Israel] will guarantee freedom of religion, conscience, language, education, and culture." Yet Israel has historically insisted on a marked representation of its Jewish character on a symbolic level (e.g., a flag with the Star of David, a national hymn that praises the return of Jews to Israel, Hebrew as the official language of the state, the national festivities and memorial days all according to the Jewish tradition). Indeed, the field of national belonging in Israel can by and large be conceptualized as the field of Jewishness, not Israeliness. Both the Law of Return (1950) and the Nationality Law (1952) categorically refer to the term "Jew"; while the first law ensures the "historic" right of all Jews to "return" from anywhere in the world to Israel, the latter stipulates the automatic inclusion of Jewish immigrants as full citizens in the state.[2]

The compatibility of a Jewish state and a democratic regime has been fiercely debated for many years in Israel. Smooha (1990) has defined Israel as an "ethnic democracy," stressing the general democratic nature of the state and its formal move to award Palestinian citizens full social and civil rights, albeit restricted political rights. Israel's refusal to give equal political rights to all its non-Jewish citizens was meant to prevent the possibility that a non-Jewish government would be elected. According to Peled (1992), restrictions on the ability of Palestinian citizens to run for political office have practically reduced their legal status to that of a "nominal" citizenship. Recognizing the overall dominance of the Jewish citizenry, some academics have charged that Israel actually constitutes an "ethnic republic" (Rabinowitz 1997, Ghanem 1998) or even an "ethnocracy" (Yiftachel 1997). These critics point to the legal framework that Israel put in place to safeguard the Jewish character of the state, at any cost.

While being Jewish in Israel is a necessary condition for belonging to the dominant national group, there is also an internal hierarchy within the Jewish dominant group. One major organizing criterion in this internal hierarchy is the perceived contribution of members to the fortification of the Jewish state. This explains, for example, the elevated status of army generals in Israeli society. A sense of superior contribution to the establishment and strengthening of the Jewish state also partly accounts for the ethnic division between "Ashkenazim" and "Sephardim" (or "Mizrahim") Jews in Israel. Ashkenazim have claimed a superior status and "first rights" in Israel because of their pioneering role in the establishment of the Jewish state. This superior status served Ashkenazim morally to cover up a blunt and institutional economic and cultural discrimination against Sephardim.[3]

The Israeli Declaration of Independence urged Palestinian citizens to contribute to the fortification of the Jewish state. "We appeal for the Arab inhabitants of the State of Israel . . . to participate in the upbuilding of the State on the basis of full and equal citizenship." This call might seem ironic, but the symbolic power of the state to shape and inculcate the categories with which citizens make sense of their realities also powerfully impinged on Palestinians in Israel. Thus, Rabinowitz (1998) shows how Palestinian teachers educate children according to the Jewish curriculum that on some remembrance days celebrates the defeat of Palestinians by the Zionist movement and later by the Jewish state. Smooha (2005) found out in an extensive survey among Palestinian citizens in Israel that 70 percent of them accept the definition of Israel as a Jewish and democratic state.

Returning to the issue of immigration, it is important to point out that in the official terminology, as well as in common idiom, Jewish immigrants to Israel are called *Olim*. The term *Olim* is taken from the Bible; it literarily means "Ascenders." It evokes the ancient custom of seasonal pilgrimage among Jews ascending to the Temple Mount. Accordingly, the ministry in charge of immigration in Israel is called the Ministry of Ascendance and Absorption (*Misrad Ha'Alia ve Ha'Klita*). At the same time, Israel unambiguously rejected non-Jewish immigration, and is especially careful in blocking the return of Palestinian refugees to the country. Israel has never had an explicit immigration law applicable to non-Jewish foreign citizens who wished to settle there. In fact, non-Jewish immigration is a category entirely missing from the state's legal terminology. In the absence of a generic immigration law, and given that existing laws refer exclusively to Jews, any immigration of non-Jews has been practically rendered a legal no-man's land for all legislative, executive, and judicial arms of the Jewish state.

Against this exclusionary ethno-religious constitution of the Jewish state, it is indeed remarkable that in the 1990s Israel officially imported one hundred thousand non-Jewish guest workers, and in addition unofficially absorbed around one hundred thousand non-Jewish undocumented migrants. We now turn to the clarification of this process.

The collapse of the Berlin Wall in 1989 and the subsequent disintegration of the Soviet Union brought about the removal of migration restrictions for Jews living in the Eastern Bloc. Consequently, massive numbers of Jews began emigrating from the different countries of the former Soviet Union (hereafter FSU). In the years prior to 1990 there was a yearly average of around 15,000 Jewish immigrants arriving in Israel from all over the world. In 1990, however, only a few months after the fall of the Iron Curtain, some 200,000 Jews migrated to Israel in just one year. In 1991, more than 175,000 Jews reached Israel; thereafter the number decreased, and it has stabilized at an average of around 60,000 per year. In the period between 1990 and 2000, Israel received approximately one million new immigrants (Central Bureau of Statistics 2002). It is important to note here that in 1989 the total population of Israel proper was 4,559,000, of whom 3,717,000 were Jewish and the rest mainly Palestinian citizens (ibid.). This means that Israel received, in a period of ten years, a number of Jewish immigrants that is approximately equivalent to one quarter of its total population.

Accommodating such high numbers of immigrants presented Israel with two pressing challenges: providing housing and employment for arriving migrants. Lacking either might have induced Jewish immigrants to leave Israel and look for other countries to settle in; this process would have been calamitous from the Israeli state's viewpoint, as it would signify its failure to fulfill the very raison d'être of the Jewish state, that is, to secure a "home" for all Jews worldwide. Ideally, the two hurdles could, to some extent, be overcome in tandem. Newly arrived migrants increased the demand for housing and therefore strained the construction industry. If qualified as construction workers, migrants could inject the sector with badly needed labor while also partly solving their own employment predicament. To understand why such a plan, which was indeed attempted by the state of Israel, has failed colossally, we must complement our view of the labor market with relevant social and cultural dynamics.

Since its very early days, the structure of the Israeli labor market clearly fits the definition of a dual labor market (Semyonov and Lewin-Epstein 1986, Grinberg 1991, 1993, Schnell 1999). The model of a dual labor market, as comprehensively elaborated by Michael Piore (1979), has been contested mainly on the grounds that divisions into primary and secondary sectors tended to be artificially drawn, ignoring the more fluid and changing character of different jobs (Hodson and Kaufman 1982). However, in Israel the distinction between sectors has been historically solidified along the lines of a national division between Jews and Palestinians, who have been engaged in a larger religious and national struggle. Unlike more elastic lines of class or pure economic rewards, the division in the Israeli labor market reflected the tension between Jews and Palestinians in Israel and the Middle East, and as such it has proven to be stable and unwavering for decades (Al-Haj and Rosenfeld 1990).

Palestinian citizens of Israel exclusively filled the less attractive jobs at the bottom of the labor market, in line with their low position within the field of national belonging. Israel has also consistently used security issues in order to limit the opportunity structure of Palestinian citizens (Rouhana 1997, Jamal 2007). After the Six-Day War of 1967, Israel occupied territories in the West Bank and the Gaza strip that had been under the control of Jordan and Egypt, respectively. Beside the many political, legal, and international issues that arose from Israel's new position in the Middle East, the pacification of Palestinians, who lived in these territories, was seen by Israel as an important task. Withdrawing from the Occupied Territories was dismissed in the context of an unresolved conflict, yet annexing them was also problematic, as it would have endangered the Jewish majority inside Israel and forced the government to legally incorporate more Palestinians or openly opt for an apartheid configuration. It was eventually the military assessment that was decisive in rejecting legal annexation, while at the same time incorporating Palestinians into the Israeli labor market. It was believed that relative economic prosperity and livelihood would enhance domestic order and avert civil unrest (see Grinberg 1993).

In 1969, Israel began recruiting thousands of Palestinians from the Occupied Territories to perform manual, low-paid jobs primarily in the construction and agricultural sectors, but also in industries such as metalwork and textile. This recruiting practice peaked in the mid-1980s, when the number of authorized Palestinian workers in Israel was around 110,000 and constituted about 9 percent of the total Israeli workforce. In sectoral terms, "Palestinians held 25 percent of Israeli agricultural jobs and 45 percent of construction jobs" (Bartram 1998: 307). Palestinians from the Occupied Territories had no political rights in Israel and were also barred from organizing themselves or becoming members of the General Federation of Laborers in Israel (*Histadrut*). This lack of political capital prevented Palestinian workers from having any bargaining power in their relations with Israeli employers. The lack of occupational alternatives in the Palestinian economy, and the fact that Palestinians were also ineligible for unemployment benefits in Israel, rendered them readily available under conditions that were the most favorable for Israeli employers. The incorporation of disenfranchised Palestinian workers reinforced the division between a primary and a secondary Israeli labor market.

In 1987, Palestinians entered a new phase in their struggle for self-determination and aspiration for an independent state. The first intifada was marked by organized resistance against Israeli military forces in the Occupied Territories, and also by sporadic terror acts committed by Palestinians against civilian targets inside Israel. Consequently, there was an increase in the Israeli army's imposition of curfews in the Occupied Territories, and other limitations on the free movement of Palestinians have been regularly enforced. Apart from the Israeli restrictions, the local Palestinian leadership often independently initiated general strikes and prevented workers from going into Israel. Subsequently, Israeli employers could no longer rely on Palestinians for a steady supply of cheap labor. A demand for the substitution of Palestinian workers got the support of yet more employers as some violent terror acts were directed against them. The pressure to find an alternative workforce was exacerbated by the fact that seasonal agricultural work cannot be put on hold, and the government's own assessment that the shortage in the labor market would lead to an economic recession and a serious housing problem for Jewish immigrants from the FSU. This last concern was politically charged, since Jewish immigrants instantly received full Israeli citizenship, including political rights. It meant that if not attuned to the needs of Jewish immigrants, the government would risk facing a protest vote from this new electoral population in the next election.

Faced with an acute labor shortage, the Israeli government sought to encourage Israeli workers to take on the jobs that Palestinians had traditionally occupied. This seemed a viable solution given that the unemployment rate among the Israeli working population in the early 1990s hovered above 10 percent. In 1992, for example, the number of unemployed Israelis reached 207,400, which is roughly twice the total number of Palestinians that were employed in the Israeli labor market prior to the break out of the first Palestinian intifada in 1987 (Central Bureau of Statistics 2000).

In an effort to attract Israelis to sectors such as agriculture and construction, the government designated jobs in these sectors as "required" jobs, and offered economic incentives both to Israeli workers who took on such jobs and to Israeli employers who hired them. The government also drew up a special scheme for recently released soldiers who entered the Israeli workforce; they were offered a monetary bonus of around US$1,500 for completing six months of work in a "required" job. Finally, the government sponsored a public campaign to revive the principle of "Hebrew labor" (*Avoda Ivrit*). The notion of "Hebrew labor" was developed in the early nineteenth century by the Zionist movement. It promoted the ideal of an independent Jewish nation that was connected to the land of Israel not just in a spiritual manner. "Hebrew labor" advocated the manual cultivation of the land, and praised physically demanding agricultural work, in contrast to the typical diasporic Jewish occupations (*luftmensch*). The modern Israeli campaign of the 1990s sought to reignite this working spirit by drawing on nationalist sentiments and solidarity. It called upon the Israeli population to participate actively in saving the national economy and demonstrating that Israel could be a self-sustaining state.

In spite of this robust attempt by the government, all methods proved futile as most Jewish Israelis firmly kept away from "Arab jobs." Some ex-soldiers took advantage of the monetary bonus but were usually ready to quit right after they were awarded the state dividend. Jewish immigrants from the FSU entered the secondary labor market, but only in small numbers and until they found a better job. These recent migrants resembled middle-class Jewish Israelis in a number of ways (a high level of human capital, political consciousness, etc.), and they were generally indisposed to act in Israel as typical migrant workers who are usually disinterested, at least initially, in the local hierarchy of jobs (see Smooha 1994, Kimmerling 1998).

The government's failure has largely confirmed the idea that wages not only reflect conditions of supply and demand, but also confer status and prestige (Piore 1979). In addition, the avoidance of certain jobs by the larger Israeli workforce, especially the unemployed portion of it, was unintentionally supported by Israel's welfare regime, which provided all citizens with health services, education, and unemployment benefits. However, it was the failure of the campaign to revive the spirit of "Hebrew labor" that delivered a bitter blow to the government efforts, as it demonstrated an apparent decline in the ability of Israel to use Zionist values as a resource for national economic mobilization among Jews in Israel.

Yet the reluctance of Israeli workers constituted only one side of the failure. The other part had to do with Israeli employers who sought to maximize their own interests. As we have seen, the hiring preferences of Israeli employers were established during the decades when an uninterrupted supply of disenfranchised Palestinian workers was available. Replacing Palestinians with unionized Israeli workers, in labor-intensive sectors, had many unwelcome consequences for employers, such as higher expectations about wages and working conditions. Unsurprisingly then, most Israeli employers endorsed importation of cheap labor from abroad as an alternative solution to the shortage of unskilled labor. Employers collectively used their powerful political lobbies in the Israeli Parliament to mobilize support for this alternative (Bartram 1998). At the same time, some individual employers sued the government, demanding compensation and legal permission to import guest workers. Employers claimed that they lacked access to the Palestinian workforce, and therefore incurred losses, as a direct result of the government's political and military actions (ibid.: 313). Employers intensified their pressure on the government by spotlighting its ineptitude at reconstructing the local labor market.

Due to concern about the Jewish character of the state, Israel was reluctant to engage in labor importation, although this has for decades been a common practice among most Western states. It was not only the bitter recognition that Israel needed to rely on non-Jewish workers in order to accomplish its goals, but the much deeper fear—based on the experiences of other labor-importing countries—that non-Jewish guest workers might eventually settle down in Israel. Most Israeli politicians considered the importation of non-Jewish workers to be an admission that the Jewish state had failed to live up to its moral and historical expectations. An ideological reluctance was shared by most political parties, but it was religious parties and their spiritual leaders that formed the most vocal and militant opposition to the idea. However, in 1993 Israel signed the Oslo Agreement that officially endorsed the "two states for two nations" solution to the Israeli-Palestinian conflict. Accordingly, Israel began adapting to the new geopolitical contingencies that such a solution implied for its economy, for example, a possible long-term separation from Palestinians in the labor force.

In September 1993, the religious party Shas decided to leave a Labor-led government, allegedly due to the far-reaching compromises that it was negotiating with the Palestinian leadership. Between 1993 and 1996 a narrow coalition government of only secular parties operated in Israel (for only the second time in Israel's history), and tellingly it was in this period that the government finally conceded and resorted to licensing work permits for non-Jewish guest workers. Nevertheless, members of the government were clearly unwilling to be seen by the public as the ones who permitted such a plan. For example, Ora Namir, the labor minister at the time, vociferously opposed the importation plan when it was debated in government, but finally voted in favor only after she explained that she was doing so "out of security considerations alone" (*Yediot Aharonot* 15.04.1994). Other ministers, including Prime Minister Yitzhak Rabin, also "argued that the government had no choice but to bring in workers if it wanted to protect the lives of Israelis" (Bartram 1998: 315). Thus, the importation of non-Jewish workers was publicly legitimized by claiming loyalty to an even greater ideal, the protection of the lives of Jews in Israel.

At first, work permits to guest workers were issued on a very limited basis and under strict control to sectors in distress, that is, primarily construction and agriculture. However, as the Israeli-Palestinian conflict worsened, and restrictions on the employment of Palestinians in Israel became more frequent, licenses were given to non-Jewish guest workers by the thousands. The government consistently and rapidly increased the number of permits more than tenfold within three years: from 9,600 in 1993 to 103,000 by 1996. From 1997 until 2005, the number of permits stabilized at around 80,000 per year. All of this led to a situation in which guest workers, and not recent Jewish immigrants or Jewish Israelis, gradually replaced Palestinians in the Israeli workforce. While the overall percentage of non-Jewish workers in Israel increased moderately (from 8.9 percent in 1990 to 14 percent in 2000), the composition of the workforce changed considerably. In 1990, the phenomenon of guest workers hardly existed: they comprised only 0.1 percent of the total Israeli workforce. This situation rapidly changed during the 1990s, reaching a record level in 1999, when 10.1 percent of the total Israeli private workforce consisted of guest workers (Central Bureau of Statistics 2002).

Unintended Consequences? From Guest Workers to Undocumented Migrants

As a latecomer to the group of labor-importing states, Israel was alarmed by the experience of other countries that eventually saw the partial settlement of guest workers. Accordingly, the government applied a highly restrictive importation mechanism that relegated most direct responsibility for the process and the needs of guest workers to private employers and mediating agencies. Thus, although formally initiating and legally regulating the importation process, the government persistently looked to minimize its direct responsibility for guest workers, who were never contracted by the state or in the public sector. Israel attempted a "legal distance" from guest workers, a distance that it saw as legitimizing a complete discrediting of any future claims by guest workers.

Work permits for hiring guest workers were commonly given for a period of one or two years, sometimes with the possibility to prolong them up to a maximum of five years. Authorized work periods were limited in order to ensure a constant substitution of guest workers that would not allow them the possibility to settle in Israel. To obtain a work permit, employers had to sign an official commitment, assuring that designated guest workers would be exclusively employed in the company and the job for which the permit was authorized. Once in Israel, the passports of guest workers were stamped with a visa, which stipulated the specific job they would be allowed to perform and indicated the exclusive employer for whom they would be permitted to work. This registration process became known in Israel as the "binding contract," as it strictly bound guest workers to the particular Israeli employer who contracted them.[4] The binding contract was counterproductive for the Israeli market, as it prohibited a flexible movement of guest workers to supply changes in demand for labor across sectors, or even among employers within the same sector. Having to import new guest workers instead of relocating dismissed ones seriously burdened the Israeli economy. Given that this and other shortcomings of the binding contract mechanism were pointed out by several Israeli academics (Drori and Kunda 1999, Schnell 1999), as well as the Ministry of Labor (2000) and the Bank of Israel (2000), it is probably safe to say that the government decided to stick to it because its restrictiveness made it less likely for guest workers to settle down in Israel.

Yet the stringent binding contract was not only hindering the Israeli economy, it was also making guest workers totally dependent on their exclusive employer for employment. Guest workers were deprived of all bargaining power. Whenever employers unilaterally decided to terminate their contract with guest workers, the work visas of the latter were instantly rendered invalid, and they were forced to leave the country. By the same token, whenever guest workers independently decided to quit their job, their visas automatically expired, and they had to return home. Guest workers thus found themselves in an extremely vulnerable position when many employers began to take full advantage of the situation, routinely violating signed contracts with guest workers and threatening that any complaint to law enforcement institutions would lead to their dismissal. Given this bureaucratic caging, guest workers in Israel could be classified as "captive labor" (Calavita 1992, see also Rosenhek 1999, Kemp 2004). In fact, in 2003 an investigation by a joint team from the International Federation for Human Rights and the Euro-Mediterranean Human Rights Network on the situation of migrant workers in Israel resulted in a report that documents the systematic and unlawful mistreatment of migrant workers, and equates the situation in Israel with "[a] contemporary form of slavery" (Ellman and Laacher 2003).

Soon after the importation of guest workers began, alarming signs for their widespread and systematic exploitation loomed. Employers commonly paid lower salaries than those that were agreed upon in guest workers' contracts, or made them work more hours for the same salary. (For more on these forms of exploitation, as well as others, see Kav La'Oved 1998, 2000, Schnell 2001, *Haaretz* 11.02.2003). Some especially ruth-less employers held up the salaries of guest workers for a few months, only to then dismiss them arbitrarily from their jobs and force them to leave the country without paying their salaries (see *Haaretz* 27.02.2002 and 10.02.2003). When guest workers refused to leave and insisted on payment, employers often resorted to the use of violence in order to get workers out of the country (see *Maariv* 15.12.1996).

Guest workers seriously feared a shortened working period in Israel since they were usually recruited from Third World countries (e.g., Thailand, the Philippines), or poor European countries (e.g., Romania, Bulgaria, Ukraine). Working abroad was often seen as a once-in-a-lifetime opportunity for such workers, who frequently paid a large amount of money to recruitment agencies in their country. To pay these agencies workers often took out a hefty loan that was to be repaid with the money earned abroad. For such indebted guest workers, not being able to complete a carefully calculated term abroad meant a full-blown economic catastrophe.

The role of mediating agencies in stimulating and perpetuating the systematic exploitation of guest workers is crucial. Mediating agencies specialized in recruiting workers and getting them from their home countries to Israel. Surprisingly enough, the services of mediating agencies cost Israeli employers nothing. This was the case because mediating agencies charged expensive fees to the workers they contracted abroad. Often working together with local recruitment agencies abroad, Israeli medi-ating agencies charged from US$3,000 (in Romania and Thailand) to US$20,000 (in China) for each contract to work in Israel. After paying local recruitment agencies and covering the expenses of getting workers to Israel, mediating agencies were still left with a hefty profit (Berman 2007, see also State Comptroller 2003). It is important to note here that charging guest workers for the right to work in Israel was unlawful according to Israel's Law of Employment (1959); however, this law was never enforced by the Israeli authorities.[5]

Several Israeli mediating agencies even paid employers for the right to import workers from abroad for them. Encouraged by rewards from mediating agencies, Israeli employers often demanded, and occasionally received, more guest workers than they actually needed, and were thus even more disposed to arbitrarily dismiss their workers. Some employers began to "sell" their guest workers to other eager employers in sectors that were not entitled, according to the official criteria, to an allocation of guest workers. While mediating agencies and employers were profiting from illicit practices, it was guest workers who paid for it; first, by paying mediating agencies thousands of dollars, and second, in being exploited by employers.

Severely criticizing the government for its ineptness in confronting the actions of mediating agencies, the state comptroller asserted that "[t]he state and its citizens suffer from these practices. . . . The financial benefits from charging guest workers with fees for coming to work in Israel creates a temptation to pressure for more work permits than is necessary, and for the unlawful dealing of work permits" (State Comptroller 2003: 649). As repeated journalistic and police investigations found out, mediating agencies powerfully lobbied the government to set higher quotas of guest workers, using bribes to officials in key ministries as one prominent means to achieve this (Kav La'Oved July 2000, *Yediot Aharonot* 07.10.2001, *Haaretz* 26.02.2002). A former adviser for the Israeli government on the issue of guest workers, Hertzel Hagai, expressed his frustration with the process, remarking in a somewhat sarcastic way that "the major profit in Israel from guest workers is coming from their very importation rather than their employment" (*Haaretz* 02.10.2002).

The state, although initiating and formally regulating the importation of guest workers, did very little to create the necessary conditions for their reception. As Drori and Kunda (1999: 6) remark, "While the number of guest workers was rising, no serious official attempt was made to promote legislation or design appropriate policies and implementation mechanisms regarding such issues as . . . regulation of employment conditions, social rights and welfare." The government's lack of involvement allowed the exploitation to intensify, as it led to a situation whereby employers, whose main interest was profit making, were given free rein in setting the working conditions that they provided for their guest workers.

For example, while Israel did have a comprehensive National Health Insurance Law, it was applicable only to Israeli residents—an unattainable status for guest workers. Thus, the ministerial directives stipulated the absolute responsibility of employers to obtain medical insurance for their guest workers. But these same directives fell short of specifying either a standard for such insurance policies or a minimal coverage perimeter. Consequently, many employers opted for the most cost-effective insurance policies, which private insurance companies were fast to specialize in drafting. The low-priced insurance policies, to be paid by Israeli employers, practically exempted guest workers from most expensive medical treatments, and allowed for their prompt relocation to their own country in cases of extreme injuries or severe sicknesses.[6]

In addition to inadequately regulating the provision of guest workers' conditions, the Israeli government made little effort to enforce some of the laws that defined their rights. For example, the Bank of Israel found that the Minimum Wage Law (1987) was rarely enforced in the case of guest workers; between 1996 and 2000 an average of 56 percent of guest workers were unlawfully paid below minimum wage. Other labor laws, like the Hours of Work and Rest Law (1951) and the Severance Pay Law (1953), were also widely violated by employers, with no serious precautions taken by the state to prevent the violations (Schnell 2001). A scrutiny of the work of civil servants in the Ministry of Labor, who had responsibility for supervising the conditions of guest workers, showed that the enforcement of guest workers' rights was seriously neglected (see Yanay and Borowosky 1998, State Comptroller 1996).

Finally, the entrenched exploitation impinged on guest workers' civil rights. For example, employers commonly confiscated the passports of their guest workers in order to exercise even greater control over them. Confiscating passports constitutes a criminal offense in Israel that carries a penalty of up to one year in prison (Penal Law, article 376-a). Israeli NGOs such as Kav La'Oved (Hotline for Workers) assisted thousands of guest workers who complained about the confiscation of their passports; nevertheless, the police took little if any action to follow up on these complaints and bring the violating employers to court. The few cases that reached Israeli courts often brought condemnation from the judges; one judge said, "[G]uest workers are not slaves; their rights, including the right to hold their own passport, must be protected" (*Haaretz* 17.02.2002). Nevertheless, Israeli authorities not only refrained from enforcing the law, but actually collaborated with employers on this unlawful practice. Officials from the Interior Ministry, who were responsible for checking guest workers' passports upon arrival in Israel, commonly returned the passports not to workers but to their Israeli employers (see Association for Civil Rights in Israel 1997).

The systematic exploitation of guest workers pushed thousands of them to become undocumented migrants. Guest workers either were forced out of their legal status by a premature dismissal or were induced by harsh exploitation to forfeit their legal status and look for alternative employment as an undocumented worker. In 2001, the Israeli Research Centre for Social Policy unequivocally stated in a special report that "[t]he blunt exploitation of legal foreign workers is so severe that it is better for them to give up their legal status and remain to work illegally." A survey by the Ministry of Labor provided strong evidence in this respect, as it found out that 73 percent of former guest workers improved their salaries once they left their exclusive employers; 45 percent also reported an improvement in the treatment they received from their new employer (Ministry of Labor 2001: 50). No longer bonded to one employer, former guest workers could offer their labor in the free market and earn competitive salaries. Moreover, employers knew that ill-treatment of undocumented workers would almost immediately lead the latter to search for a better employer, thus significantly narrowing their risk of exploitation. Many employers commonly exercised in their working relations with undocumented workers what we can call "utilitarian opportunism"; that is, employers treated them with fairness and even kindness, which ensured workers' continuous employment under conditions that were very profitable for employers. Interestingly, the same Ministry of Labor survey discovered that 48 percent of all undocumented workers had been employed in the construction sector, which was also the chief sector for the employment of legal guest workers. Thus, improvement in the conditions of undocumented workers often occurred within the same sector in which they had worked as legal guest workers.

From an economic point of view, this dynamic in the Israeli labor market could occur only if there was an ample unanswered demand for undocumented workers. Indeed, this was precisely the case, as the government quota for the importation of guest workers only partially provided a solution to the demand for cheap labor among Israeli employers. Israel originally decided to allocate permits for guest workers only to employers who were, according to official records, heavily dependent on legal Palestinian labor before the outbreak of the first intifada. However, it is estimated that in the early 1990s around fifty thousand Palestinians regularly worked in Israel without official permits (Schnell 2001). Since employers of undocumented Palestinians could not put forward to the government their demand for guest workers, they instead introduced it directly into the informal labor market of undocumented migrants.[7] In addition, in 1996 the right-wing Likud party formed a new coalition government together with two religious parties. The new government curbed the number of authorized guest workers and even decreased it in subsequent years.

Another dynamic that shaped demand for undocumented workers was the emerging demand among Israel's middle classes for domestic cleaners and servants. In the mid-1990s, as a step in the privatization of the health service sector, the Israeli government authorized families with a debilitated member (usually an aged person) to import caregivers.[8] The number of authorized permits for overseas caregivers increased from 4,300 in 1995 to 30,000 in 2001, a 700 percent rise (Ministry of Labor 2002b). Most caregivers were women, mainly recruited from the Philippines and Romania. They regularly resided with the hiring family. It often was in the mutual interest of both sides to expand caregivers' tasks to include domestic work for extra payment. While this was an informal practice, it was often propagated by mediating agencies, which commonly advised families to pay their caregiver a supplement of just US$50 for extra housekeeping services (Kav La'Oved October 2000). As the conversion of caregivers into overall domestic servants became commonplace, it also appealed to many middle- and upper-class families that did not have a debilitated member in the house. This demand for domestic servants was then transmitted into the informal labor market, and was met by scores of undocumented migrants as well as legal caregivers who decided to leave their exclusive employer. One survey among the Israeli middle and upper classes showed that 55 percent of these households employed domestic workers (*Yediot Aharonot* 30.12.2002).

Enter a Third Party: Undocumented Migrants Reaching Israel

In the early 1990s, when the government recurrently debated and constantly delayed its decision to import non-Jewish guest workers, there were signs that the market was beginning to embrace its own informal solution to the demand for cheap labor. In 1990 the state comptroller had already reported the emergence of undocumented migration of non-Jewish workers to Israel. In response, the Israeli Parliament swiftly moved to pass the Foreign Workers Law: Unlawful Employment, which defined the criminal aspects and the corresponding penalties for those who engaged in the unlawful employment of non-Jewish migrant workers. Nevertheless, an increasing number of undocumented migrants reached Israel from 1993 onward.

Most undocumented migrants entered Israel on a legal tourist visa and then overstayed it. Israel faced particular difficulties when trying to tighten its visa and entrance regime for tourists. Apart from the fact that tourism was a vital source of national income for Israel, the religious significance of the Land of Israel, especially for Christians, made it problematic to prevent entry of those who wished to visit it for allegedly religious purposes. A much less popular way for undocumented migrants to enter Israel was by trespassing its national borders, or by using falsified documents. These options were initially only rarely used, not least because of Israel's international image as a beleaguered country that exercises tight border controls due to its sensitive security situation. Nevertheless, by 1995 it became known that human-traffickers operated, mainly from Egypt, to help undocumented migrants stealthily cross the border into Israel (*Maariv* 21.09.1995, *Yediot Aharonot* 13.11.2002 and 23.05.2003).[9]

While the exact number of undocumented migrants in Israel has been widely contested and politicized, since the mid-1990s most estimates put the number at between 100,000 and 150,000 (see State Comptroller 1997, Schnell 1999). The relative ease with which tens of thousands of undocumented migrants entered Israel and found jobs should be evaluated in light of an Israeli blind-eye policy. The government found it a convenient intermediate solution to deal with the steady flow of undocumented migrants into the country. Officially deciding to limit the number of guest workers, the government still sought to avoid harming the national economy and avert political pressure from employers' powerful lobbies. While undocumented migrants satisfied the demand for cheap labor, the government could expediently present itself not as the cause of this development but rather as its victim.[10] Furthermore, from the perspective of a Jewish state that feared the settlement of guest workers, "admitting" undocumented migrants seemed less problematic since they were strictly defined as deportable illegal trespassers. It was thus that the government deliberately adopted a "symbolic policy," that is, officially appearing restrictive but unofficially allowing undocumented migrants' entrance and work. The adoption of "symbolic policy" by states in the case of undocumented migrants is of course not unique to Israel; it can be found in the United States (cf. Cornelius, Martin, and Hollifield 1994) and different countries in Europe (cf. Bade 2004).

While the government always vowed to expel tens of thousands of undocumented migrants, in practice, as table 2.1 illustrates, deportations were actually very limited until the end of 2002.

Table 2.1. Deported Undocumented Migrants 1995–2001

Year	Number of deported undocumented migrants	Percentage of total undocumented migrants
1995	950	2%
1996	950	1.3%
1997	2768	3.1%
1998	4037	3.8%
1999	4615	3.8%
2000	742	0.5%
2001	1915	1.4%

Source: Ministry of Labor 2002a.

Only a tiny fraction of the total undocumented migrants was deported each year prior to 2002. Deportation campaigns were undermined primarily because consecutive governments failed to budget for a necessary extra police force, juridical personnel, and detention facilities. One high-ranking police officer described the governments' recurring deportation plans as "amusing." Expressing his profound disillusionment, the police officer explained that "these plans by the government can only work in theory. Without the corresponding budgets there is no chance to deport thousands of illegal foreign workers" (*Yediot Aharonot* 03.01.2002). In addition, Israeli NGOs contested the legality of every step in the expulsion procedure for undocumented migrants. Using qualified lawyers and insisting on migrants' rights under both Israeli law and international conventions, NGOs managed to slow down deportation significantly. The lengthy legal procedures that the NGOs forced on the state led to congestion of migrants in detention facilities, which sometimes stalled the whole campaign.

In many of the conversation I had with Latinos, the ease with which they could enter and find work in Israel was noted. Latinos clearly had the impression that Israel was not enforcing a strict entry regime. With respect to the Israeli deportation policy, notwithstanding the devastation experienced by individuals who fell victim to it, most Latinos considered it to be a "symbolic policy"; Latinos understood that Israel was mainly paying lip service to its commitment to the Jewish character of the state. Here is, for example, how Juanito, a 29-year-old Chilean undocumented migrant, put it:

> I don't think they [Israeli authorities] really want to get us out of here. I'm
> in this country for nine years and I never had a problem finding a job or
> renting a place. In these nine years I've only seen more and more Latinos
> arrive, and they all find jobs. They [Israeli authorities] know we are here,
> they even know where we live. But they know we do the jobs that they
> [Israelis] don't want to do, so they don't mind that we are here. Of course

I'm afraid that they [Israeli police] will pick me one day, but I keep telling
myself that the chance is very small, especially if you know how to keep safe.
It might not seem like that, but I always keep my eyes open when I'm
walking on the streets.

Differences between estimates of the number of undocumented migrants in Israel
were significant, and at times they translated to around 5 percent of the total Israeli
workforce. There is a universal difficulty in recording the number of undocumented
migrants, who in self-interest try to stay out of the purview of state officials and
circumvent all attempts to monitor them. However, it seems that the state of Israel
never genuinely attempted to keep an accurate record of undocumented migrants'
numbers. Indeed, every agency that has tried to produce estimates has pointed to the
inadequate database managed by the state. For example, the Bank of Israel (2000)
remarked that "the lack of organized statistics regarding foreign workers from overseas is limiting the reliability of the data." Given that collecting and maintaining exact
data was important for, among other things, assessing the structure and composition
of the labor market, it is indeed striking that Israel never seriously established an
orderly record. Leaving aside allegations of corruption among officials, I suggest that
vagueness best suited the government's blind-eye policy. Having this kind of uncertainty about the exact number of undocumented migrants allowed the government to
underestimate the number of undocumented migrants, fend off political opposition,
and appear to the public as fighting and containing the phenomenon.

Yet on the ground, a different reality was taking shape. Undocumented migrants
reached Israel from all corners of the globe. In the year 2001 the number of countries
of origin of deported undocumented workers from Israel stood at ninety (Ministry of
Labor 2002a: 5). Kav La'Oved, an Israeli NGO which worked closely with undocumented migrants, produced the following estimate, given in table 2.2, for the composition and number of undocumented migrants in the year 2000.

Importantly, the data in table 2.2 include both undocumented migrants and guest
workers who lost their legal status. Indeed, a survey among undocumented migrants
discovered that 53 percent used to be legal guest workers (Ministry of Labor 2001).
Since Israel rarely recruited guest workers from the Middle East, Latin America, or
Africa, these groups mostly represent undocumented migrants. From other countries,
there was an official recruitment of guest workers, and we can therefore reliably
assume that many undocumented migrants from these places were former guest
workers.

The exact number of Latinos in Israel is disputed, just like all other estimates
regarding undocumented migrants. In table 2.3 I present my own estimate for the
number of Latinos according to their countries of origin, and the relative proportion

Table 2.2. Non-Jewish Undocumented Migrants in Israel

Countries of Origin	Number of Migrants	Relative Proportion
Jordan, Egypt, Morocco	30,000	21.3%
Former Soviet Union	30,000	21.3%
Philippines, Thailand	25,000	17.7%
Romania	15,000	10.7%
Latin America	12,000	8.5%
China, India, Sri Lanka	10,000	7.1%
Africa	10,000	7.1%
Bulgaria, Hungary, Poland	5,000	3.5%
Turkey	4,000	2.8%
Total	141,000	100%

Source: Kav La'Oved, May 2000.

Table 2.3. Latino Migrants in Israel

Country of Origin	Number of Migrants	Relative Proportion
Ecuador	5,000	38%
Colombia	4,500	35%
Chile	1,200	9%
Peru	1,200	9%
Bolivia	500	4%
Venezuela	250	2%
Brazil	250	2%
Argentina, Paraguay, Dominican Republic, Mexico	100 (tens of migrants from each of these countries)	1%
Total	13,000	100%

Source: Author's Estimate

of each national Latino group. My own estimate is informed by a number of other estimates (Kav La'Oved 2000, Kemp et al. 2000, Schnell 2001, Alexander 2003), as well as one additional source. During fieldwork in Ecuador I was able to access the official records of the Ecuadorian National Institute of Statistics and Census regarding the number of Ecuadorian tourists traveling to and from Israel between 1996 and 2001. It is reasonable to assume that the gap between these two figures largely indicates Ecuadorians who stayed in Israel as undocumented migrants. The more accurate data that I obtained in the case of Ecuadorians also helped me in calibrating other estimates about the number of Latinos in Israel.

It is important to note that the total number of Latinos, as well as the size of the different national groups, was in flux across the years. My estimate is for the year 2002, and as such it documents the situation just before the massive deportation of undocumented migrants in 2003 drastically changed the number and composition of Latinos in Israel. Migrants from Ecuador and Colombia constituted the two major Latino national groups. Colombians generally arrived in Israel before Ecuadorians, and they certainly constituted the largest group of Latinos throughout the 1990s. It was mainly from 1999 that the number of Ecuadorians significantly increased, gradually turning them into the largest Latino group in Israel. Chileans, although relatively not a large group, were considered (in their view and in that of most other Latinos) to be the pioneering Latino group in Israel.

Another important characteristic of Latino immigration to Israel is its gender composition. From my fieldwork experience, there appeared to be a balance between male and female migrants among Latinos. I found further validation for my observation in the official Ecuadorian data regarding the gender of tourists who left for Israel. Given the low recorded number of tourists returning from Israel to Ecuador, we can assume that most Ecuadorian tourists were undocumented migrants to-be. The gender composition of Ecuadorian tourists to Israel in 1999 stood at 56 percent female and 44 percent male; in 2000 almost similar rates, 55 percent female and 45 percent male, were recorded; and in 2001 54 percent were male and 46 percent female (Ecuadorian National Institute of Statistics and Census 2003). There is good reason to assume, as my observations also support, that the gender composition among Ecuadorians was indicative also of the composition among other Latino groups.

According to a comprehensive Israeli survey (Ministry of Labor 2001), in the year 1999 some 77 percent of all undocumented migrants were men, compared with 87 percent in 1998. The substantially more balanced gender composition among Latinos has primarily to do with the fact that most Latinos were employed as domestic workers. Israelis, at least initially, preferred to employ women for this type of job. Thus, female Latino migrants were often more likely to find a job in Israel than their male counterparts. This induced many Latino couples to emigrate together to Israel, or with a short interval between their separate migrations. The overall tendency of Latinos to settle in Israel could thus be seen as an outcome of, as well as a reason for, the more balanced gender composition among these migrants.

Finally, in a survey that was conducted among seventy-seven Latinos in Israel, the reported level of education was on average twelve years, and half of the respondents mentioned working in white-collar occupations in their countries of origin (Kemp et al. 2000). Women showed a lower level of education (11 years on average) in comparison to men (13 years), most likely because many of them were homemakers or held blue-collar jobs. The same survey also reported that 80 percent of the respondents were between twenty and forty years old, with an average age of thirty-four. From my own survey and observations, a similar picture emerges about the socio-economic characteristics of Latinos. Interesting, however, is the closer examination of the age distribution of Latino migrants to Israel. Since there are no official Israeli records on this, I again find it useful to analyze the data of the Ecuadorian National Institute of Statistics and Census regarding tourists traveling to Israel in the years 1999–2001. According to this data, 52 percent of all Ecuadorians traveling to Israel were aged between twenty and thirty-nine. In addition, 15 percent of all Ecuadorian tourists were children, and another 15 percent were people older than fifty. As I describe in detail in chapter 4, many Latinos who had initially left their children in their countries of origin later sought to reunite their families by bringing their children over to Israel. Grandparents commonly became the guardians of migrants' children. When Latinos moved toward an advanced settlement in Israel, they were reluctant to travel back to their countries of origin in order to fetch their children. Latinos feared that leaving Israel as undocumented migrants would prevent them from re-entering it (as was often the case). Instead, parents often paid "carriers" to take their children to Israel. Grandparents were regularly used as carriers, which largely explains the relatively high percentage of Ecuadorian tourists above the age of fifty. My observations during fieldwork suggest that while most children remained with their parents in Israel, most grandparents returned to their countries of origin after a few weeks.

Beyond and beneath the Jewish State: Responses from NGOs, the Media, and Public Opinion

While few undocumented migrants were deported, the rest increasingly settled down in Israel, establishing elaborate communities and networks. In 2000, a survey among undocumented migrants in south Tel Aviv discovered that 33 percent had already been living in Israel for more than five years, and 42 percent expressed intentions to remain in the country in the coming five years (Schnell 2001: 17). What Israel feared most also began to materialize; namely, undocumented migrants started their own social, religious, and political organizations. Israel's democratic characteristics distinguish it from countries such as Singapore and the Gulf Monarchies that have similar restrictive labor importation schemes and deportation policies (Castles and Miller 1998, Massey et al. 1998, Kemp 2004). Israel has historically adhered in its internal politics to democratic procedures, freedom of speech, and the establishment of a viable and independent civil society. Indeed, the settlement of undocumented migrants was largely facilitated by the work of independent civil actors (e.g., Israeli NGOs, the media, and academics) that made extensive use of Israel's democratic characteristics. Civil actors assisted non-Jewish migrants in demanding their rights under Israeli laws and international conventions to which Israel had committed itself.

Some existing NGOs, which had been actively protecting Palestinians' rights in Israel, diverted much of their efforts to protect the rights of non-Jewish migrants. New NGOs that opposed the Israeli immigration regime were also established throughout the 1990s especially for fighting the exploitation of non-Jewish migrants. On the most practical level, NGOs provided badly needed services to migrants. The Association for Civil Rights in Israel and Kav La'Oved (Hotline for Workers) offered free judicial advice and official representation in courts for migrants whose labor and civil rights were violated. Physicians for Human Rights opened a clinic in the heart of south Tel Aviv where doctors and nurses voluntarily gave medical treatment to migrants who lacked adequate (or any) medical insurance. Finally, Hotline for Migrant Workers in Detention visited arrested migrants in prison, verified the legality of their arrest, and helped them to pursue their rights.

NGOs regularly appealed to Israeli courts, challenging the overall legality of Israel's labor importation scheme. In their legal appeals, NGOs often included references to an international discourse of human rights (Cornelius, Martin, and Hollifield 1994, Jacobson 1996, Sassen 1999), and more particularly to some international conventions to which Israel is a signatory. These include, among others, the Migrant Worker Convention (1975) of the International Labor Organization (ILO) and the United Nations International Convention of the Rights of all Migrant Workers and Members of their Families (1990). Indeed, most improvements in the conditions of non-Jewish migrants in Israel were achieved due to the work of NGOs. For example, Hotline for Migrant Workers in Detention effected a formal change in the period in which arrested migrants must come before a judge, from fourteen to four days. Physicians for Human Rights pressured the government to assume responsibility for setting an official standard for health services that private insurance companies must include in their policies for guest workers (Filc and Davidovich 2005).[11] Finally, in 2000 a joint appeal by six different NGOs to the High Court of Justice eventually forced the government to amend the Foreign Workers Law in ways that defined the rights of guest workers with more precision and allowed them to find another employer in case they were arbitrarily and prematurely dismissed by their exclusive employer.[12]

While Israel officially refused to deal with the provision of non-Jewish migrants' needs, an in-depth study into the approach of officials in the welfare system revealed that "the state apparatus does not function in a homogeneous mode" (Rosenhek 2000: 22). Already in the early 1990s, before there was any policy toward undocumented migrants, some officials made decisions on the ground to assist non-Jewish migrants with health services. Nurses in family and health clinics (*Tipat Halav*) provided medical attention to pregnant women and their babies, while many hospital physicians broadly interpreted, in the case of undocumented migrants, the notion of "imperative medical care" under which they are obliged to treat patients regardless of their (lack of) insurance coverage. Social workers also attended to problems brought to them by families of undocumented migrants.

Notwithstanding a fissure in the official policy of the state, local municipalities needed to deal with the issue in a more concrete way. Municipalities could not ignore the needs of settled undocumented migrants, for humanitarian reasons as well as the fear that neglecting the issue could lead to social, sanitary, and other hazards for all residents. The situation was most acute in Tel Aviv, where the majority of settled undocumented migrants resided. Estimates put the number of non-Jewish migrants in Tel Aviv at around sixty thousand. Of this number, 80 percent were estimated to be undocumented (Alexander 2003: 121). This residential concentration turned south Tel Aviv into a migrant enclave during the mid-1990s. The municipality of Tel Aviv moved steadily from an informal provision of services for undocumented migrants toward a more formal policy for what it conceptualized as a permanent, rather than a transient, phenomenon (Alexander 2003). Over the years the municipality of Tel Aviv urged the national government to assume ultimate responsibility for undocumented migrants and draft national policy on the issue. Tel Aviv also demanded reimbursement for services it provided locally to undocumented migrants. The government's firm reluctance to cooperate with such demand eventually led the mayor of Tel Aviv, Ron Huldai, to declare the city's "independence" from the state. In 1999, Tel Aviv unilaterally established the Aid and Information Center for the Foreign Community, known in Hebrew by its acronym MESILA. In his speech at the inauguration of MESILA, the mayor clearly challenged the Israeli government and spotlighted its deficient policy, when he told a crowd of municipal workers, civil activists, and undocumented migrants, "Approximately 200,000 foreign workers reside in Israel, many of them without permits. This disturbing statistic requires a policy response at the national level . . . we can no longer stand aside. We can no longer turn a deaf ear to their cry . . . if we continue to turn a blind eye these problems will only increase" (quoted in Alexander 2003: 142). MESILA reacted regularly to requests for help by migrants, but it also proactively engaged in reaching out to migrants, finding out their needs, and initiating programs to improve their situation. For example, MESILA offered free professional courses for migrants who ran clandestine crèches (childcare centers) for children of undocumented migrants. MESILA was also interested, in sharp contrast to the national government, in the emergence of leadership among communities of undocumented migrants. It was believed that communication with, and assistance to, these communities could be more effectively channeled via representative leaders. Accordingly, MESILA organized community-leadership trainings for potential leaders from different migrant groups.

Given the accommodating initiatives taken by Israeli NGOs and MESILA, the settlement of undocumented migrants and the formation of communities with varying degrees of organizational structure were further facilitated (Schnell 1999, Kemp et al. 2000, Rosenhek 2000, Alexander 2003). It is important to reiterate here that what largely brought on this particular settlement of undocumented migrants was, paradoxically, their "illegality," which in terms of the restrictive Israeli migration regime meant a relative liberty to organize their communities and cooperate with supportive Israeli civil actors as well as ordinary Israelis.

We should finally consider Israeli general public opinion, as a larger context for legitimization in which the exclusion-inclusion battle of non-Jewish migrant workers was conducted. The Israeli media was by and large committed to exposing the problematic position of non-Jewish migrants, feeding the public debate with graphic reports as well as in-depth articles. Several documentaries and investigative programs revealing the exploitative situation of migrants were broadcast on national and commercial channels. Some Israeli journalists also actively assisted non-Jewish migrants with political organization and later even mediated between them and Israeli officials, in order to find ways to regularize their situation (Kemp et al. 2000: 106). Notwithstanding occasional articles that reinforced stereotypes about groups of migrants (e.g., Thai migrants' alleged habit of hunting and eating dogs), the media stressed from time to time the positive sides of non-Jewish migration to Israel. For example, beginning in 1996 the most popular local newspaper in Tel Aviv featured a permanent column called "The New Tel Aviv-ians" (*Ha'Tel Avivim Ha'chadashim*). As its title implies, the column sought to promote the incorporation of non-Jewish migrants, elaborating on their social and cultural activities and their enrichment of the city life. Other attempts to communicate more broadly and humanely the experiences of non-Jewish migrants included some theater plays portraying migrants' lives and a commercial film about the life of a Christian undocumented migrant from Africa, *James' Journey to Jerusalem*, which was screened in cinemas across Israel.

Public opinion in Israel was also initially considerably supportive and tolerant of non-Jewish migrant workers. In 1995, a survey among Jewish Israelis found a majority (79 percent) expressed widespread appreciation for guest workers for saving the Israeli market from its dependence on Palestinians (Bar-Tzuri 1996). Moreover, 75 percent thought that "foreign workers" were unfairly exploited, and 87 percent believed that suitable living and working conditions had to be secured for them. In addition, 55 percent were willing to live in the same neighborhood together with "foreign workers." These findings arguably reflect open-mindedness and tolerance of non-Jewish migrants among Israelis.[13] High numbers of intermarriages between Jewish Israelis and non-Jewish migrants are also indicative of this kind of openness. In 1996, only three years after guest workers and undocumented migrants first reached Israel, an estimated four thousand such marriages took place (Shuval and Leshem 1998).[14]

This openness of many Jewish Israelis can be attributed to the fact that in the case of guest workers there was no concrete animosity that could justify indifference to their systematic exploitation. In the case of Palestinians there was a degree of correspondence between their ill-treatment and a popular negative image. Some Jewish Israelis clearly held prejudiced views about foreign workers, but tellingly, those who came in contact with non-Jewish migrants held more positive views of them. Accordingly, the residents of Tel Aviv, where most undocumented migrants resided, displayed the most tolerant attitude toward non-Jewish workers (Nathanson and Bar-Tzuri 1999). What certainly also prompted these supportive attitudes was the practical fact that many Israelis directly or indirectly benefited from the work of non-Jewish migrants. The following remark, which a shopkeeper in south Tel Aviv made to me, reflects this general practical attitude:

> What does it matter if you are Jewish or not? There is no difference, trust
> me; they [Jewish Israelis] left and these guys [non-Jewish migrants] came,
> but it is just the same. You know what? It is even better; Israelis make a lot
> of fuss in the shop; these guys, they buy what they need without all the
> hassle.

The pervasive and normative nature of the immigration experience in Israel has also induced this tolerant attitude toward non-Jewish migrants. Israel has seen the ongoing immigration of Jews from countries worldwide. In 1995, 39 percent of all Jews in Israel were foreign-born (Shuval and Leshem 1998: 3). Being an immigrant, or growing up in an immigrant family, is therefore widespread in Israel. Jews from different origins have regularly brought to Israel their distinctive rituals, customs, culinary traditions, and so on. Accordingly, it is not odd for Israelis to interact with migrants who, for example, speak Hebrew with an accent or have not yet completely assimilated to Israeli society and "culture." Yet for many decades, the state of Israel strictly adhered to the "melting pot" assimilationist model. This was seen as a crucial part of Israel's nation-building process; Jewish immigrants were expected (or it was even demanded of them) to discard their cultural distinctiveness and wholly embrace the ethnic identity of the "new Israeli" (see Eisenstadt 1967). Although Israel extensively invested in facilitating and garnering national support for the cultural assimilation of Jewish immigrants into Israeli society, this process has always been lengthy and incomplete. Moreover, as many critics in Israel point out, the Israeli "melting pot" was largely a Eurocentric project of the Ashkenazim elite that aimed to define their own characteristics as the dominant ones in Israel and to subjugate Sephardim Jews under this hegemonic national identity (e.g., Shohat 1992, Shenhav, Hever, and Mutzafi 2002).

Notwithstanding its critique, the limitations of the Israeli assimilationist project were visibly demonstrated in the immigration and integration of black Ethiopian Jews in the 1980s. The Jewishness of Ethiopian migrants was widely questioned by Israeli officials, and they faced widespread institutional discrimination. The systematic discrimination of Ethiopian Jews on a cultural (racial) basis bitterly testified to the largely imaginary amalgamating capacity that Israel has denoted to its ethno-religious definition for belonging in the Jewish state (Ojanuga 1993, Kaplan and Salamon 2004). Yet it was the arrival of close to one million immigrants from the FSU in the 1990s that most evidently challenged the official Israeli assimilationist model (Lissak and Leshem 1995). Given their proportion in the total Jewish Israeli population (close to 25 percent), immigrants from the FSU have constituted a powerful political and cultural group that overtly resisted acculturation in Israel (Siegel 1996, Ben-Rafael 2007). This trend was reinforced by the fact that, as DellaPergola (1997) has documented, tens of thousands of those who entered Israel from the FSU were actually not Jewish. An estimated 30 percent consisted of non-Jewish spouses and children who were officially recognized by the state of Israel and received legal status as residents (see Al-Haj and Leshem 2000). Consequently, many non-Jewish and Jewish immigrants from the FSU have chosen to speak Russian and preserve their "culture" in Israel.

Notwithstanding such cracks in the seemingly unified Jewish Israeli society, an analysis of Israeli public opinion cannot disregard the underlying national sentiment of most Jewish Israelis, who see themselves not only as members of the state of Israel but also crucially as belonging to a Jewish nation. This sentiment is overwhelmingly prevalent among many Jewish Israelis, including most secular ones (Cohen 1995). It was also this sentiment that the Israeli government used when it sought to legitimize its massive deportation campaign. The government has regularly alleged that non-Jewish migrants are corrupting the Jewish character of the state, as well as increasing unemployment among Israelis. It is fair to assume that many Israelis were influenced purely by the state's rhetoric, while others, especially unskilled Israeli workers, might have actually suffered from competition with an increasing number of non-Jewish migrants. Indeed, it was found that disadvantaged populations in Israel (those with low income, those with low education, the unemployed, and Israeli Arabs) were most likely to endorse economic discrimination against guest workers (Semyonov, Raijman, and Yom-Tov 2002). Disadvantaged Israelis clearly perceived guest workers as a threat to their economic interests. However, the research further discovered that Jewish Israelis expressed significantly more hostility toward guest workers than did Arab Israelis, although the latter were more prone to suffer from competition with guest workers. It was thus concluded that the attitudes of Jews are also motivated by

> [s]entiments which are entirely exogenous to labor market competition . . . [and are largely explained by] the ideological commitment (among Jews) to preserve the Jewish character of the State . . . non-national workers are evaluated not only as economic competitors, but also as a threat to the very essence of the social and political order of the state and to its national (Jewish) identity. (Ibid.: 428)

On the other hand, NGOs also used as a moral resource in their public campaigns the particular diasporic Jewish history of ethnic discrimination and religious prosecution, in order to highlight the ethical inadequacy of Israel's treatment of non-Jewish migrants. The Hotline for Migrant Workers adopted as its motto the following biblical verse: "Thou shall neither vex a stranger, nor oppress him: for you were strangers in the land of Egypt" (Exodus 22:21). This verse appeared on every official communication of the NGO. In reaction to Israeli deportation campaigns, some undocumented African migrant leaders also stressed the Jewish history in an attempt to appeal to the sensitivity of Jewish Israelis with respect to religiously based expulsions (see Kemp et al. 2000: 109, and Sabar 2004).

In 2002, when Israel moved toward the massive deportation of undocumented migrants, the rhetoric that was used by some politicians to frame the debate was radicalized even further. For example, speaking at Bar-Ilan University, Eli Yishai, the chairman of Shas and interior minister, told a crowd of students, "Israel is rapidly losing its Jewish demographic majority in the country, as it turns into an immigration country." He added that the number of non-Jewish workers in Israel had steadily increased, and that according to the data of his ministry tens of thousands of non-Jewish migrants had become permanent residents in Israel by marrying Israeli citizens (*Yediot Aharonot* 13.06.2002). It should be noted here that such statements by religious parties were unacceptable for many in Israel and were vigorously denounced by some politicians, journalists, and academics. For example, Natan Sharansky, the deputy prime minister at the time, avowed that the statement by Eli Yishai "emits a bad smell of racism"; Yossi Sarid, the opposition chairman in Parliament, said in response that "Shas is the number one enemy of the Jewish State"; while another MP, Roman Bronfman, suggested that "Yishai must face trial on the ground of not conforming to the norms and laws as the Interior Minister" (*Maariv* 25.11.2002).

Israeli public opinion, however, was proven to be highly responsive to the state's nationalistic rhetoric, which portrayed non-Jewish migrants as an alleged religious and demographic threat to the Jewish state. Deterioration in support for non-Jewish workers was ongoing among the general Israeli public (Nathanson and Bar-Tzuri 1999) as well as among the residents of south Tel Aviv (Schnell 1999). I find the following reasoning, given to me by a middle-class Israeli in Tel Aviv, representative of the views of many Jewish Israelis with respect to the position of non-Jewish migrant workers in Israel:

> I have nothing against them as people. In fact, I fully understand that they
> want to come here to achieve a better life for them and their families. I even
> have respect for them. And they are good people. But they knew from the
> first day that this is a Jewish state and therefore they can never really
> become citizens here or something like that. So when Israel decides that

they have to leave, they have to respect it. And if they don't, you can't blame
Israel for picking them up and sending them back. They knew that these
were the rules of the game here.

Israeli public opinion about non-Jewish migrants can therefore be characterized by a
distinctive duality. On the one hand, most Jewish Israelis recognized as unfair the
exploitation of non-Jewish migrants, and supported better conditions for them. On the
other hand, the vast majority of Jewish Israelis firmly endorsed the need to maintain
Israel's Jewish character. In a much deeper sense, therefore, most Israelis conceived of
the settlement of non-Jewish migrants in Israel as a contradiction in terms.

Chapter Three

Destiny and Destination

LATINOS DECIDING TO LEAVE FOR ISRAEL

If you had told me a year ago that I would be
living and working in Israel, I would have said you
were a lunatic, I didn't even know where Israel
was on the map.

—*Patricio, 36, undocumented Ecuadorian migrant
in Tel Aviv*

Undocumented migrants from Latin America face impediments beyond Israel's categorical rejection of non-Jewish migrants, notoriously tense military situation, and threat of acts of terror. Israel has no historic connections (economic or cultural) with Latin American countries of the kind that might stimulate large-scale migration, and the geographic distance between them is great. Embarking on such a transatlantic trip not only is intimidating for many undocumented migrants, but is also a big commitment, since return is uncertain. Nevertheless, beginning in the early 1990s, the haphazard immigration of a few Latinos to Israel subsequently generated a significant chain-migration that induced the remarkable spread and intensification of transnational social networks within a span of less than five years. How did Israel become a popular migration destination for thousands of people in Latin America?

Latinos who decided to go to Israel mostly came from a low-middle-class background. In their country of origin, they often resided on the outskirts of the capital city, or other big cities and towns, where they usually occupied menial or semi-professional jobs in the private sector and/or the informal economy. Many of them came from families that, a generation ago, had migrated internally from the rural area of the country to an urban setting. Indicative of this latter characteristic is the fact that many Latinos in Israel came from a major urban center in an agricultural region of their country, for example: in Ecuador, from Cuenca and Loja; in Colombia, from Cali and other towns in the Valle del Cauca; in Bolivia, from Cochabamba.

From the migration stories of Latinos it became clear that not all of them could easily be categorized as economic migrants. Some Latinos were driven by a religious fervor regarding the Holy Land, while others apparently decided to emigrate in a rather spontaneous and intuitive way, basing their decision on little knowledge about Israel. While the immigration of most Latinos to Israel was facilitated by transnational social networks, some Latinos conducted their migration in an individual and isolated fashion with no solid ties to such networks. The significant number of "atypical" migrants I encountered in Israel made it empirically inadequate merely to cast them aside as exceptions. I therefore present an analytical framework in which different types of migratory motivations can be accounted for. Rather than identifying different "push-pull" factors, I construct a typology of the motivational structures and the decision-making processes that stimulated Latinos to choose Israel as their destination. I distinguish three prominent processes: economic, religious, and spontaneous. After laying out this typology I introduce the concept of a "migratory disposition" in order to account for people's immersion in an emigration environment and the ways in which they make sense of their position in it. This approach is meant to advance our understanding of potential migrants' decision-making processes, and more particularly to elucidate cases in which migrants' decisions to emigrate appear spontaneous, irrational, and isolated. A better understanding of Latinos' motivational structures will also lead to a more nuanced understanding of the particular life strategies that they adopted in Israel.

The Potency of Migration: The Emergence of Transnational Social Networks around Rudimentary Connections

According to world-system theory (Portes and Walton 1981, Castells 1989, Sassen 1988, 1991), the establishment of transnational migration networks largely follows historical (often colonial) ties, as for example between England and India, Portugal and Brazil, and France and Algeria. Given such ties, migration is said to be facilitated by the fact that citizens in former colonies often speak the language of the colonizer state and are aware of, and intrigued by, employment opportunities in these richer countries. Yet, there are no substantial connections between Israel and Latin American countries of the kind that world-system theory points to.

More recently, global paths of capitalist penetration (multinationals, outsourcing, etc.) are taken to be essential in the enhancement of cultural ties and the formation of bi-directional channels for the transfer of capital and commodities, which subsequently also give way for the migration of labor. However, as Bartram (1998) indicates, Israel had very few economic ties with most of the countries in Latin America from which undocumented migrants originated. Moreover, even when Israel officially began to import guest workers, it never recruited laborers from Latin America.

Notwithstanding the lack of historical or extensive economic ties between Israel and countries in Latin America, in the early 1990s transnational social networks were quickly established and rapidly consolidated by Latino migrants who reached Israel. Transnational social networks were initially established in a somewhat informal fashion. Given their recent emergence, I was able to trace their origins and identify five major nodes around which these networks emerged.

First, in Israel there are hundreds of kibbutzim—agricultural communities that have been ideologically established under communist ideas by European Jews. Under the slogan "workers of the world unite," kibbutzim have regularly received non-Jewish voluntary workers from all over the world into their communities. "Volunteers," as they are commonly called, receive a special visa for a period of six months to stay and work in kibbutzim across Israel. In the last two decades, the economic incentive behind "volunteering" has become clearer, as kibbutzim have recruited workers willing to perform hard manual jobs for practically no payment ("volunteers" receive free accommodation, food, and some minor pocket money for recreation). Some of the first undocumented Latinos in Israel started off as "volunteers." After completing their term in kibbutzim, they decided to overstay their visas and look for undocumented employment opportunities.

Second, in most countries in Latin America there is a Jewish community, and in some countries also a more recent community of Israeli migrants. Affluent Jewish and Israeli families often employ domestic workers and nannies from among the non-Jewish native population. When some of these families decided to immigrate (or return) to Israel, they sometimes brought with them their loyal domestic workers. This was often done in an informal way; that is, families did not obtain official work permits from the Israeli authorities but simply asked their workers to embark as tourists on the same flight to Israel. I met several female migrants who came to Israel in such a way from Chile, Bolivia, Venezuela, and the Dominican Republic. The nature of their job as live-in domestic workers usually protected these migrants from police inspections.

Third, some Jews and Israelis in Latin America (as elsewhere around the world) married non-Jewish partners from the local community where they lived, worked, or traveled. Some of these mixed couples then chose to live in Israel. During my fieldwork I met two non-Jewish spouses, one from Argentina and the other from Ecuador, who took advantage of their unique legal and integrated position in Israel to establish an informal "recruitment agency." They advertised the employment opportunities in Israel among non-Jewish people in their countries of origin. Advertisement was done either by these spouses on visits back home or by collaborators (often relatives) in countries of origin. These spouses offered to supply potential undocumented migrants with the know-how in Israel for a sum of US$2,000–4,000. One of these entrepreneurial migration brokers even deceitfully promised some migrants she would get them legal work visas for an extra fee.

Fourth, Israel has been selling military equipment, ammunition, and technology to various countries in Latin America as elsewhere in the world. Israel also occasionally trains foreign military units. For example, when Israel sold a fleet of combat jets to Ecuador, it also trained Ecuadorian pilots for a few months in Israel. Some wives of these pilots accompanied their husbands during their stay in Israel. As one of them told me, she and some of her friends began to work informally as hourly-paid domestic cleaners in a city close to the military base where they were stationed.

Finally, some small-scale Israeli private companies have targeted the markets of countries in Latin America; for example, "Israriego" supplies agricultural products, such as irrigation systems, and "Solarium" is active in the installation of solar heating systems across the north of Chile and in Bolivia. Although the presence of Israeli companies in Latin America was very limited, I met three Latinos who had worked for an Israeli company in their country of origin, and after learning about opportunities in Israel decided to go there.

The successful haphazard immigration of a few Latinos generated a significant chain-migration that induced the remarkable spread and intensification of transnational social networks within a span of less than five years. Pioneering Latinos often called on their families, relatives, and friends to join them in Israel. Pioneers quickly disseminated information about opportunities in Israel, and often extended a helping hand to assist others financially with their migration trip. I met a few pioneering Latinos who were each responsible for the subsequent migration of around fifty more undocumented migrants from the pioneer's place of origin. Migrants who reached Israel through these initial networks most likely disseminated further information about Israel among more people back home.

The rapid establishment of extensive transnational social networks between Israel and countries in Latin America, around the above-mentioned rudimentary connections, is indicative of the general "migratory potency" of people in Latin America.[1] Yet not all people who were located within these evolving transnational networks decided to emigrate to Israel. On the other hand, some people who had no concrete ties to such networks and simply heard tempting stories individually decided to embark on a migration trip to Israel. In the next section I seek to anchor an abstract "migratory potency" in the actual ways in which Latinos were swayed to emigrate to Israel. I thus depict ethnographically three major types of decision-making processes that influenced the considerations of migrants.

A Typology of Migrants' Decision-Making Processes

In the last decade Latin America experienced an "exodus" of emigrants, as the *Economist* (23.02.2002) called it in an article that reported some six hundred thousand people left Colombia and some five hundred thousand people left Ecuador in less than three years. To put these figures in perspective, in the case of Ecuador, for example, the number of emigrants amounted to some 10 percent of the economically active population in that country (Ecuadorian National Institute of Statistics and Census 2003). As immigration increases and accelerates, it also often diversifies. Jokisch and Pribilsky (2002) have documented the new ways in which Ecuadorian migration diversified over the last years. They accounted for the changing ethnic and gender composition of migrants, as well as for the propagation of new migration destinations that have been massively targeted by Ecuadorians since 1998 (such as France, Italy, and the Netherlands). As I argue, what has also significantly diversified is the decision-making processes that induced a growing number of people to emigrate (see Kalir 2005).

In the following typology of migrants' decision-making processes, each type highlights a dominant motivation that led Latinos to choose Israel as their destination, and a distinctive way of operationalizing the migration trip. This typology is analytically useful for differentiating between migrants. It consists of ideal-types; that is, it generalizes and compartmentalizes more complex lived forms. These ideal-types, thus, do not represent migrants but rather dynamics that influenced migrants and directed them toward the adoption of a certain migratory strategy. In practice, some migrants were influenced by a combination of overlapping dynamics. Stressing that I distinguish decision-making processes rather than types of migrants, from now on I employ the shorthand of "economic," "religious," and "spontaneous" migrants.

Economic Migrants

Most Latinos in Israel were driven by economic incentive, looking to improve their lives via immigration. Latinos could easily triple their monthly income by working in Israel. Moreover, immigration to Israel was not so costly in comparison with some other migration destinations in North America and Europe. The total amount one needed for migrating to Israel stood at approximately US$4,000. The Israeli authorities regularly required tourists from Third World countries to be in possession of a return ticket to their country of origin, hotel reservations for their visiting period, and financial proof of their ability to sustain their stay in Israel. Either joining an organized tour or independently booking a roundtrip flight and a hotel in Israel cost approximately US$2,000 for people in Latin America. To demonstrate financial solvency tourists needed to have another US$2,000 with them in cash; this extra amount was known among Latinos as *para la bolsa* ("for the wallet"), and it constituted an integral part of the preparation for an undocumented migration. Although Israeli officials did not always carefully inspect all entering tourists, most undocumented migrants to-be preferred to take no risk and fulfilled all requirements in order to enhance their chance to enter Israel.

Latino migrants (and non-migrants for that matter) often commented that the difficult economic situations of their home countries drove many people to desperation. I found a prevailing consensus among Latinos in Israel about the discouraging and worrying long-term prospects that their countries offered to those who stayed behind. Indeed, there can be little doubt that economic conditions in Latin America have served in the last decades as classical "push factors" (Larrea 1998, Kyle 2000, Jokisch and Pribilsky 2002). Latin American countries have suffered greatly from what is notoriously known as the "lost decade" of the 1980s. It is largely against this backdrop that we should view the massive emigration from Latin America in recent years.

Undocumented migration in particular has expanded greatly since the 1980s (Cornelius, Martin, and Hollifield 1994, Harris 1996). According to neo-classical economic theory in migration studies, undocumented migrants take into account the risk that their migration entails and the relevant losses that a potential deportation would cause them. If they positively evaluate their chances, they are likely to emigrate (Borjas 1990). The risk of deportation in the 1990s was not high (around 2 percent a year; see table 2.1). In addition, unlike in their own countries, Latinos in Israel enjoyed full employment. I rarely came across unemployed Latinos; an ample demand for unskilled labor ensured that Latinos could always find jobs and enjoy a steady monthly income. This is rather a distinctive characteristic of the Israeli context; in the Netherlands, for example, a survey among undocumented migrants found that one third of them were without employment (Van der Leun 2003). As one economic migrant from Colombia squarely put it: "Israel has a very good reputation as a migration destination among Latinos."

Nevertheless, from their remarks on their background and the economic incentives that induced them to emigrate, it was clear that most Latinos in Israel did not suffer acute economic circumstances in their countries of origin. They mainly came from a low-middle- and even middle-class background, and they were not poor according to either any official measurement or their own perception of their situation. These observations are in line with other research on international migration, which shows that it is hardly ever the very poor who make it abroad (Massey and Espinosa 1997). As I discovered in Israel, from an economic perspective Latinos were mostly driven by a strong sense of "relative deprivation," that is, people's urge to better their situation not only in absolute terms but, and sometimes even mainly, in relative terms compared to their significant reference group of relatives, neighbors, or community members. The notion of "relative deprivation" was first developed by the "new economics of migration" approach. This more sober attempt to integrate social aspects into economic accounts has marked a substantial advance from a time when a reduction of homo sociologicus to homo economicus prevailed, with a reigning model of rational individuals striving to maximize returns for labor (Sjaastad 1962, Todaro 1969, 1976, Bowles 1970).

Undeniably, improvements in the material conditions of migrants and their families were shown to have a noteworthy influence on the desires of other households with regard to migration (Massey et al.1993). It seemed that the material achievements of emigrants set a benchmark against which most non-migrants measured their own situation. From this perspective, the impetus for many potential migrants was not strictly harsh economic conditions, but rather their desire to achieve the kind of wealth other migrants had attained.

Consider the following migration story of Jason, who immigrated to Israel from Ecuador when he was twenty-five years old. In Ecuador, Jason made his living by holding two jobs; during the daytime he was a salesman in a shop for musical instruments, and at night he worked as a technician at a local radio station. He earned a reasonable salary in Ecuadorian terms (US$250/month in 1997), which allowed him to respectably support his wife and two sons. Jason made his decision to migrate, after one of his meetings with his *tio*. The term *tio*, literally translated as uncle, is more generally used in Latin America to refer to a relative or an acquaintance. Jason's *tio* was a rather distant relative, whose migration history turned him into Jason's favorite self-assumed uncle. Jason's *tio* had been in Israel twice (he was deported once). He earned sufficient capital to buy a brand new pickup truck and build a house. Here is how Jason recalled an ordinary but crucial visit to his *tio*:

> I remember this one day that I went to visit my *tio* in his new house. That night on my way back home, I just felt it was enough. I thought I couldn't go on busting my ass just to keep my family at a very basic level. I wanted to be able to buy my children nice clothes, I wanted to have a car and I wanted to have my own house! Is that too much? Tell me!

Jason's last sentence was said in a rhetorically furious tone, and he clearly became agitated as his pre-migration sensations were evoked. I once directly asked Jason if his situation in Ecuador was dire. Jason then plainly explained it to me:

> In Ecuador I was working two jobs; I wasn't earning bad but it didn't buy me a good life. You always live from hand to mouth; you just fill holes all the time and you can never save money. At a certain point the option to migrate looks much better than anything you would ever succeed to achieve in Ecuador.

As it became clear from my conversations with Jason, it was not only the migration of his *tio* that set an example for him. Although nobody from his immediate household had ever migrated, Jason was living in an environment of migrating people. The ex-manager in the radio station where Jason used to work had migrated to the United States. On his visits to Ecuador, the ex-manager often invited Jason for a night out, for which he normally picked him up in his fancy car. Furthermore, many of Jason's former classmates also left Ecuador, mainly to the United States, but some also to Europe. This is how Jason made sense of the situation evolving around him, as he once told me over a cold beer on a hot summer night in Tel Aviv:

> The basic idea to migrate I simply got from the fact that many people I knew had done so. We used to be a big group of friends, doing everything together, you know, hanging out, playing, smoking, getting chicks. Slowly, more and more people migrated, and then you start hearing all these stories about their successes. Later on you see them coming back for a visit, and they buy a new car and even a house. You then understand that these are not just stories; you don't just hear about it but you also see it with your own eyes.

Jason pointed two fingers at his eyes and with an oppressed anger continued:

> You know what they do? They buy the newest car and then when they go back they just leave it standing in the garage of their parents so it will wait there for them till their next visit.

Jason, although by now a successful migrant himself, was clearly annoyed by these material reminders of the wealth made by migrants from Ecuador.

Economic migrants commonly planned and coordinated their migration to Israel well in advance. They made essential use of both their household resources and their social location in a transnational network stretching between their country and Israel. Economic migrants deliberated with members in their household about who should emigrate. Often one parent went abroad, leaving the other to take care of the children. However, it was also common for the two parents to emigrate together, or with a short interval between their separate migration trips. In these cases, they usually left the children under the care of their grandparents, aunts, or uncles.

Religious Migrants

Latino migrants to Israel were Christians. While some tended to merely consider Christianity as part of their cultural upbringing, others were deeply religious. In a survey conducted among seventy-seven Latinos in Israel, 20 percent mentioned "religious reasons" for choosing Israel as their destination (Kemp et al. 2000). In my own survey among sixty-five Latinos an even higher percentage (32 percent) acknowledged that their idea to immigrate to Israel was, at least partly, religiously motivated. Indeed, some of the holiest sites for Christianity are located within Israel: Jesus' birthplace in Bethlehem; the Church of the Divinity in Jerusalem; the Jordan River where Jesus was baptized; and the Via Dolorosa where it is believed that Jesus marched with the cross on his back before his crucifixion. These sites are of the highest importance for many Christians worldwide, who yearn to visit them at least once in their lifetime.

Given that religion was in a broad sense on the minds of many Latinos, I more specifically distinguish here as religious migrants only those Latinos who strictly met the following two requirements. First, they had been members in religious communities in their country of origin, and conceived their religious motivation to be a central one. Second, they operated their migration to Israel via their connection to a transnational religious network. This definition thus excludes, for example, many Latinos who were basically economic migrants but who mentioned the religious attraction of the Holy Land as an encouraging extra incentive. It also leaves out some Latinos who had immigrated to Israel not because of a religious motivation, but subsequently appreciated and mentioned the religious value of Israel as a reason for being there.

As it were, most Latinos who met the definition of religious migrants were members of evangelical churches. Latin America, which has often been called the Catholic continent, has experienced since the 1970s a significant expansion of evangelicalism.[2] A steady increase in the number of people across Latin America who turned to evangelicalism has been well documented by various scholars, whose book titles have declared *The Explosion of Protestantism in Latin America* (Martin 1990) or rhetorically posed the question, *Is Latin America Turning Protestant?* (Stoll 1990). Bastian (1993) also reviews what he calls "the Metamorphosis of Latin American Protestant Groups" and a move away from a "Catholic monopoly." Evangelical churches mainly appeal to the majority of low-middle-class people in Latin America. These churches offer their members not only spirituality and a strong sense of community, but also some practical assistance in, for example, finding jobs and providing education to their children.

The importance of Israel and the Jewish people in the teachings of certain evangelical churches is prominent; salvation would come, so it is believed, through the Jewish people, and it is, accordingly, the duty of Christians to support Israel and Jews. Furthermore, Israel is seen as a special place where the work of God is most evidently being performed. Thus for evangelicals to be in Israel is a virtue in itself, given the presence of God. In chapter 6 I describe the expansion of evangelical churches among Latinos in Israel. It suffices here to mention that ten evangelical churches were established in south Tel Aviv alone in the first five years after undocumented immigration from Latin America began. With their establishment, evangelical churches served, among other things, as crucial nodes in transnational religious networks, which connected different countries in Latin America with Israel. These religious networks induced and facilitated the immigration and initial settlement of hundreds of religious migrants.

For decades many travel agencies in Latin America have specialized in organizing tours for pilgrimages to Israel; although these tours were commercially offered to a wider public, a special focus has always been given to Christian believers. Recognizing the increasing participation of evangelicals in these tours, many travel agencies began to particularly target pastors in evangelical churches in the hope that they would bring in clients. Some agencies offered to let pastors join tours for free as spiritual guides (in addition to the regular tour guides that agencies provided), or paid them a commission (of around US$100) for every customer they brought in. Pastors then had an economic interest in offering these tours to their members.

In the mid-1990s these organized pilgrimages became increasingly popular among a growing number of undocumented migrants as a means for safely entering Israel under the trustable guise of religious tourists. Accordingly, a thriving industry of travel agencies emerged all across Latin America. These agencies organized pilgrimages to Israel, and promoted them as a means for (undocumented) migration to a rich country. These (migration) tours, which cost around US$2,000, became very popular, not least because they were relatively cheaper than a payment to human traffickers for getting to other migration destinations (mainly the United States).

Many members of evangelical churches, who might have already considered migration on other grounds, were also tempted by the opportunity to emigrate to Israel together with their "sisters" and "brothers in faith." Recognizing the desire of many members to remain there as undocumented migrants, some pastors straightforwardly informed their followers about evangelical churches in Israel that would be happy to assist them with their settlement there. Pastors knew that a failure to satisfy their followers' migratory desires could cause some of them to defect to churches where migration to Israel was a dominant topic. Indeed, some pastors who had successfully organized a few tours to Israel gained a reputation beyond their own congregation, and members from several other churches in the same area sought to join their tours.

Pastors who were involved in religious transnational networks to Israel increasingly emphasized in their sermons the religious significance of the Jewish people, and enthusiastically shared with their followers spiritual impressions from Israel. Here is how Rodrigo, a 54-year-old Ecuadorian pastor who had been to Israel, preached to a crowd of around four hundred followers in his church in Guayaquil:

> The work of God is evident in every corner in the whole universe, but I am telling
> you, brothers and sisters, if you want to feel the work of God, if you want to indulge

in His presence, then you should head to Israel. There, in the midst of the Jewish people, you will experience the glory of God in its fullness. It is a beautiful and spiritual country, which finds itself at the moment in a difficult situation. But it is even under these difficulties and conflicts that one can so clearly see that God is with the Jewish people, and so should we be too. Glory to God! Amen!

Spiritually encouraged by pastors and assisted in practical needs by religious transnational networks, evangelicals commonly felt confident about migration to Israel. Some evangelicals even came to see it as their destiny. Revealingly, they talked about their migration in the passive form, stressing that they were brought to Israel by God. The way Jehovana, a 27-year-old devoted evangelical from Bolivia, narrated her migration story to me is representative in this sense:

> One day the pastor told us we should talk and pray to God at night, asking him directions with regards to our future. Then at church the pastor gave us a piece of paper and asked us to draw whatever vision we had. I saw a strong yellow light, mountains, and a very strange shape of land. I therefore drew a kind of map with mountains in it. What I drew looked very strange to me until the pastor saw it and told me it was the map of Israel. I was astonished. . . . I never before in my life saw the map of Israel . . . it then became clear to me that my destiny was in Israel but I had no concrete idea about it. After a few months I decided to move to Cochabamba and open my own evangelical library there, but it didn't work out as well as I thought. By coincidence, the congregation I assisted in Cochabamba was organizing a tour to Israel and the holy sites. They asked me to join them, but I hadn't enough money to pay it. I went to two preparatory meetings of the group that intended to go on the tour, thinking I might somehow get the money at the end. But two weeks before the departure when the travel agency had to order tickets for us I told them I couldn't make it. Then two incredible things happened. The lady from the agency called me up and offered that I would only pay half the price if I was willing to serve as a co-guide on the tour. She knew that I had a lot of knowledge about the Bible. But even with the discount I was still short of the needed amount. Then my brother came over to pay me back US$300, which he had borrowed from me some months before to buy a car for his work. All of a sudden I had all the money. It was clear to me that this was the work of God, and that he was directing my life towards Israel. In couple of weeks I left for Israel with the group, and since then I am here. It is amazing, it is the best thing that ever happened to me.

Jehovana, like almost everyone else on her tour, stayed in Israel. At the end of the tour the group was brought to an evangelical church in Tel Aviv. A special service was performed in their honor, followed by an informal social gathering. It was then, after talking with the local pastor and other Latinos who were already established in Israel, that most members in the tour definitively decided whether they wanted to remain or return back home. Concrete arrangements for initial accommodation were habitually offered by members in Israeli evangelical churches to those who decided to stay.

Spontaneous Migrants

Spontaneous migrants regularly featured a rather unusual combination of three characteristics. First, they were not embedded in any significant way in a transnational social network that connected them to Israel; that is, they knew practically no one in Israel, or at best had a very weak connection there. This feature seems even more peculiar when considering that Israel's conflictive and dangerous security situation is known worldwide. One thus expects potential migrants to choose Israel as their destination only after carefully considering their chances and relying on an established network that could guarantee at least some economic safety and social familiarity. Nevertheless, it appears that evidence for this pattern of "networkless" migration is found among Latino migrants to other destinations as well; for instance, Lincango (2001) observed that "[h]aving family established in Spain with knowledge about migrating, housing, and job opportunities facilitates emigration, but has not been a prerequisite. Some emigrants have departed without family or friends waiting for them; others have gone with only loose connections in Spain" (quoted in Jokisch and Pribilsky 2002: 84).

The second feature characteristic of spontaneous migrants, which derives largely from the first one, is that they based their decision to emigrate upon very little information about Israel. Spontaneous migrants commonly described their decision as intuitive. As one migrant brashly put it: "To tell you the truth, I didn't know anything about Israel before I came here; it was simply that my friend told me about the opportunities here and I thought, 'well, why not?'" When one listens to spontaneous migrants, it seems that they made their way to Israel almost arbitrarily. Their decision to emigrate to Israel was triggered by stories that they heard about the destination from an acquaintance or distant relative who had been there. These stories apparently ignited their imagination regarding their possible migratory future, and heightened their actual ambition to undertake this option.

> I always wanted to go to the U.S. but it cost a lot of money to get there. . . . I also thought of migrating to Spain; it costs much less and you don't need a visa to enter [this was in 1997]. But I heard that in Spain there were too

many Ecuadorians already, so there was a lot of competition and you couldn't earn so much money. Then someone told me about the great opportunities in Israel; he said that it was easy to enter, that you could earn a lot of money, and that it costs relatively little to get there. I then felt that this was for me and decided to come here. (Jeffrey, 29-year-old undocumented Ecuadorian migrant in Israel)

The largely unpremeditated decision of spontaneous migrants seems to be characterized by a sense of hastiness and thrill. Although some of them clearly pondered migration for a very long time, they often had no concrete plan to realize their ambition prior to their sudden decision to leave. Notably, most spontaneous migrants were young, either in their late teens or early twenties, although a few were in their thirties. Some even expressed astonishment about their own actions: "If you had told me a year ago that I would be living and working in Israel, I would have said you were a lunatic; I didn't even know where Israel was on the map" (Patricio, 36, Ecuador).

Given their location outside transnational social networks, spontaneous migrants operationalized their migration trip individually; that is, they received no financial help nor facilitating know-how from established migrants in Israel. Moreover, no one was there in Israel to receive and help them with the initial arrangements and adaptation process. Spontaneous migrants thus borrowed money from their families or from loan sharks in order to pay for their migration trip. They regularly joined organized tours to Israel, often religious ones. Spontaneous migrants also often traveled to Israel in pairs, in order to alleviate their loneliness and expected unfamiliarity in destination.

Finally, the third feature typical of spontaneous migrants was a lack of consultation and deliberation with their family and household. Spontaneous migrants typically informed their families about their decision to migrate just before they were about to realize it. According to these migrants, their families were often struck by, and opposed to, the idea. Here is how Pepe, a 31-year-old Ecuadorian migrant, recalled it:

When I heard about the opportunities in Israel I decided to come here . . . when I told my family I was leaving, my wife, my sons, my parents, they all told me that I was crazy to leave behind my business and go to Israel, but I thought I had to try it.

I was greatly concerned with substantiating my perception of spontaneous migrants' uniqueness. I wanted to make sure that it was not simply subjectively portrayed in certain ways by migrants and reproduced by me. I therefore followed up, during my fieldwork in Ecuador, on the stories of some Ecuadorian migrants I had come to know in Israel. I visited their families back home and inquired about the views of family members regarding their relatives' emigration to Israel. The following examples are representative of the kind of reactions I encountered. Here is how Fernanda described the departure of her husband to Israel:

> One day he came back home and announced that he was leaving for Israel by the end of the month. He said it was for us, that he would finally be able to make a lot of money and provide for us in a good way. I was shocked and afraid; first I thought that he was drinking and just talking out of his drunkenness, but later I understood he was serious, and within a month he borrowed money from a filthy loan shark and left.

And here is Maria's view of her brother, who one day informed his parents and her about his imminent departure to Israel:

> It was out of the blue for us; he never discussed this with any of us before, and we never heard him talking about Israel. We were very surprised and worried; we tried to talk him into taking some more time for looking carefully into his decision, but there was no one to talk to, he was so decisive.

My conversations with families of some spontaneous migrants reaffirmed and resonated with the stories I had directly heard from migrants in Israel. These families were taken by surprise as they were faced with an already-made decision to migrate. Families often complained that they were not consulted, but were only asked to help finance the migration trip. One can possibly argue that it was perhaps the threatening image of Israel as a dangerous destination that deterred many Latinos from telling their families in advance about their plan to go there. However, during fieldwork in Ecuador I found out that this pattern of non-consultation with one's family was present among migrants to other countries as well. More families told me of a member in their household who had migrated to other destinations, mainly to the United States and Spain, in the same abrupt fashion.

Notably, spontaneity and a lack of consultation with one's family have been identified before as characteristics of the migration of some Latino men, mainly young and unmarried (Escobar-Latapi et al.1987, Davis 1990, Hondagneu-Sotelo 1994). This migration pattern, however, was usually found in a context whereby a concrete invitation to migrate was presented to someone by his brother, father, or uncle, who was already established as a migrant abroad. The spontaneity involved in these decisions was thus usually "[t]he result of a social opportunity which must be grasped and acted upon immediately, before it vanishes" (Hondagneu-Sotelo 1994: 96). I therefore stress that those whom I distinguish as spontaneous migrants took their decision to migrate *without* having any invitation extended to them from established migrants, who might have also offered to facilitate their migration trip and initial adjustment to the destination.

Nine of the sixty-five Latinos whose migration stories I studied featured all three above-mentioned characteristics. These nine consisted of one unmarried woman and eight men; five of the men were single and three were married; of the married men, two had children at the time they decided to leave for Israel. All migrants came from an urban origin and were typically lower-middle class. They commonly held jobs in the industrial and service sectors. Although my sample might not be representative, it is certainly indicative of this new type of spontaneous migrants.

This emerging reasoning by spontaneous migrants about migration is new, not only in the sense that it did not exist some ten years ago, but also in terms of its incompatibility with the existing body of migration theories. The significance of this new type of migration is intensified by the fact that it regularly generates further migration in its more established forms. Thus, each new migrant is a potential pioneer, encouraging and facilitating the migration of relatives and friends. This was certainly true in the case of most spontaneous migrants in Israel. Understanding this new migration is thus important for grasping the volatile expansion of new migration destinations worldwide, and the rapid consolidation of transnational networks around them.

Before attempting an explanation, let me reiterate that there were many overlaps between the three types of migrants I presented. To mention only one example, there were economic and spontaneous migrants who pretended to be religious migrants, and sometimes even ended up in this category once in Israel; there was also diffusion in the opposite direction, that is, religious migrants who "lost the way" once they experienced new ways of life in Israel and deserted their religious community.

The Development of a Migratory Disposition

I have distinguished and described three ideal-types of Latino migrants to Israel. This was useful for highlighting the diverse motivational structures of migrants, and it will also be instrumental for my task in the rest of this book, namely, to describe the life strategies and adaptation process of Latinos in Israel. In the rest of this chapter I elaborate on what I believe to be the common thread that interlaced the motivation of all three types of Latino migrants: their personal readiness to engage in international migration or, in other words, their embodiment of migratory potency.

The concept of migratory disposition helps account for the increasing propensity of many people in Latin America to embrace migration opportunities as life strategies. The motivational structure of potential migrants is explained according to this notion by complementarily accounting for their embeddedness in a social and physical environment, which is being dynamically transformed by migration-related developments. At the heart of this argument rests the idea that the multiple ways in which people in emigration regions are being exposed to the effects of international migration renders them disposed to this option. This exposure may take different forms: it can be encountered visually or socially and culturally grasped. Yet in all its forms it significantly shapes people's perception not only in conscious and calculative ways, but also, importantly, in an intuitive, emotional, and involuntary fashion.

The notion of a migratory disposition helps us understand the impulsiveness that is closely associated with the emigration of spontaneous migrants, but that to some degree could also be detected in the conduct of some economic and even religious migrants. The concept of migratory disposition stresses the fact that many people in Latin America are inclined and minded to emigrate, and would decide to migrate under an influence that can sometimes appear to be very limited in its significance.

In the next section I theoretically elaborate on the need for, and meaning of, the conceptualization of a migratory disposition. I identify and depict four processes that significantly induce the formation and inculcation of a migratory disposition. I thus focus on people's perceptions of, and reactions to, migration-driven changes, first in their material environment and second in their socio-cultural environment. Third, I highlight an emerging notion among potential migrants with regard to the functionality of transnational social networks, and fourth I describe the ways in which the intense commodification of the migration process has reshaped many people's consideration of this option. Equipped with the notion of a migratory disposition, I finally proceed analytically to account for what is seemingly a spontaneous and isolated decision that some Latinos took with respect to immigration to Israel.

Migratory Disposition: A Theoretical Conceptualization

The dominant focus in migration studies on families, households, and transnational communities has greatly overshadowed some of the more subtle new ways in which the overall impact of migration can sway more people to make the crucial decision to emigrate. Significantly, it has diverted social scientists' attention from the more encompassing and formational influence that the phenomenon of migration has had on all kinds of potential migrants. I espouse a more generative tendency (Bourdieu 1977), attempting to integrate changing structures and their interaction with, and influence on, the actions and perceptions of people living in emigration regions.

On the most abstract level, the idea of "time-space compression" (Harvey 1990) has clearly impacted and transcended people's perceptions of strict territorial and cognitive boundaries that perfectly match those of nation-states (Appadurai 1996). During the last two decades, cheap international airfares and new communication technologies have facilitated movement across national borders and the creation of dense transnational social networks and practices (Castells 1996, Hannerz 1996). The logic of late capitalism is seen as proliferating and enmeshing economic currents, cultural transmissions, and human mobility, to an extent that reorders the familiar and lived reality of many people worldwide. Consequently, this reconfiguration on a global scale forcefully leads people everywhere to rethink their personal position and to readjust their life strategies. Yet, rightly pointing out that these innovations are out of reach for an impoverished majority of people worldwide, critics have highlighted the largely misleading liberalizing, open-for-all sense that underlies such approaches toward globalization-led and transnational opportunities (Massey et al. 1993, Ong 1999).

Constructivist theories in migration studies have more specifically attempted to accommodate the conjunctures and interplays between changing macro structures and local social processes. This trend has been predominantly evident in the development of a cumulative causation theory. At the core of this theory lies the idea that "causation is cumulative in that each act of migration alters the social context within which subsequent migration decisions are made" (Massey et al. 1993: 451). This encompassing theory thus somehow eclectically bundles different insights from the changing organization of agrarian production (Massey and Garcia-España 1987) to the new distribution of income and human capital (Stark 1991), and from the distribution of land (Mines 1984, Wiest 1984) to a rising "culture of migration." This last component is meant to capture the fact that "As migration grows in prevalence within a community, it changes values and cultural perceptions in ways that increase the probability of future migration" (Massey et al. 1993: 452). At an individual level, it is argued, the "tastes and motivations" of migrants change as they are exposed to Western societies, while at a societal level "migration becomes deeply ingrained into the repertoire of people's behaviors, and values associated with migration become part of the community's values" (ibid.).

Such a cultural conceptualization of migration is certainly a step in the right direction, yet it is still deficient. It promotes a rather passive notion of migrants as actors who are captured in a thick web of norms and values that somehow forcefully channel them toward migration. I therefore suggest the concept of migratory disposition to account for the propagation of the migratory practice among many people from the low-middle class in Latin America. This concept stresses the propagation of a formational process through which people's perceptions develop as they actively attempt to make sense out of structural, cultural, and social transformations that rapidly change their familiar reality. A concept of disposition dialectically stresses both the significance of social structures in (in)forming people's inclinations and the novel ways in which people make sense of and interpret the reality they experience. It thus endows actors with a resourceful capacity rather than a mechanical, normative set of reactions to particular circumstances. At the same time it also clearly indicates that actors are constrained in the possibilities that they see in front of them, and that they are likely to prefer.

Following Bourdieu (1977), a disposition, the constitutive component of habitus, "[e]xpresses first the result of an organizing action . . . it also designates a way of being . . . and in particular, a predisposition, tendency, propensity, or inclination" (Bourdieu 1977: 214). Importantly, a disposition is made out of "[s]chemes of perception and thoughts . . . inscribed in the body schema and in the schemes of thought, which enables each agent to engender all the practices consistent with [that] logic" (ibid.: 15). Thus the distinctive dispositions of a certain group, although "having been constituted in the course of collective history, are acquired in the course of individual history and function in their practical state, for practice" (Bourdieu 1984: 467). Dispositions are further being "acquired in social positions within a field and imply a subjective adjustment to that position" (Harker, Mahar, and Wilkes 1990: 10). If we think here of the "field" as life strategies for successful economic subsistence in the context of emigration regions, then a migratory disposition alludes to the subjective perception of people with regard to the possible adjustments of their personal position in relation to their social and economic environment.

My descriptions of the four processes that contribute to the creation of a migratory disposition are based primarily on ethnographic material from my fieldwork in Ecuador. However, I also draw on information I gathered from interviews with other Latinos in Israel as well as secondary sources.

The Material Environment: The Omnipresence of Migrants' Economic Achievements

Constant immersion in an environment that represents migrants' positive achievements is one of the main forces that shape a migratory disposition. To a large extent this insight has been integrated already into the conceptual elaboration of "relative deprivation" (Stark 1984, Stark and Taylor 1989, 1991), that is, people's desire to better their standard of living in relative terms, comparing their material situation to that of migrants and their families (Massey et al.1993).

Perhaps the most obvious change in the material environment of Ecuador can be found in its transformed housing landscape. A simple glance from a higher point in any emigration town or village reveals the incredible number of gigantic new villas with glamorous modern architecture that seem to pop up like mushrooms after the rain. This architectonic renaissance is due to a construction extravaganza by the many migrants who left in recent years. A stroll through the streets of such places divulges the sharp change as old adobe-made houses still stand, in marked contrast next to luxurious new villas that are often garnished with new cars in their private parking lots, and sometimes even with a swimming pool in the spacious backyard. One of my informants now lives in one such booming small town on the outskirts of Cuenca, Ecuador's third largest city. As I walked uphill through the town's winding streets, the reformed urban passage was evident from every curve. Looking at the houses, I thought that it seemed that a street from a rich residential suburb in the United States was stitched into an Ecuadorian village. Luxury cars roamed through the town's muddy roads, which, being a public property, did not receive the same enormous investment as the private houses lining it.

The other notable change in the material environment of such towns is the establishment of new upscale shops in the city center and shopping malls. These shops often cater to the rich consumerist tastes of wealthy migrants and their families; for example, chic hairdressers with big neon signposts announce "The Los Angeles Style" or "The Miami Cut," making clear their cultural orientation and source of inspiration. The same goes for the "John F. Kennedy" pharmacy, the "One Night in New York" nightclub, and the "Just like in the USA" fashion boutique. Many shops sell the latest electronic goods, such as flat-screen televisions and computer monitors, huge refrigerators and flashy mobile phones. Although these businesses are open to everyone, it is well known which clientele they serve. The price lists usually deter most non-migrants from shopping at these stores, although they do occasionally enter them out of curiosity.

Exchange houses, courier services, and long-distance telephone centers are other types of businesses that exclusively provide for migrants and their families. Their proliferation during the last years has been immense and escapes no one's eyes. These businesses are set up on almost every major street of cities and towns across Ecuador, and it is now also the case that a Western Union outlet can be found in even some of the remotest villages in the country, sticking out among the few basic shops in the parish. Such exchange houses, where migrants' families come to collect remittances sent to them by their relatives abroad, are highly noticeable, as heavily armed guards normally stand outside, protecting their exclusive costumers. Courier services, such as Quishexpress in Ecuador, announce their diverse services and goods on big billboards across towns: two-day delivery service to migrants abroad; letters and videos; bottles of Zhumir (a national alcoholic liquor).

The constant daily exposure to a material environment shaped by migrant influences unquestionably crept into most non-migrants' frame of reference, shaping their disposition toward migration. But migration experiences are only selectively represented in a visual sense; that is, when a migrant has failed abroad and the construction of a big new house and a new consumerist lifestyle do not follow, it is usually only close relatives and friends who get to know about it. Thus, non-migrants in the home community may see the effects of only successful migrations, which generate a myriad of potent symbolic representations for non-migrants to witness. The ingrained effect of this new material environment is even detectable in young children's perspectives, as a question posed by a 6-year-old girl to her mother vividly reveals: "When will Grandpa go to New York so that he can build us a new house?" (quoted in Wamsley 2001: 160, my translation). Indeed, livelihood and migration have been coupled in the minds of adults as well as teenagers and children. As one Latino in Israel told me, his children used to come home from school frustrated, asking his wife and him to buy them the trendy goods that their affluent classmates, children of migrants, enjoyed. Thus, breadwinners' sense of relative deprivation is replicated in the experiences of all their family members.

The material presence of absent migrants surely gives non-migrants the feeling of missing out on an enormous opportunity. For example, Jason's strong sense of deficit persisted despite his above-average salary and standard of living. Separately, the material aspirations that drove him to leave his family and country might seem a bit far-fetched; after all, how many Ecuadorians, or for that matter, people in the West, have their own house by the age of twenty-five? His skyrocketing desires are understandable only against the backdrop of an environment filled with migration-related representations, which set a common point of reference for most non-migrants. The American dream is no longer transmitted to people in emigration regions solely through telecommunicated images, as migration theories would have it; instead, desires are driven by very physical and corporal material transformations that impinge on people's own immediate surroundings.

The Social Milieu: The Glorification of Migration and the Emergence of a New Class

An important feature in a "culture of migration" is the establishment of international migration as "the right thing to do," mainly for young men but also for women in certain places that experience sustained emigration (Massey et al. 1993, 1994). Turning the act of migration into a modern "rite of passage" implies that norms and social pressure are exercised by society to push certain members into making the decision to migrate or run the risk of being socially sanctioned and looked down on as "lazy, unenterprising, and undesirable" (Reichert 1982). Although the power of social sanctions and norms should not be underestimated, focusing solely on this aspect of the migration process renders involved actors devoid of agency. It portrays migrants as peons forced to move in a particular direction on the local-global chessboard of migration. It is by paying attention to complementary positive attributions, which are conferred on migrants by their societies, that we can see how non-migrants come to actively desire migration.

Of importance in this respect is a process in which migrants and migration experience are being hyped, celebrated, and even glorified. On a national level, the state of Ecuador has officially celebrated the *Día del Emigrante* (Day of the Emigrant) for over a decade. This day, which is celebrated nationwide on the third Sunday of September, marks the recognition and support given by the nation to its migrants. The Día del Emigrante started as a single day but now stretches for almost a whole week. Apart from a presidential message, municipalities, schools, and churches prepare festivities and hold meetings around different relevant themes. In one pamphlet made for this occasion, the main objective was written in bold letters on the first page: "Dedicating a special time of grace to celebrate and pray for our migrant brothers and sisters."[3]

On a communitarian level, religious emigrants are often offered a special Mass and a blessing prior to their departure. Moreover, once they are abroad their congregation often prays for them whenever they are in trouble or face difficulties. While in Ecuador I participated in a few religious services in evangelical churches, where families communicated the difficult situation (sickness, unemployment, etc.) of their relatives abroad to the pastor, who in turn dedicated a special collective prayer for their well-being. For people in the audience this was a tangible and powerful demonstration of the importance ascribed to migrants by the community. Secular migrants also habitually enjoyed a big fiesta when they departed, and they received a hero's welcome upon their successful return. Non-migrants often gathered around returnees or visiting migrants, who told stories from their migration destination. As I observed on numerous occasions, these tales were greatly appealing. Non-migrants also clearly desired the company of migrants.

It should be noted here that there were also cases in which former migrants refused to assume this role. Some returnees deliberately distanced themselves from non-migrant former friends. They maintained an affluent lifestyle and aspired to become part of the upper class. Indeed, migrants and their families constituted a new social and economic class in Ecuador. Many migrants from a lower-middle-class background, who had thrived abroad economically, enjoyed an improved status and standard of living upon their return. Migrants' families that had stayed back home usually also enjoyed many material improvements. Ecuadorian migrants were commonly called *residentes* (residents). This title colloquially referred to their civil status in another country, mainly in the United States. Even when migrants never achieved legal residency abroad, the term was still used to indicate their established migratory status. Many returnees lived in superior houses, often in emerging nouveau riche residential neighborhoods. They dressed in the latest fashion, and they wore expensive ornaments and accessories.

It can be argued that a migratory sub-culture has been created in emigration countries like Ecuador. This sub-culture is reflected not only in material representations and a consumerist lifestyle, but also through language skills acquired abroad. The fact that it has become rather easy to recognize *residentes* illustrates the notion of a tangible new migration-driven class division. The following incident illustrates the rift that was sometimes created between *residentes* and the ones who were left outside the migration boom. Referring to his former classmate who had just passed us in his lavish car, my informant mournfully commented:

> Since he returned [from the U.S.] he has become a real *aniñado* [snob]; if he sees me he hardly nods his head and he never stops and chats. I used to play football with him, we were good friends, but now he only hangs out with other ex-migrants.

In the mass media, the special place of migrants in the chronology of the country was evident. National newspapers, such as *El Comercio* and *El Universo*, had a daily migration section with sizable articles on relevant topics, as well as public letters sent by migrants to the editor. Special transnational radio programs, such as *Añoranzas* (Homesickness), broadcast "migrants' voices," as migrants in different countries called in and publicly delivered messages to their loved ones in Ecuador or expressed their longing for their motherland. Other programs, such as *Callos y Guatitas* (named after a popular dish made of tripe), offered both migrants and potential migrants the possibility to solicit information on various migration-related issues from experts in the studio. It also provided a channel for migrants to publicly share their personal experiences. Furthermore, on television there were soap series and other dramatic series, such as *La Vida Real* (The Real Life), where migrants were often the protagonists. On many of these different media channels migrants often discussed their hardship abroad, for example, experiencing discrimination and exploitation or painfully longing for families and friends. Nonetheless, these communications were regularly tainted with a strong sense of empathy toward migrants, and their experiences were largely romanticized even when heartbreaking.

A similar thing occurred on the musical scene, where many songs were written about migration. These songs compassionately portrayed migrants' sufferings, and turned them into folkloric, heroic figures. Some bands also identified with migrants through their names, for example, *Emigrantes Latinos* (Latino Migrants) and *Los Emigrantes* (The Emigrants). Songwriting can also be seen as part of a larger process whereby the role and place of migrants is inscribed into the historic national narrative. Moreover, in many music shops there was a surge in the sale of Ecuadorian traditional music, especially for migrants to take on their journeys. The covers of many of these musical compilations make direct reference to migrants; for example, one cover features an emotional departure scene at the Ecuadorian national airport.

Thus, in countries like Ecuador a multilevel process of positive recognition and even glorification of migration and migrants takes place. Migrants are being transformed into new role models, and they enjoy the solid support, and often envy, of the whole nation. While positive ascribed status was perhaps not alone sufficient reason for embarking on a migration trip, it certainly excited and ignited the imagination of many, especially young, people who had already pondered migration on other grounds. Here is how one Ecuadorian, who migrated alone to Israel when he was only twenty years old, reflected on what drove him to leave: "I was so energized just imagining myself as a migrant; I was thrilled by the opportunity to have this special experience."

Finally, it is worth mentioning that the development of a *residentes* class also increased the propensity to migrate among people who traditionally belonged to the middle class. Claudia, who came from a solid middle-class background and migrated to Israel all by herself, is a case in point. When I asked about her rather surprising decision to migrate she told me:

> Before I migrated to Israel I never really thought about migrating
> anywhere. On the contrary, I mean, you see all these *residentes* with their
> new wealth and to be honest it is quite appalling; they drive these big cars
> and they wear all these golden shackles and these trendy clothes but you see
> that they have no style. Like my ex-landlady used to say about them—"a
> monkey dressed up fancily is still a monkey." I never meant to be one of
> those! It's like an epidemic, they are everywhere—for example, the
> nightclub where my friends and I used to hang out became filled with *hijos
> de residentes* [sons of migrants]. They spend a lot of money on drinks, but it
> is a problem for the owner 'cause then people like my friends and me stop
> coming. I know it sounds racist; I am sorry but that is really what I think,
> everyone has his place.

Within middle-class circles the term *residentes* was almost always pejoratively used to refer to indigenous people who managed to elevate their socio-economic situation and infringed on the middle and upper classes. People like Claudia were highly irritated by the "invasion" of *residentes* into their spaces (discos, bars, shopping malls, etc.). Upset by what they perceived with distress as a destabilization of traditional class boundaries, the more established middle class regularly denigrated *residentes*, but at the same time began to consider migration as the way forward.

The New Functionality of Transnational Social Networks

While the application of a crude cost-benefit theory suggests that most individuals in less-developed countries would be economically better off by migrating abroad, often the involved costs, risks, and non-monetary concerns of leaving one's family and familiarity behind keep many at bay. In this respect, migration theories point us to transnational networks as commonly mitigating these upheavals (Portes and Basch 1985, Massey et el. 1998, Glick Schiller, Basch, and Blanc-Szanton 1992, Basch, Glick Schiller, and Szanton Blanc 1994). By having families and communities stretched between countries of origin and migration destinations, potential migrants can significantly lower involved risks and costs, and also enjoy the comfort of being received by a familiar face who facilitates and cushions the hardship involved in a necessary occupational and cultural adaptation into new societies (Hugo 1981, Massey 1990a, 1990b, Gurak and Caces 1992, Portes 1995).

Moreover, since the late 1970s, a more holistic approach, "the new economics of migration," has rightly called attention to the fact that decisions to emigrate were often taken by families or even extended households. This approach looked at the process of migration as a survival strategy on the family level, and illuminated how households diversely allocate their labor resources to counter institutional deficiencies in governmental provision of insurance, welfare, credit, and so on (Mincer 1978, Stark 1984, Stark and Bloom 1985). More elaborate research projects into the complex threads and functionality of the relational configuration of families yielded great insights for the ways in which decisions are being taken with regard to who migrates (and who stays put), when, and where (Wolf 1990, Grasmuck and Passer 1991, Hondagneu-Sotelo 1994, Hugo 1994).

Most Latino migrants to Israel made their decision to migrate together with their families, and they operationalized it via transnational social networks that incorporated their households. Migrants typically received financial assistance from their network of relatives and friends in Israel, who usually also provided practical answers to questions about undocumented migration (e.g., when was a good time to arrive; from which border one should cross into Israel; what answers one should give if examined by the border police). The connection to a social network in Israel was also, of course, crucial for the reception of a new migrant and the initial accommodation process.

Nevertheless, some migrants, mainly spontaneous ones, operationalized their migration largely outside the realm of transnational networks. They typically based their decision to go somewhere on information they had about the opportunities there. Sometimes they also obtained a superficial link to someone they did not personally know, as in the case of one spontaneous migrant to Israel:

> When I made my decision to leave, a friend of mine gave me a telephone number of his friend in Israel whom I could contact and ask for some help in finding accommodation and a job. He also told me to go on Saturday to the Dolphinarium Park to meet other Ecuadorian migrants.

The classical function of transnational networks in lowering migrants' risks and costs did not apply in the case of these particular migrants. We could of course stretch the concept of a network to encompass the operationalization of migration by migrants whose only connection at their destination was a telephone number of a person they never personally knew; yet such an exercise is likely to leave us with a very formless and abstract concept of a network.

The other alternative is to think of the functionality of networks in a new way. Given that networks have externally expanded and internally condensed, there is a qualitative change in their function for many potential migrants who at the point of decision stand outside them. Migration theories claim that networks expand to encompass more and more segments of society and that "eventually, knowledge about foreign locations and jobs becomes widely diffused, and values, sentiments, and behaviors characteristic of the core society spread widely within the sending region" (Massey et al. 1993: 453). Although this is undeniable, it is my contention that what is also being importantly diffused by networks nowadays is not just knowledge about foreign locations, which is still closely associated with a rational choice that follows from it, but rather a sense of confidence. This sense of confidence is noticeable in at least two ways. First, there is a prevalent confidence among many potential migrants that if so many people around them have already successfully migrated, then they can do the same as well. This confidence, although always mixed with a degree of wariness, was very common among Latinos in Israel. Especially, spontaneous migrants were explicit about their belief that given the number of people around them who had migrated, there was hardly a question about their own ability to accomplish the same undertaking.

Second, a feeling of confidence is not limited to one's own proficiency; some potential migrants who are not directly linked to a network seem to be also increasingly confident about their ability to draw on some essential resources from an existing community of their compatriots abroad. There is a strong notion among potential migrants regarding the connectivity and receptivity of an "imagined" (to borrow Benedict Anderson's concept) Ecuadorian community in foreign destinations. This perception of anonymous solidarity among compatriots who share a similar fate abroad is then fueling the courage first to migrate and only later, once at the destination, to establish ties with a community and social network. In Israel, this strategy was proved to be rightly adopted by new migrants, who found their way to the heart of the Ecuadorian community in Tel Aviv soon after their arrival. New migrants admitted that it took them some effort but that eventually they found a room in an apartment rented by compatriots and were given information about job opportunities from their new friends.

The idea that a transnational space exists out there and that one can easily make contact with a diasporic community is being consolidated by a widespread acquaintance with certain places in foreign destinations where it is known that compatriots gather (e.g., certain parks where people get together on weekends; churches where compatriots congregate for a Mass delivered in their native language; restaurants and streets where traditional food is served). Information about these centers, such as Parque del Lago in Madrid or Plaza España in Barcelona, is by now well known and easily discovered by a migrant. In Israel I witnessed this dynamic during the weekly Latino football tournament held on Saturdays in the Dolphinarium Park in Tel Aviv. In recent years this event became a popular meeting point for Latinos. While the game was played on an improvised pitch, some migrants sold traditional Latino dishes and drinks from makeshift stalls set up around the field. Groups of Ecuadorians and other Latinos used to sit around and enjoy their day off.

It was common on these occasions to see recently arrived migrants approaching their compatriots, presenting themselves, and asking if they could join the group. They were often warmly welcomed and were asked about the latest news from back home. During these group outings newcomers were regularly given necessary information about the local scene. Occasionally I saw how immediate offers for *cupos* were made to newcomers, and exchanges of telephone numbers followed. A *cupo* is the term used for a bed or a "slot" in an apartment that is shared by a few Latinos. This is a standard scheme for accommodation whereby one migrant, usually with some experience in the host country, signs a contract for renting an apartment, which is normally divided into four to eight *cupos* (depending on its size). *Cupos* are then offered to friends or otherwise put on offer in the informal Latino housing market. The quality and price of a *cupo* vary according to the number of inhabitants in the apartment, its location, and other such factors. Notably, this practice of *cupos* is based on the idea that migrants do not exclusively search for accommodation through family ties or classical networks, but that they also increasingly individually share a place with other compatriots. In turn, the *cupos* scheme, by creating an informal public housing market, enhances the migration of individuals who can count on their chances to find accommodation without an actual connection to a particular network.

There is indeed a highly developed notion of connectivity bounded by anonymous solidarity among compatriots in migration destinations. The very existence of vibrant transnational communities in migration destinations disseminates the idea that one can simply link up to and mobilize an "imagined" social capital from such established networks. This notion of an ever-expanding transnational space is vividly reflected in a remark made by one of my informants, who was deported to Ecuador after six years in Israel. Now contemplating migration to another destination, where just as in Israel he had no established network to draw upon, Roberto noted, "No matter where I choose to go next, by now there must be some Ecuadorians in every corner of the world."

Some networkless migrants tried to alleviate their initial loneliness by convincing a good friend or a relative to join them. If they were successful, then their migration was no longer strictly individual, but it was still networkless. Another way in which some migrants dealt with the initial difficulty of undertaking migration alone was by thinking of those who might follow in their footsteps. Here again there is a strong sense of confidence that if migrants are successful then some of their relatives and friends will soon follow. This conviction was indeed proven right in the case of most spontaneous migrants in Israel.

Understanding the logic behind the motivation of some potential migrants to operationalize networkless migration might partly account for the failure of restrictive migration policies in some receiving countries. In recent years many Western countries adopted new immigration policies, curbing the ability of settled immigrants to expand their community through, for example, family reunification and marriages with foreign citizens. Notwithstanding the overall effects of such policies, what I have described as "the new functionality of networks" clearly indicates that by now transnational networks and communities serve as magnets and facilitators for potential migrants who are not operating their migration from within them.

"To Buy or not to Buy?": Migration as a Commodity

The propagation of courier services, which connect nearly every town in Latin America with every migration destination, has clearly allowed Latinos not to depend on a transnational social network for managing both the transfer of remittances to relatives and the reception of letters, videocassettes, and other goods. However, transnational networks also play an important role in operationalizing the migration trip itself, which is usually very expensive, and in the case of undocumented migrants can also be risky. Within transnational social networks, established migrants often lend money to, and share know-how with, potential migrants. In this respect, the commodification of the migration process is a significant development that has reduced the essentiality of social networks, as it largely facilitates and robustly disseminates the idea of migration as an independently achievable project for potential migrants.

Historically, legal migration has always had a twin in the form of undocumented migration, which in its modern form has been widely assisted by an illicit "migration industry" (Harris 1996). In Latin America the migration industry is doggedly operated by *coyotes* (guides for illicit journeys across national borders) and financially managed by *chulqueros* (loan sharks). Until recently it used to be rather complicated to contract the service of *coyotes,* as one needed certain knowledge and contacts in order to approach these semi-Mafioso people. However, particularly during recent years, there has been a marked expansion in the accessibility of these illicit services to a much wider public. While in Ecuador, I asked a friend if he could arrange for me a meeting with a *coyote*. It did not take more than a phone call to set a meeting for the following day. It seems that the whole secrecy surrounding this business has evaporated into the thin air of strong demand and weak enforcement by corrupted authorities (for more see Kyle and Liang 2001). *Coyotes* appear to have lost their fear and are quite recognizable by the public. This trend is also amplified by the growing respectability that many Ecuadorians ascribe to these providers of human international mobility. The reasoning offered by the sister of one Ecuadorian migrant who used a *coyote* to get to the United States is illustrative:

> I think they [*coyotes*] do nothing wrong, what do you think? There are so
> many people here whose best option is to migrate, but they cannot do it
> because of the system. So *coyotes* are providing this service; it is true they
> ask a lot of money, but they also take a high risk themselves and have to pay
> many people along the way.

Another example of the trivialization of *coyotes* in Ecuadorian society is demonstrated by the following anecdote. While in Cuenca, I joined children from one school on a trip marking the end of the year. As the bus, which was taking us to a nearby natural reserve, passed by a huge luxurious villa the children put their heads out of the windows and repeatedly yelled, "Here lives the *coyote*." When I inquired of the teachers in the bus whether there was truth to the children's chants, they offhandedly nodded their heads in confirmation while one teacher casually let slip, "They [*coyotes*] are everywhere."

In Latin America, decisions to migrate with *coyotes* are predominantly taken by people striving to reach the United States. Nevertheless, in recent years I met and heard of a growing number of Latinos who had used the services of *coyotes* in order to reach different destinations in Europe. In the mid-1990s the "*coyote* business" even reached Israel, with special traffickers illicitly bringing undocumented migrants into the country from Israel's border with Egypt. Potential Latino migrants also frequently finance their migration trip by taking loans from *chulqueros*, as was the case for many Ecuadorian migrants to Israel. The common execution of migration in such a fashion promulgates among many people the idea that migration can be realized by one's own self-determination. The migration industry has altered the overall meaning of migration, which although very expensive is now within the reach of many ordinary people, who otherwise find themselves outside the circle or network of migration.[4] Having migration shelved as a product with a price tag attached to it renders it devoid of the social relationships that traditionally formed the most crucial part of the undertaking. Hence, commodification not only directly facilitates the possibility to independently migrate, but also transforms a highly social decision and propagates among many people the very powerful notion of becoming, as it were, masters of their own destiny.

Explaining a Hasty Decision

I have demonstrated how different complementary processes and practices have jointly contributed to the inculcation of a migratory disposition into the governing mindset and the decision-making process of many potential migrants. This idea of a migratory disposition can help us understand the apparent abruptness and impulsiveness that is closely associated with the emigration of many Latinos, especially spontaneous migrants. There are two possible ways to account for this peculiar conduct of migrants.

First is the rising importance of the *tio-coyote* duo for potential migrants who redefine their significant kinship lines according to a "migration experience" parameter. Potential migrants who are located outside transnational networks often reach out to distant relatives with migration experience and discuss their plans with them. It is thus that some potential migrants largely substitute a practical and emotional reliance on their close family, with confidence and inspiration from *tios*. This ability to lift distant relatives and acquaintances to a level of close *tios* is a great illustration of Mark Granovetter's (1973) notion regarding "the strength of weak ties," and a fulfillment of David Kyle's (2000: 84) more recent related hypothesis: "[T]o the extent that the primary group is not able to provide all of the social and physical resources needed for out-migration in a particular setting, weak ties to external resources will play a crucial role in the migration process." Concurrently, *coyotes* symbolize for potential migrants the possibility to operationalize migration without having to be dependent on one's family or on a link to a transnational network. Migrants thus do not have to plan their migration together with their families, nor do they need to rely on them for its execution. In their mind, potential migrants can simply go at any given moment to the nearest "*coyote* agency" and purchase the desired migration trip.

The second way to account for migrants' impulsiveness pertains to the emotional aspect implicit in the notion of a disposition. The formation of a migratory disposition clearly implies a cognitive process or a drift whereby people's views are being outwardly reshaped, and their awareness about migration options is raised as they become more susceptible to them. At the same time, it also entails an embodiment, that is, the internalization into one's sense-making mechanism of a particular way of thinking about opportunities and devising life strategies. Such an internalization influences not only calculative practices but also bodily feelings and emotionally driven desires. It is thus that the very prospects of migration can produce a particular excitability or evoke certain emotions in potential migrants, which in some constellations might lead to an abrupt decision to emigrate.

A disposition thus involves an affective process whereby potential migrants develop a "deep feeling," to quote one of my informants, toward the migratory option.

For example, the constant confrontation with migration-driven wealth generates not only jealousy in potential migrants such as Jason, but also agitation, frustration, and even rage. On the other hand, individuals are enthused by a range of stimulations as they imagine their future as migrants. Jason "felt," as he put it, that he was taking the right step, and it was probably no coincidence that he made his actual decision just after a visit he had paid to the luxurious house of his *tio*. As another informant described it, Jason was "ecstatic" when he decided to migrate to Israel.

Instead of looking at migration as becoming "the right thing to do" (Massey, Goldring, and Durand 1994), alluding to economic and cultural dynamics, we should also consider that migration has an affective influence on disposed people, and it largely becomes "the thing that feels right to do." Although it might seem merely a matter of semantics, this is a qualitative divergence, conceptualizing migration, among other things, as an affectively informed decision. Put metaphorically, the formation of a migratory disposition leads people to have their finger readily set on a migration trigger. It is often then enough for a seemingly negligible event, which evokes an emotional (negative or positive) response, to make people pull the trigger. Thus, what might appear to be an abrupt and hasty decision is actually only the tip of the iceberg: a culmination of a lengthy process whereby the idea to emigrate has been entertained not only knowingly but also involuntarily and intuitively, even when it was never verbally articulated.

PART TWO

Chapter Four

Shifting Strategies

FROM THE ACCUMULATION OF MONEY TOWARD
THE ACCUMULATION OF BELONGING

We work here like blacks so that we can live there like whites.
—*Pedro, 33, undocumented Peruvian migrant in Tel Aviv*

Israelis are the Latinos of the Middle East.
—*Guirremo, 29, undocumented Colombian migrant in Tel Aviv*

All three types of Latino migrants in Israel originally conceived of their immigration as a springboard to a better future in their countries of origin. They sought to accumulate a certain economic wealth that would allow them to reposition themselves and their families back home. In order to achieve their goal as quickly as possible, Latinos initially lived frugally and saved as much as they could. Driven by a clear economic ambition, Latinos were inclined to take on whatever jobs they were offered. Most of these jobs were in the cleaning sector, and for Latinos, mainly men, to perform them was psychologically challenging. This challenge was exacerbated by Latinos' larger need to deal emotionally with the experience of displacement and, most acutely, with the separation from their families. A major predicament for Latinos in this respect was the fact that they operated in a constrained transnational space, in the sense that it was practically impossible for them as undocumented migrants to re-enter Israel once they left it.

Within a few years in Israel, most Latinos achieved the economic goal that they had set out to accomplish via immigration. Moreover, Latinos enjoyed what they considered to be a high standard of living, a rich recreational scene, and good relations with Israelis. In spite of their undocumented status, many Latinos who managed to avoid police inspections were able to regain a sense of normalcy in their life in Israel. Latinos could rent apartments, receive mail, open bank accounts, give birth in Israeli hospitals, attend churches, go out to salsa clubs, and pursue other ordinary activities. Boosted by their success, and deterred by the idea that once they left Israel it was for good, most Latinos opted to prolong their stay. Many Latinos thus reconsidered the temporariness of their immigration plans and gradually contemplated settling down in Israel as a long-term strategy.

As Latinos came to desire long-term settlement in Israel, new economic, familial, and emotional orientations emerged. Prolonging their stay often led to the formation of new families. Latinos also commonly solved their experience of displacement by bringing their families to Israel. Here again Latinos felt encouraged when they discovered that their children could be insured under the Israeli national healthcare system and enrolled in Israeli state-sponsored schools. Latinos were enthusiastic about integrating their children into Israeli society. They often gave their children Israeli names, urged them to pick up Hebrew, and instilled in them their strong desire to settle down in Israel. This distinctive approach of Latinos, which was very different from the one adopted by many other undocumented migrant groups, stemmed largely from their belief that the legalization of their status in Israel was most likely to occur through the successful social integration of their children.

Whether consciously or intuitively, Latinos' shifting orientations often went along with their strivings for enhanced cultural assimilation in Israel. As I follow closely the lives of Latinos in Israel, from finding their first apartment and job up to their advanced settlement, it will become evident that Latinos employed much creative agency in accommodating to their developing situation. At the same time, it will also spotlight how the "cracks" between the state and society in Israel, between formal exclusion and practical inclusion, affected the perspective of Latinos and induced their inclination to belong and settle down in the country. I begin, however, by defining with more precision the Israeli context as a constrained transnational space that interdicted a back-and-forth movement between Israel and Latin America. The limited transnational mobility of Latinos first augmented their experiences of displacement and loss, and later compounded their emotional and economic gravitation toward long-term settlement in Israel.

Constrained Transnationalism

Transnationalism has cast in new light the experience of migrants who seek their fortunes abroad. The development of transnational social networks has outdated conceptualizations of migrants' place according to a dichotomy of "here" versus "there." Changes in the organization of space have had a considerable effect on the formation of a transnational perception, adopted by many transmigrants, which transcends strict geographical and cognitive boundaries of nation-states. A good example of this transnational perspective is given by an El Salvadorian migrant to Los Angeles. When asked why he remained in the USA, although being subjected, according to his own account, to discrimination and an inferior position, the migrant responded, "I really live in El Salvador, not in L.A. When we have the regular fiestas to collect funds for La Esperanza, I am the leader and I am treated with respect. . . . In L.A. I just earn money, but my thoughts are really back home" (quoted in Portes 1999: 466).

During the last two decades, new communication technologies (Castells 1996) and cheap international airfares have facilitated the compression of space and time (Harvey 1990). The creation of dense transnational social networks has facilitated the accommodation and integration of migrants, and allowed migrants to mitigate their experience of displacement in novel ways. Until recently, most displaced people could make sense of their loss mainly by nostalgically referring to the places and people they left behind. Nowadays, migrants can often travel back and forth in a transnational space. The growing global circulation of people, newspapers, TV channels, cuisine, and so on has led to the formation of global flows that Arjun Appadurai (1996) has neatly captured with the suffix "-scape," as in ethnoscape, mediascape, and ideoscape. These scapes transcend territorial borders of nation-states and permit migrants to recreate and reproduce their cultural environment abroad. Transmigrants can nowadays maintain close contacts with their countries of origin. The dimension of these contacts can stretch all the way from private family engagement to a more collective socio-cultural one, including political activities (Portes, Guarnizo, and Landolt 1999, Vertovec 1999).

As Gupta and Ferguson (1992: 9) claim, "something like a transnational public sphere has certainly rendered any strictly bounded sense of community or locality obsolete. At the same time, it has enabled the creation of forms of solidarity and identity that do not rest on an appropriation of space where contiguity and face-to-face contact are paramount." It is thus that many migrants perceive their private and collective reality not exclusively in terms of the space where they reside but also, and at times even mainly, in terms of the effect that they have on the places they left. The establishment of transnational social networks clearly testifies to the agency and capacity of transmigrants creatively to confront nationalism and restrictive policies. Transmigrants contest and transcend states' exclusionary national logic, which is under pressure given the increasing fluidity of a progressively more globalized world (Gilroy 1987, Bhabha 1994, Clifford 1994, Appadurai 2002). As Ong (1999: 15) puts it: "freedom from spatial constraints becomes a form of deterritorialized resource that can be deployed against the territorially bounded nation-state."

The situation of many undocumented migrants presents a constrained variant of this evolving transnational model. "Illegality" should clearly be considered for its implications on the more limited position of undocumented migrants. Much attention has been given to the ways in which illegality complicates migrants' efforts to organize politically and be legitimately recognized as actors in the internal politics of their host state (Soysal 1994). The political dimension of Latinos' organization in Israel will be discussed in the next chapter; here, however, I would like to highlight the spatial dimension of undocumented migrants' "illegality" and the ways in which it shaped the life strategies of Latinos in Israel.

In the most practical sense, illegality significantly hampered the ability of undocumented migrants in Israel to travel back and forth in their established transnational networks, in order to visit their families, take part in crucial events, and take care of their investments. This condition of constrained transnationalism constituted a major reason for many Latinos successively to prolong the duration of their stay in Israel. Some migrants did try, and sometimes even succeeded, to re-enter Israel after they had left it. Yet re-entering Israel was always considered highly risky, and so most Latinos were very reluctant to leave, and to jeopardize their successful settlement in Israel. In fact, most of the Latinos who attempted to re-enter Israel were deportees.

From the late 1990s, officials at Israeli international border gates were specifically instructed to inspect the passports of departing tourists in order to detect those who had overstayed their visas for a substantial period. These tourists were then considered to be undocumented migrants, and their exit from Israel was handled as a deportation procedure; that is, officials signed their passports with a deportation stamp that denied them any future entry to Israel for several years. Even when officials failed to detect undocumented migrants who left Israel, the very fact that a migrant's passport contained Israeli entry and exit stamps, with an interval between them that exceeded the length of a tourist visa, precluded the possibility of these individuals' re-entering Israel without raising suspicion. Therefore, undocumented migrants, either caught and deported or voluntarily exiting Israel, were prevented from re-entering Israel.

Consequently, a cat-and-mouse game developed between undocumented migrants and the state of Israel. While migrants developed several tactics to re-enter Israel, the state gradually moved to upgrade its control system to foreclose such possible re-entries. The most common way used by migrants to re-enter Israel was the following: upon arrival in their countries of origin they declared their passport to have been lost, stolen, or damaged, and they requested to be issued a new passport. New passports were of course "clean" of all Israeli stamps, and contained a different serial number and a recent photo, which made it all the more difficult for the Israeli officials at border ports to detect that these passports corresponded to former undocumented migrants. This method was widely employed by migrants in the late 1990s with some success, not least because of Israel's blind-eye policy with regard to undocumented migrants. Yet in the year 2000 the state of Israel extended its record of undocumented migrants who exited its borders to include in addition to their passport number also their full name, date of birth, and other possible indicators that were unchangeable in new passports.

To overcome the improved ability of the Israeli authorities to detect undocumented migrants, Latinos commonly re-entered Israel with new passports via peripheral border crossings: either by land from Egypt (and sometimes also from Jordan), or by sea on cruise ships that sailed from Greece and docked in Haifa. Undocumented migrants looked to take advantage of the fact that the records in Israeli border ports were not synchronized. Given that migrants mostly left Israel by air via the international airport, they were registered as undocumented migrants only in the database at this port. The most popular way among Latinos was to book an organized tour that combined a visit to both Egypt and Israel, but that first landed in Cairo, and only after a few days in Egypt continued into Israel by land via the remote border crossing in the Sinai Peninsula. I found an indication for the popularity of this alternative itinerary in the official records of Ecuador, which registered a rise in the number of Ecuadorian tourists traveling to Egypt from a single person in 1998 and only four in 1999 to 132 in 2001 (Ecuadorian National Institute of Statistics and Census 2003). Unless Egypt experienced a meteoric rise in its popularity as a tourist destination for Ecuadorians, it is more likely to assume that the higher number of travelers in 2001 represents undocumented migrants who were on route to (re-)enter Israel.

In 2001 Israel computerized and synchronized its database with all its national border ports. Consequently, from 2002 onward a re-entry into Israel largely ceased to be an option for undocumented migrants. Some undocumented migrants still attempted to enter Israel by illegally crossing its borders with the help of smugglers, or by purchasing and using false documents. Nevertheless, from my experience very few Latinos were involved in such illicit attempts.

Initial Settlement: "I only want to complete my mission"

Most Latinos in Israel originally conceived of their immigration as a springboard for a better economic future in their countries of origin. "I only want to complete my mission" (*Solo quiero cumplir mi meta*) was a sentence I repeatedly heard from Latinos who had never consciously contemplated settling down in Israel as a long-term strategy. Most Latinos hoped to earn much money, commonly over a period of around three years, in order to reposition themselves back home. Operationalizing their migration with a timeframe in mind induced a general sense of urgency in most Latinos, who looked to work intensively and to minimize their expenses in Israel. Initially, Latinos typically lived frugally in Israel to maximize their saving capacity; for example, they lived in overpopulated apartments in the cheapest neighborhoods of Tel Aviv, cooked basic food, limited costly recreational activities, and bought second-hand clothes.

For some migrants the sense of urgency was initially exacerbated further by the fact that they had borrowed money to finance their trip to Israel. Most Latinos did not have the necessary capital (around US$4,000) to finance their migration. Economic and religious migrants who operated within transnational social networks were commonly given an interest-free loan by their established relatives in Israel. This loan was to be repaid once a migrant began working in Israel. Other migrants, mainly spontaneous ones, needed to borrow money, often in the ""gray" market, paying an extortionate interest of around 10 percent a month to *usarios* (loan sharks). In order to rid themselves as quickly as possible of their burdening loan, many Latinos wired back the US$2,000 *para la bolsa* immediately after successfully entering Israel. Yet the money *para la bolsa* often not only served to prove their financial solvency to Israeli officials in border ports when entering, but also was their means of subsistence in the first weeks before they could start counting on a steady local income. Therefore from the moment Latinos entered Israel, an hourglass began counting down the time they had left before exhausting their initial resources. Finding a job and cheap accommodation was crucial for newcomers. Latinos commonly drew on their transnational social networks and local communities for assistance. However, Israeli real estate and employment agencies were also very active in meeting migrants' needs.

Finding a Place to Live

Most Latinos, just like other undocumented migrants, initially chose to live in the poor neighborhoods of south Tel Aviv, where cheap apartments could be rented. Living in south Tel Aviv was also convenient, as the central bus station was located in this area, providing easy access for migrants, who mostly had to reach their workplaces in north Tel Aviv or the suburbs around the city. The fact that the first undocumented migrants settled in this area, and began establishing ethnic niches, also created momentum that later attracted subsequent migrants.

South Tel Aviv has traditionally been the residential area for lower-class Israelis. Some parts of this area are infamous for their concentration of prostitution and underworld activity. While considered poor by Israeli standards, apartments in south Tel Aviv all have modern electricity and sewage system, a bathroom with hot water, a kitchen with an integrated gas cooking apparatus, and even a connection to satellite cable TV that can receive channels in the Spanish language from around the world. Such living standards match the ones that are mainly found in middle-class neighborhoods in Latin America, and they normally exceed the ones Latinos enjoyed before emigrating to Israel. Most Latinos thus considered the living conditions in south Tel

Aviv to be more than reasonable, sometimes even luxurious. In addition, it is in south Tel Aviv that the last remaining industrial workshops can be found; the rest of the city has been swept by post-industrial economic activities. Here again, while for Israelis south Tel Aviv is considered an underdeveloped area, for undocumented migrants it offered semi-professional employment opportunities.

Renting an apartment as an undocumented migrant in Israel was not at all problematic. Israeli law did not stipulate the responsibility of homeowners to verify the legal status of people to whom apartments were sublet. Undocumented migrants could even receive mail at the address where they rented an apartment (although many feared a link existed between the Israeli postal service and the police). In principle, undocumented migrants could sign contracts directly with Israeli homeowners; however, such direct connections were largely hampered by the inefficiency of Israelis' directly advertising among undocumented migrants and migrants' fear that publicly posted offers, for example on street corners, were a police trap. As a result, real estate agencies became vital in bridging this gap, often employing an Israeli who spoke the language of migrants. Recognizing a profitable business opportunity, agencies approached low-class residents in south Tel Aviv with an offer to rent their apartments from them for an attractive sum. Many poor residents saw these offers as a chance finally to move out of their shabby neighborhood and into a better area. Real estate agencies then sublet the apartments to undocumented migrants at much higher prices. The effective work of agencies produced an exodus of Israelis from apartments in south Tel Aviv into better neighborhoods, ensuring a supply of accommodation for undocumented migrants, whose numbers in this area gradually increased and were estimated in the year 2000 at around sixty thousand (Schnell 2001).

Migrants commonly redesigned the interior of apartments to accommodate more roommates; sharing an apartment with four to eight migrants (depending on the size of the apartment) usually ensured a reduced price of around US$120 per month for each person. Yet signing a contract with real estate agencies was often a tricky undertaking for several reasons. First, contracts were written in Hebrew, and agencies often inserted clauses in small print that gave them an absolute right to end the contract at a short notice, or raise the rent if they so wished. Migrants thus needed to have a good knowledge of Hebrew, or an Israeli friend who was willing to assist them with the revision of the contract before they signed it. Second, agencies regularly demanded a deposit of several hundred dollars, as insurance in cases of damage to the apartment or a delay in payment of the rent. Finally, in case of conflict with sub-lessees, agencies often threatened to report undocumented migrants to the police, although in practice they hardly ever did so, fearing damage to their reputation with other potential clients.

For all these reasons it was normally veteran migrants who took on the responsibility of signing contracts with agencies, and the rewards for these migrants were multiple. Veteran migrants could choose their roommates, and they were able to dictate general codes of conduct inside the apartment, for example, rules about smoking, drinking alcohol, or inviting guests after a certain hour at night. Moreover, sharing overpopulated apartments with complete strangers naturally led roommates to have occasional quarrels. Latinos knew that tension must be eased and peacefully resolved since violent clashes could easily lead to police intervention. When such conflicts erupted, renters of apartments were in a powerful position to decide whether someone had to leave the apartment. Finally, when renters offered living spaces (*cupos*) in the Latino informal housing market, they often looked to make some profit by charging roommates a relatively higher price. This capitalistic attitude of some veteran migrants toward newcomers has been reported in many migratory contexts, and it has been shown that solidarity among compatriots can even turn into exploitation in some cases (Mahler 1995, Kwong 1997). This was certainly the case among many Latinos in Israel.

Yet living in south Tel Aviv involved a paradoxical risk. Because residential conditions there suited and attracted so many undocumented migrants, the Israeli police focused most of their operations during deportation campaigns in this part of the city. Moreover, some of the poor and elderly Israeli residents of south Tel Aviv stayed in their apartments, mainly because they did not have the energy to move out. These residents largely perceived the "invasion" of undocumented migrants into their neighborhood as another hazard that was inflicted on their already deteriorated living environment. Some residents even organized and jointly submitted to the mayor of Tel Aviv a letter that detailed their complaints: criminality had increased, many new brothels and bars were established, migrants often got drunk, and they lived in overpopulated apartments and thus increased pollution and noise. I got to see this letter, which was handwritten and contained many spelling errors that clearly reflected the poor educational background of the residents who wrote it. Notwithstanding generally calm relations with undocumented migrants, some of the remaining Israeli residents in south Tel Aviv grew frustrated and bitter, and they sometimes called the police to complain about their undocumented neighbors.

In order not to upset their Israeli neighbors, many undocumented migrants exercised much caution in their conduct at home, for example, making as little noise as possible, not littering, and promptly paying for all house-related services. Many Latinos used to hang Israeli flags on their windows and balconies, and glue on their front door nationalistic stickers, which were occasionally distributed as part of the political propaganda of right-wing parties in Israel. These stickers often contained the Israeli flag and a slogan such as "Stand Up for Israel," "I Do Not Have Another Country," or "The Nation is with the Golan." (The Golan Heights is a territory that Israel captured from Syria in the Six-Day War of 1967 and has occupied since.) Latinos believed that having such stickers on their door would sidetrack police inspections and promote friendly relations with their Israeli neighbors.

However, the risk involved in living in south Tel Aviv induced some, mainly settled, undocumented migrants to move out of this area. This tendency was very pronounced among Latinos. As some of my informants told me, they felt castigated in south Tel Aviv due to the "undocumented" reputation of the area. Latinos were aware that they were probably among those who stuck out least as undocumented migrants in Israel, and so they felt that the police often were disposed to inspect them simply because they lived in south Tel Aviv. Latinos widely believed that by moving out of this area they would significantly increase their chance to avoid police inspections.

Some Latinos moved to more spacious, air-conditioned apartments in the richer neighborhoods of north Tel Aviv, while others left Tel Aviv for its nearby suburbs. Latinos who guarded their expenses usually moved to cheaper working-class suburbs such as Hulon and Bat-Yam, while those who looked to upgrade their living conditions moved to the middle-class cities of Hertzelia and Raanana. Initially a move out of Tel Aviv almost completely protected undocumented migrants from police inspections, but with the establishment of the Immigration Police in 2002, control was broadened to include Tel Aviv's satellite suburbs.

Finding a (Better) Job

Given their urgent economic needs, Latinos' first job was the most important one, but it was also often the most demanding and psychologically challenging one. The spectrum of jobs for Latinos in Tel Aviv was very narrow. Most women were employed either as domestic cleaners or as nannies (which usually also included domestic work), while some also worked as office cleaners. Many women in Latin American countries do not hold paying jobs but are still traditionally responsible for running the household. Thus, for many female migrants working outside the house for payment was a new experience. This experience was mostly positive, but many women found it difficult to work under the supervision of Israeli bosses, especially if they were men.

Latino men were mostly employed as cleaners of offices, restaurants, and private houses. A few of them were hired for semi-skilled jobs such as blacksmiths, painters, and carters. Even though men usually knew what kind of jobs awaited them in Israel, to perform them in reality was mentally taxing. This was especially the case among men who had held respectable, although financially unrewarding, jobs in Latin America (e.g., teachers, clerks, tellers). Cleaning was particularly demeaning for many Latino men because it was seen as a feminine job. Some men initially declined cleaning jobs or quit them after a week or two. Nevertheless, operating under financial pressure, they quickly had to come to terms with the reality that the employment opportunity structure in Israel presented them. After two months, newcomers were willing to take on "whatever job," as one Latino put it. In the case of Latino couples, men also had to deal with the new position of their spouse. Some Latino women told me they felt emancipated by their new status as equal providers, as one of them related:

> In Ecuador I didn't have a say in the running of our lives. Now my husband
> knows that he can't simply order me around; he has to consult me about
> our plans and way of life. I can see he doesn't like it but he has no choice. I
> earn even more than he does! (Lucia, 28, Ecuador)

For men, dealing with empowered wives was made all the more difficult given the prevailing gender norms in Latin America (often referred to as "machismo"). It sometimes generated tension in their personal relationships, which occasionally led to domestic violence (although I do not claim to know to what extent the new position of women contributed to this).

Having to take on what were widely considered to be humiliating jobs certainly reinforced the inclination of many Latinos to initially conceive their migration as limited by time. Latinos endured this situation due to their desire to "complete my mission" (*cumplir mi meta*) and the significantly higher salary that they received. Latinos earned an average salary of US$800– 1,000 per month (in the late 1990s), which was commonly quadruple what they had earned in their own countries.

The economic and social desire of Latinos to improve their position within the Israeli informal labor market added to the significance of social networks. Information about attractive employment opportunities was usually distributed within close circles of relatives and loyal friends. This dynamic had a crucial impact on Latinos who relied on their relatives and friends for asking Israeli employers whether they had, or knew of, an available job. Increased knowledge of the local market and command of Hebrew often allowed veteran Latinos to develop good relationships with Israeli employers and to achieve better working conditions. This is in line with similar findings among undocumented migrants in other settings (Bailey 1987, Massey 1987, Borjas 1990). Veteran Latinos evidently enjoyed this authority and the respect from newcomers whom they assisted in finding jobs. This kind of assistance always implied a pending debt toward the more established migrants and the buttressing of their elevated status.

There were also numerous Israeli employment agencies that specialized in mediating between undocumented migrants and local employers, who did not always know how to find each other. In this way, even spontaneous migrants with no existing network in Israel could usually get a job from one of the many agencies that were spread throughout south Tel Aviv. However, given that the employment of undocumented migrants was unlawful, agencies hardly ever documented their engagements with migrants in a contract. As a result, undocumented migrants had to trust the integrity of agencies, which were often run by Israelis who looked precisely to exploit this situation. Employment agencies commonly charged up to 50 percent of the salary that Israeli employers were willing to pay undocumented migrants for their work. It gave much incentive to both employers and undocumented migrants, once the initial contact was established between them, to cut out the mediation fee of employment agencies. This indeed frequently occurred, to the detriment of agencies, and it only enhanced their economically predatory conduct in the period that their control of migrants was effective.

Although their employment opportunities were limited, Latinos established a hierarchy of jobs that were roughly scaled according to four parameters: payment, physical demand, autonomy at work, and the relationship with Israeli employers. While the first two parameters are straightforward, the latter two call for some clarification. Autonomy at work was a status sign because it usually indicated that workers were experienced and trusted by their Israeli employers. For example, office cleaners enjoyed complete autonomy in performing their job; they were usually given a key to the office they were responsible for cleaning, so that they could access it after work hours when it was empty. This meant that their employers completely trusted them.

Latinos attributed perhaps the highest status to jobs that facilitated the development of warm and friendly relationships with Israelis. Such relationships were valued because they offered significant advantages for the life strategies of undocumented migrants. Incorporating Israelis into their social networks boosted Latinos' general confidence with respect to their long-term settlement in Israel. Emotionally, it provided them with a sense of social integration and a feeling of acceptance. Instrumentally, by developing good relationships with employers, migrants lowered the chance that they would suffer from exploitation, and increased the chance for improved working conditions. Supportive Israeli employers also occasionally mediated (without pay) between Latinos and Israeli homeowners. When such mediation was successful, migrants could save a lot of money on rent, and they also enjoyed more tranquility, knowing the homeowner personally rather than dealing with a real estate agency. Finally, friendly relationships with Israelis occasionally led to romantic relations. For many Latinos who were desperately looking for an Israeli partner, the enhancement of this opportunity was invaluable.

Latinos often competitively compared their jobs, and in particular the relationships they established with their Israeli employers. The following is a colorful example of this practice. In an eatery in south Tel Aviv, a conversation about work developed between four Ecuadorian friends. Jeffrey boasted that he had already quit his job three times, only to return each time after his employer begged him to come back on improved terms. Although Jeffrey was a cleaner in an automobile workshop, he stressed that his boss often taught him and even allowed him to practice some professional repair work. It was precisely the professional aspect of his job that Ramirez then chose to highlight in response to Jeffrey's comments:

> I am in charge of painting the varnish on all the furniture in the workshop;
> I have a professional job. The big boss trusts me with closed eyes; he also
> asks me to supervise the job that the other painters do. They can't do
> without me in the workshop; if I miss a day the work just piles, the
> workshop is paralyzed.

Not certain whether his statement left a strong enough impression, Ramirez quickly added, "They know that with me they can't mess around, they give me much respect, they treat me like an Israeli worker." He then drew our attention to the fact that he was wearing a training suit of Maccabi Tel Aviv (the city's popular basketball team), and continued, "when the games of Maccabi are broadcast live on the television they [Israelis] invite me to watch it with them. And you know how they call me, they call me Rami, that's an Israeli name." Israeli employers often used nicknames for their loyal workers, and in the case of some Latinos, employers modified their names to sound like Israeli ones; for example, Ramirez became Rami, Roberto became Robi, and Rebecca became Rivka.

As Ramirez paused to take a bite from his pita bread, Vicente, who worked as domestic cleaner for a very rich and famous Israeli family, quickly intervened:

> Ah, that is nothing, my boss buys me presents for my birthday. They also
> give me presents for my daughter. When I work in the house I'm allowed to
> open the fridge whenever I want and take a cold drink or something,
> without asking anyone. I sit there at the table to eat lunch together with
> them every day. I am like family there. They also always try to help me
> practice my Hebrew. [Vicente then turned to me and said,] You say it,
> Barak, who is speaking the best Hebrew here among us? Ah?

Before I could even answer, Vicente pulled out from his wallet a photo showing him next to his famous employer.[1] "You see here I am with my employer, you recognized him right?" Vicente proudly asked me. "Every Israeli who sees it, will know for which family I'm working," he asserted. A few Latinos who worked for Israeli celebrity families all carried photos taken with their employers. They proudly showed these photos in public. It was as if a photo with an Israeli celebrity was a kind of an informal ID card issued by society, and a substitute for the most desired official ID that was never issued by the state.

Domestic cleaners, and even more so nannies, were probably in the best position to develop warm and trustful relationships with Israeli employers. I encountered, for example, many cases in which employers assisted their Latino domestic workers to find better accommodation in a better neighborhood, directly from a homeowner they personally knew. Many employers also encouraged their domestic workers to learn Hebrew and patiently practiced with them. Some employers even promised their Latino workers to help them out in case they would be arrested by the police. Although this was often an empty promise, I know of a few cases in which Latinos' employers did their utmost to convince the police to release their detained employees and were even willing to pay a bail to have them released from detention.

Jeffrey, who felt he was losing the competition, lashed out at the rest: "But you are illegal like all of us; tomorrow they can decide to fire you, or the police will pick you up and throw you out of the country." Ramirez angrily replied, "I am here already for eight years; nobody can do anything to me." He then looked at me and asked rhetorically in Hebrew, "And who will do my job anyway if they take me out? Israelis don't want to do this job, right?" He pointed his finger to the sky and continued, "We have a permission from God to work here." Ramirez was not a religious person, and his remark was said more in reproach against the fact that he could not legalize his status, although he had conducted his life in Israel in a full sense for eight years already. Seeking reassurance for his secure position in Israel, Vicente immediately asked me, "If you were a policeman walking outside here looking at me, could you tell that I was illegal?"

This elaboration on the hierarchy of jobs among Latinos is not meant to romanticize the rock-bottom, dead-end type of jobs that they occupied in Israel. Latinos knew they were employed in jobs that Israelis, even unemployed ones, were not willing to take on. My intention is to emphasize the ways in which Latinos attempted emotionally to divorce themselves from the demeaning status conferred on them by their jobs. This was especially the case when Latinos prolonged their stay in Israel, and had to face the perpetuation of their position in the labor market. The creation of an internal Latino hierarchy clearly served to alleviate this predicament. Migration literature often focuses on a comparison of migrants' earnings to those of the native population (Chiswick 1978, Piore 1979, Borjas 1987, Dustmann 1993). Although often offended by it, Latinos understood that they were not competing for employment with the native Israeli population, and thus looked to elevate their position and status by drawing internal comparisons with other undocumented migrants.

The following is a vivid example of the way in which Latinos compared their position with that of other undocumented migrant groups. I once went together with Ernesto, a veteran Ecuadorian migrant, to do some shopping for the weekend at the Carmel market. When we passed by a fish store, Ernesto drew my attention to it and with a clear sense of satisfaction told me that this was his first workplace in Israel. "It was awful, you see the Chinese guy there, I was just like him." Ernesto pointed to a worker at the back of the store who was using a knife in order to clean fish. He then recalled the working conditions there with marked disdain:

> You have to work here every day from six in the morning until half-past seven in the afternoon, and at the end of the day the owner also wants you to sweep up the whole store. He pays you two dollars [U.S.] an hour, which for me in the beginning still looked like a lot of money. Today I would not do this work for anything in the world.

Ernesto then pulled from his jacket a bundle of keys to the offices he was cleaning at night. He jingled them in pride and, like a self-made man who had managed to advance in the ladder of status, stated:

> Now I am my own boss! And I earn almost double than what I used to get here. It is hard here [in Israel] in the beginning but if you are smart you find your way up. Only a few years ago we [Latinos] were in the place where the Chinese migrants are today.

Dealing with Displacement: Coping Strategies

Most Latinos in Israel enjoyed what they considered to be a high standard of living, a very handsome salary, and the possibility to save a substantial amount of money. Furthermore, after the initial stage of paying off debts, many Latinos diverted an increased portion of their time and resources to recreational activities. Yet, however positive their experience, most Latinos found it extremely difficult to overcome the separation from their families. Migrants' longings were a source of much agony and pain, which was normally suppressed but on certain occasions surfaced and seemed to be emotionally devastating. At this point in their migration trajectory, Latinos felt most strongly their "double absence," to use the term of Sayad (1999); while they were not fully integrated as immigrants in Israeli society, they still painfully experienced the dislocation from their home society.

This longing for one's family was probably most acute in the case of migrants who left their children back home. Most migrating parents maintained weekly telephone contact with their children, but it usually only enhanced their pain rather than alleviating it. I regularly witnessed parents burst into tears as they talked to their children on the phone, leaning their wet cheeks against the Perspex partition of a telephone booth in a calling center, often holding a photo of their child in their hands to provide a fuller dimension to the conversation. Latino families seemed to be emotionally closely bound together and the breakup that immigration forced on them was a source for much suffering and misery to all parties involved. Leaving one's elderly parents behind was also heartbreaking for many Latinos. Mercedes reached Israel from Bolivia with her husband, Julio, and later they also brought over their son, Samuel. Nevertheless, Mercedes could not find peace as she was constantly worried about her father:

> I used to visit him every week. His house would get dusty, but he wouldn't even notice. He is an old man. So I would clean the whole house, and then I would cook for him and we'd sit together and eat. Ay, my beloved father, I miss him so much.

I tried to comfort Mercedes by saying that her sisters were still in Bolivia, and they surely took care of their father, but Mercedes was inconsolable:

> No, no, they don't take care of him like I do. He is a sick man, he needs his medicine. I used to look at his drawer to check if he had all the medicine, and if not, I would go and buy it for him. They are all very busy, they don't take care of my papi like I did. You know every night in bed I think of him and cry. I try to keep my tears inside but they just drop into the pillow.

Her husband, Julio, who sat with us, nodded in confirmation, as Mercedes burst into tears. The experience of displacement and loss certainly constituted a mental challenge for most Latinos. It sometimes even appeared to be traumatic, as was found in other migratory contexts (see Portes and Rumbaut 1996: ch. 4). The emotional experience of loss and displacement led Latinos to develop private and collective coping strategies that were adjusted to their particular constrained transnational position in Israel.

When Vicente and Blanca emigrated from Ecuador they left their children, Genesis and David, who were four and two years old, respectively, with their grandparents in Guayaquil. The couple operationalized their migration within an established network that included close relatives. In settling down they also received much assistance from their relatives. Vicente and Blanca both found jobs in the cleaning sector, and they earned "an incredible amount of money," as Vicente once described to me. Vicente quickly made some friends from the many Ecuadorians in his age group who lived in the same neighborhood, and the couple began to regularly take part in all sorts of social activities that were organized by the Ecuadorian community. In many ways the story of Vicente and Blanca was the story of a smooth migration. Yet the couple found it enormously difficult to bear the distance from their young children.

In the apartment that they shared with four other Ecuadorians, Vicente and Blanca's room was filled with photos of their children. On many occasions when I visited the couple in their apartment, they played for me the latest video of their children. Videotapes were often sent to Latinos so that they could closely follow the development of their children and have a tangible image of the improvements to which their remittances contributed. Videos typically showed children in their daily lives: dressing up for school, playing with a new toy, or sitting in front of a new television set or a computer.

Although watching these videos was precious to Latinos, it was also very painful. Blanca would burst into tears with the very first images of her children, and Vicente, who initially would try to keep himself firm, also usually ended up crying. Some Latinos sent videotapes to their families back home, showing the kind of lives they had in Israel. Popular items on these videos featured a trip to Jerusalem, a shot of the modern skyline of Tel Aviv, or a relaxing time on a sunny beach or in a park. Latinos also often used videos in order to directly "talk" to their children, congratulating them for their birthday or telling them to behave well and do their homework from school.[2]

Exchanging videotapes was a private coping strategy; there also existed collective practices that were meant to alleviate Latinos' experience of displacement. The most prominent collective coping strategy took place in the regular practice of *reuniones,* that is, social get-togethers of a group of relatives and friends who sat down together to enjoy traditional food, listen to music, and in many cases also slowly sip whiskey or other liquor for many long hours. *Reuniones* were normally held in people's apartments at weekends, and in order not to burden the host with the necessary preparations, each guest would habitually bring a bottle of liquor, a few cans of beer, or something to nibble. Conversations in *reuniones* included all sorts of issues: from attractive job opportunities and gossipy stories about other compatriots to the new methods that the Israeli police used to apprehend undocumented migrants (a topic on which my contributions were highly appreciated). Latinos commonly got nostalgic in *reuniones,* and easily recalled stories and memories of family members and friends whom they left behind. It was in this sense that *reuniones,* which were always considered a recreational activity, often took on the form of an emotional support group.

Vicente often organized *reuniones* in his apartment for a group of Ecuadorians. He invited his relatives who also lived in Tel Aviv, and some of his Ecuadorian friends. Vicente had a guitar at home, and during *reuniones* at his place someone would always at a certain point pick up the guitar to play familiar Ecuadorian songs. Guests typically joined along in singing, and it was normally not long before they all got emotional. Some people would start crying, and others would embrace their partners, whispering comforting words in their ears. The crying was not limited to women, as some of the most macho men also often shed tears and sometimes even collapsed in the arms of their partners, friends, or simply those who sat next to them. An occasional funny remark would evoke somewhat agitated laughter that would then quickly give way again to the general melancholic atmosphere. This collective singing, crying, and laughing could easily last until the early hours of the morning. Some people would slowly start leaving, while others would stay to sleep over on mattresses in the living room.

Such emotional *reuniones* clearly constituted a type of collective healing practice for dealing with the experience of displacement. Some of the songs Latinos chose to sing at *reuniones* were written in their home countries. These songs treated the experience of migrants with much compassion and sympathy, and often even portrayed migrants in heroic fashion. The following is my translation of two songs that were often played and listened to by migrants at *reuniones*. The first one is an Ecuadorian popular song.

Mother, Prepare My Suitcase	Madre, Prepara Mis Cosas
Mother, prepare my suitcase	Madre, prepara mis cosas
for I must depart	porque tengo que partir
to look for new opportunities	a buscar nuevas fortunas
although leaving tears me apart	aún que me cuesta salir
I can only ask you:	solo te digo:
"Don't forget, and give me your blessing"	"No olvides, y dame tu bendición"
Yet my destiny takes me	Pero el destino me lleva
and I must follow it	y junto a él yo me voy
it is heartbreaking to see a mother	que triste ver a una madre
as she sits down to cry	cuando se pone a llorar
over a son she adores	por este hijo que adora
and will never return	y no ha de volver jamás
From a distance I still see my hometown	Y mi ciudad a los lejos se ve
ah, sadness overwhelms me	ay, que tristeza me da
knowing I left everything behind	al saber que dejo todo
mother, fiancée, and home	madre, novia, y hogar

The second song was often played at *reuniones* of Colombians:

The Emigrant	El Emigrante
Yesterday early morning	Ayer muy de mañanita
I had to leave my land	tuve que dejar mi tierra
with my soul shattered	con el alma echa pedazos
to my mother I said farewell	me despedí de mi vieja
I told her: "don't suffer mother	Le dije: "no sufras madre
for soon I will be back,	que muy pronto he de volver,
I'm going to earn money	me voy a ganar dinero
to put you all on track"	para poderlos mantener"

My wife constantly wept	Mi esposa quedó llorando
and only said to me as I left:	y me dijó al partir:
"Come back soon my life"	"Vuelve pronto vida mía"
I felt inside me death	Que sentí yo he de morir

My brothers so beloved	Mis hermanos tan queridos
accompanied me as I departed,	me fueron a despedir,
my children were still sleeping	Deje mis hijos dormidos
I almost felt like dying	Casi me sentí morir

To an involuntary exile	A un exilio involuntario
my poverty condemned me	me condeno la pobreza
I know my country is rich	siento mi patria tan rica
yet I had to leave for other lands	tuve que irme a otras tierras

Several salient issues can be detected from these songs and the context in which they were written and played. Most notably, these songs convey the pain and sadness that engulf emigrants as they cut themselves off from their beloved families and countries. Taking into account the dramatic character of poetry, it is still very clear that the experience of immigration as communicated in these songs (and many others) appears to be enormously difficult if not traumatic. A prominent theme is migrants' preoccupation with their destiny and the misery their departure inflicted on their loved ones. There are repeated figurative references to the separation from children and spouse as a killing experience.

While in the first song the force driving people out of their countries is vaguely termed as "destiny," in the second song poverty is condemned for sentencing people to "an involuntary exile." In Israel, Latinos perceived their migration with a sense of a mission (*cumplir mi meta*), which often developed against a backdrop of relative deprivation as opposed to absolute deprivation. In this sense most Latinos can be seen as "voluntary migrants" who seek in migration a way for securing a certain standard of living for their families. Yet with its potential to be traumatic the idea of voluntarism has its flipside; that is, migrants' perception that they voluntarily inflicted misery on their families can cause serious psychological distress and a guilt complex. Migrants' anguish is thus exacerbated by the fact that in an attempt to better the lives of their loved ones, they actually caused them much pain.

Songs not only poetically reflected a difficult reality, they also functioned as a creative force in at least two ways. First, they allowed for migrants, as individuals who suffered loss, to express and share their feelings in a joint healing process. By engaging in an aesthetic activity, the most common, but suppressed, feelings were given expression and served to create an affective space for consolation, solidarity, and emotional relief (see Baumann 1987: 173–83). It was further a space where "individuals and groups of individuals try to make sense of the profusion of things that happen to them" (Geertz 1976: 1478). Important to note here is the ritualized character of *reuniones,* and the integral role that music played in them. It is largely the patterned form of *reuniones* that facilitated, mediated, and normalized the affective release of emotions by participants who might otherwise, in different settings, remain restrained.

The creative force of songs played in *reuniones* emanates from the fact that they were written, recorded, and also widely played in migrants' home countries. The production of these songs thus symbolically bespoke the reconstructed space devoted to, and occupied by, absent migrants. In a way it bestowed on migrants a place in the national narrative of their countries of origin. While migrants often made sense of their migratory experience in relation to their effect on people in their countries of origin, these songs confirmed for them that people back home also understood their own reality in direct relation to migrants.

When I visited Vicente in Ecuador two years after he had been deported from Israel, I could see the enduring meaning that Latinos attributed to these songs. One day as we were driving in the taxi that Vicente now owned and operated in Guayaquil, he put on a cassette that featured many of the songs that he and his friends had sung in Israel during *reuniones.* Vicente told me that he enjoyed playing these songs as they now nostalgically reminded him of his time in Israel. "It also often provokes passengers to ask me whether I used to be a migrant, and I like to tell them about it," he explained, and a bitter mellow smile spread on his face.

Prolonged Settlement: Shifting Material
Investments and Emotional Orientations

Most Latinos managed to achieve the mission they had initially set out to accomplish when embarking on a migration to Israel. Many of them were able to save a considerable amount of money, which they typically remitted to families and invested in their countries of origin. It was precisely their success in Israel that largely induced most Latinos to prolong their stay in Israel. Latinos who managed to avoid deportation considered themselves fortunate, and they were thus disinclined to leave Israel voluntarily. Most espoused the following logic to account for the prolongation of their stay in Israel:

Once we leave Israel it is for good. What will we do if we go back now? What is the use? We won't find jobs that pay like the ones we have here. We better stay so long as we can and take full advantage of the opportunity we have. (Fernando, 32, Colombian)

Latinos who supported their children and/or parents were worried that their return home would mean a return to a lower standard of living. "We work here like blacks so that we can live there like whites": this remark was made by one of my informants from Peru, who decided to extend his stay in Israel. Leaving aside the racial connotations in the sentence, the double use of "we" is indicative of migrants' bifurcated perception regarding their place. Migrants were fully aware that maintaining the lifestyle of their families was conditioned on the uninterrupted supply of remittances:

> When I came here I left my children with my parents and promised to send them money for taking care of the children. My three children are now all going to good schools, they wear nice clothes, and I would like them to go to the university. If I return today, I will never be able to afford a good education for my children, my savings would be eaten up within couple of years . . . and my parents . . . I can't just say "thank you" and stop supporting them, so where will I get the money for all this if I return now? (Ángel, 41, Ecuadorian)

Some Latinos also thought it was important to remain abroad because of their crucial role in helping out their family members in times of severe health problems that required a costly treatment. For example, when Linda's mother got seriously ill and needed an urgent operation, Linda's sister in Colombia informed her that the operation cost US$3,000 and expected her to send the money:

> I have two more sisters and a brother, but they never migrated. I am the only emigrant in my family and therefore have much more money than they do. In cases like this the family expects that the migrant would help out, and that is what I'll do.

Juan, Linda's husband, fully supported her, and he added in a tone that conveyed both compassion and a clear sense of superiority:

> If the rest of the children in Colombia put together all of their savings they probably can't give their mother more than US$1,000. That is why it is customarily up to migrants who made it to help their families. We have our savings and it is in such cases that we must be there for our loved ones. Let's be frank about it, if it wasn't for us Linda's mother could never undergo this operation and would probably die. Last year my sister got very ill, and we also paid her treatment and saved her life.

Enhancing the well-being of their relatives conferred much status on migrants and made them feel vitally needed. It compounded and perpetuated their sense of mission as their immigration also served as an insurance policy for relatives back home (Massey 1990a).

It was common for Latinos who reconsidered their migration plans to protract their stay in Israel by one additional year each time. "Next year we definitely go back" was a common sentence that I repeatedly heard from Latinos who had achieved the economic aim they had set to accomplish via immigration to Israel. This "myth of return" is widespread among migrants in countries worldwide (see Cohen and Gold 1996, Rodriguez Garcia 2006, Bolognani 2007). However, it usually refers to legal migrants who recurrently prolong their stay, each time with another milestone in mind, for example, a substantially better economic position back home, the formation of family, or the end of children's educational term (see Baumann 1996: 54). Latinos' prolongations of their stay in shorter intervals, typically of one year, probably reflected the uncertainty undocumented migrants faced in planning their future. Not knowing whether settlement in Israel was a realistic option, Latinos arguably tried to convince themselves, as a defense mechanism, that their return back home was still imminent. Yet the prolongation of their stay produced some powerful dynamics that gradually reshaped their outlook, and gravitated their financial and emotional orientations toward Israel.

From an economic perspective, after the subsistence of migrants' families had been secured at a considerably higher level, Latinos normally looked to invest their savings. Latinos preferred investment was in real estate; either rebuilding their own dwelling back home, or more commonly purchasing a new apartment, house, or land. Real estate property was considered not only a safe investment, but also a useful one for migrants who had left behind their family. Families could then move to the new house, enjoy improved facilities, and save the cost of rent in case they had rented a house. Having said that, during my fieldwork in Ecuador I saw a few houses that were built or bought by the relatives of Latinos in Israel, and stood completely empty. This was mainly the case where both parents emigrated, leaving children with their grandparents, who often preferred staying in their own homes despite offers to move and inhabit newly bought houses. The most striking example of such a "ghost house" I encountered in a village outside Cuenca. It was a very nice and spacious two-story house that was built right next to the old house of the grandparents, who were left to raise the four children of Esperanza and Alberto when they left for Israel. Although the old house was small and damp, the grandparents refused to move into the new house. The four children would go every day to clean the new house and work in the small garden at its side. Looking at the care with which the four children worked in and around it, I thought the house seemed more like a giant altar where the achievements of the parents were worshiped and their absence mourned.

Some Latinos, often after successfully investing in real estate, looked for other investments. Putting their money in savings accounts was never their preferred choice, not least because of their mistrust of the banking system. Chronic fraud scandals and a series of bankruptcies in some of the most respected financial institutions across Latin America fostered much contempt toward banks. For example, in 1999 one of Ecuador's most popular banks (Filanbanco) suddenly closed its operations and froze all accounts of its beneficiaries. Consequently, an enormous fraud scheme was revealed, and hundreds of thousands of Ecuadorians, including migrants, lost most of their savings. Moreover, banks could hardly protect their clients' savings from sudden devaluations in local currencies that so often struck Latin American countries, sometimes halving the real value of money in a matter of a few days. Ecuador in 1996, Brazil in 2001, and Argentina in 2002 are examples of such extraordinary devaluations.

Establishing a business in their home country was an investment option that some Latinos considered. Yet because of their inability to travel back home and oversee the establishment of a business, migrants needed to work with a partner in their home country. Clearly, trust in one's partner was crucial to this kind of "entrepreneurialism by remote control." I knew a few Latinos in Israel who invested in such partnerships, for example, in running a restaurant or a bus line. Yet migrants were often lured into fictitious investments, which eventually turned out to be schemes that would simply allow "partners" to pocket some of the migrants' wealth. For example, Elsa accused her brother-in-law of robbing her of money, by convincing her to invest in a frozen yogurt business that allegedly failed. When I met Elsa's brother-in-law in Ecuador and mentioned to him her grievances, he aggressively told me in an accusatory tone:

> She should be ashamed for blaming me for this. She has all that money and
> still I tried to help her with investing it here in Ecuador, and what do I get?
> Accusations that I stole her money. You know what, I don't want to say
> anything about it any more. . . . She should perhaps have thought to give
> her family more money in the first place instead of investing it for herself.
> To tell you the truth, I am not even sad anymore that she lost her money.
> Let's see her now taking care of her money herself from Israel.

Limited and risky investment opportunities enhanced an already existing tendency among veteran Latinos to divert increasing portions of their savings and earnings to improving their standard of living in Israel. Probably sensing a drift in their orientation toward increased settlement, these Latinos looked to normalize and improve their lives in Israel. As mentioned earlier, many veteran Latinos moved out from south Tel Aviv in search of a better and safer living environment. It was also common for veteran Latinos to move to an apartment with more space and fewer roommates. Most Latinos also increasingly participated in the elaborate recreational scene that provided ample opportunities for leisure, solace, and the development of romantic relations. All these readjustments reflect the transition in Latinos' perception from "*quiero cumplir mi meta*" to a prolongation of the migratory phase, and a long-term settlement.

Some Latinos began to engage in what seemed to be conspicuous consumption, for example, shopping for clothes in fancy fashion shops, going out to eat in expensive restaurants, connecting their apartments to satellite cable TV, and buying lavish electronic devices, such as DVD players, MP3 players, and expensive mobile phones. Veteran migrants also increasingly consumed Israeli music. They bought Israeli CDs, which gradually replaced Latino ones on shelves in their apartments. I provocatively asked some of my close informants, who were engaged in this more consumerist lifestyle, if it was worth the effort to work so hard and then spend most of their salaries on items that were apparently insignificant for their future lives. In response some Latinos explained to me that they were, as one of them put it, "sick and tired of only working here for having a better life one day in the future." Another informant was unequivocal about the changing orientation of veteran Latinos: "We work very hard and we deserve to enjoy our life here; you can have a very good life in Israel, and there is no reason why we should prevent ourselves from it." Possessing lavish personal electronic gadgets and a fashionable wardrobe not only contributed to Latinos' satisfaction and self-esteem, but also rendered them even less detectable to the police. Moreover, adopting a lifestyle that they perceived to be Israeli (and Western) clearly enhanced Latinos' sense of cultural integration and belonging.

Veteran Latinos steadily got accustomed to their way of life and learned to enjoy Israel, not only as a place to work, but also as a place to live. Remarks of veterans about their lives in Israel included positive references to varied aspects: the climate ("it's sunny here almost every day"); the food ("first I hated hummus and pita, but now I really love it"; "turkey meat is so cheap here you can afford to eat it everyday"); the scenery ("Israel is the most beautiful country in the world"); the personal safety ("in my country you can't walk alone in the park, sometimes not even during the day; in Israel you can walk everywhere at anytime"); and the mentality of Israelis ("you shout a lot and you quickly get upset but beyond that you are very nice people"; "I think the Israeli mentality is very similar to the Latino mentality, you work hard but you like to enjoy life"; "Israelis are the Latinos of the Middle East"). This sampling of Latinos' impressions captures the reconstruction of Israel as an encouraging setting for veteran Latinos who now admittedly and consciously contemplated settling down in Israel as a long-term strategy.

Yet the most decisive factor that led Latinos to consider an enduring stay in Israel concerned the birth of children and the reunification of families. Latino couples who met and married in Israel or emigrated together before having children often eventually decided to reproduce while in Israel. Couples also sometimes experienced unplanned pregnancies and then decided to keep the child. Family formation and the birth of children enhanced Latinos' determination to root themselves in Israel. However, when pregnancy and/or the delivery were difficult, or even traumatic, it sometimes facilitated a decision to leave Israel voluntarily and return home.

Married Latinos who had migrated alone also sometimes got romantically involved with someone in Israel. "It is the power of life," Sergio, a veteran Chilean migrant, declared as he explained to me his intention to marry Talia, a Colombian woman he had met in Tel Aviv. Sergio was a married man; he had migrated to Israel in 1991, leaving his wife and three children behind. Talia was not the first girlfriend that Sergio had in Israel, but his relationship with her was serious. In 2002 Sergio married Talia in a Catholic Church in Jerusalem, and a year later their daughter, Abigail, was born. The couple was determined to stay in Israel "forever, if possible," as Sergio put it. While Sergio did not want to live in Colombia, he was also very reluctant to return to Chile, where he would have had to face the legal and practical consequences of his "old" marriage.

The prolongation of migration and the consequent formation of a second parallel household by married migrants who lived for a long period separately from their spouse was not an uncommon phenomenon. Although a migrant could covertly maintain two households, it more often led to the breakup of the "old" household, especially when children were born into the "new" household. Migrants who deserted their "old" household often left a dependent family emotionally wrecked, with no regular income. In Ecuador I met Lupe, whose husband, an undocumented migrant in the United States, left her after eleven years. Lupe was sitting at the front door to the house she built with the money her husband remitted; she was clearly still angry, although the separation had occurred more than two years before:

> That's how it is. They find there a young woman and forget about their
> home. It is one thing that he left me, but he has two children. He's a father,
> he has responsibility. What am I supposed to tell his children, ah? Well, they
> know. They know about their father. I had to say something when he
> stopped sending money. Now I'm old and I don't have work. This house is
> the only thing I have.

Yet those who stay behind, mainly women, also sometimes take on a new partner after some years of solitude. When rumors about the spouse's new relationship back home find their way to migrants abroad (and they usually do, due to intense social control), it also often leads the infuriated migrant to cut all contacts. In this sense, the formation of new households by those who remained back home can also lead to the prolongation of migrants' stay abroad.

In Israel, many veteran Latinos who had left families back home finally decided to reunite their family in Israel, bringing their spouse (when the spouse was not in Israel already), children, and sometimes even parents. A distinction should be drawn, in the process of family reunifications, between the case of young parents with small children and that of more mature couples with grown-up children. In the latter case, parents basically judged that emigration to Israel was strategically right for the independent future of their adult children. They thus enthusiastically told their children about the economic opportunities and the kind of life one can have in Israel. Parents commonly offered to finance their children's migration trip and promised to facilitate their initial adaptation in Israel. Adult children, in their late teens and early twenties, could then evaluate their parents' offer in view of their particular situation in the country of origin and make their decision. Adult children who came to Israel could also, at any given moment, independently decide to return home if they did not like it in Israel.

Reuniting one's family in Israel was a very different undertaking when it involved small children. In a practical sense it necessitated a more complex and costly operation. As a rule, Latinos in Israel preferred not to risk going back home to get their children. They thus needed a third party, a "carrier," who would travel together with their children to Israel. The choice was usually for a grandparent, an aunt, or an uncle. Parents financed the trip for their children and the accompanying adult, or sometimes even two adults, for example, in case the two grandparents insisted on flying together. The overall investment in bringing over children to Israel cost between US$5,000 and US$10,000, depending on the number of passengers, country of origin, season, and so on.

Reunification operations that involved small children were always risky. For most "carriers," but especially elderly ones, a trip to Israel was their first encounter with an airplane and with border officials; they were often intimidated by the whole plan, and thus were prone not to hold up under moderate verbal pressure from Israeli officials to reveal their intentions. Children too, no matter how well they had been coached, were disposed by their natural innocence and excitement to give information about their expected reunification with their parents. In cases that aroused the suspicion of Israeli officials, children and their "carriers" were sent back on the first scheduled flight to their country of origin. Bringing in children became even more difficult after 2000, as Israel paid special attention to preventing family reunifications. Officials at border controls were instructed to interrogate unusual combinations of children traveling with adults other than their own parents.

Failed reunification attempts were emotionally devastating for Latinos. Here is how one exasperated mother, Rosa, expressed her despair after an unsuccessful attempt:

> I don't know what to do, I can't take it any more. My little boy was one year
> old when we left Ecuador; he is now almost five and he doesn't even know
> me. Ay, ay, [burying her head in her hands and then wiping the tears] I
> can't believe it, my children were already here in Israel, only some
> kilometers away from us and we couldn't even see them. . . . I don't know

what we should do. We must return now [to Ecuador], but there isn't much we can offer them back there, and by now we are so well established here in Israel.

Rosa was clearly in an emotional turmoil. Her hands were shaking and she could not stop sobbing. A failure to bring their children was a full-blown setback for Latinos, who often became demoralized about, and disillusioned with, their long-term prospects in Israel. Some Latinos then seriously contemplated a return home, while others decided to have children in Israel.

Notwithstanding the involved difficulties in bringing small children to Israel, some Latinos also seriously doubted whether they were able to fulfill both roles as parents and providers in the challenging and significantly pricier Israeli environment. Here is how Sonia, a 29-year-old Ecuadorian, expressed her hesitation in this regard:

> You know how it is, we both work all day and the children will have to stay alone in the *guardería* [childcare center] sometimes for twelve hours a day . . . and it is so expensive to maintain a family with two children here in Israel that we will probably not be able to save any money. Like that we can't advance. . . . In Ecuador the children are happy, they are together with their grandparents, they can play with their cousins, and we can here save enough money to give them everything they need there. It tears me apart not to be with them, but maybe it is better like that. I don't know what we should do.

Infants and children younger than six were habitually kept at *guarderias*—improvised Latino kindergartens operated by some undocumented female migrants who gave up their pay with Israeli employers for running this rather profitable business. For each child, parents needed to pay the *guardería* US$100 to US$150 per month, excluding food and drinks. Parents could usually bring their children to a *guardería* as early as 6 AM and pick them up until 6 PM. Extra hours were commonly charged at a rate of approximately US$4 an hour. Dozens of *guarderias* operated across south Tel Aviv, either in the apartments of those who ran them or in the basement of the building where they lived.[3] Indeed some operators of *guarderias* renovated the interior of the basement in their building to accommodate more children. The use of communal basements for entrepreneurial aims was mainly practiced by Latinos who lived in buildings that were mostly inhabited either by other undocumented migrants or by veteran migrants who established good relationships with their Israeli neighbors, who were asked for their consent about the usage of the mutual basement.

Yet Latinos were not always able to choose whether they wanted to bring small children to Israel; the decision was sometimes imposed on parents by the reluctance or inability of children's guardians to continue raising them in countries of origin. The parents then needed either to return and take care of their children or to bring them over to Israel. Much has been written about the difficulties of second and third generations of migrants in adapting to their host societies. Much less focus has been given to the adaptation of children to irregular familial configurations and the emotional devastation inflicted upon them by their parents' emigration. The departure of even one parent often causes severe problems in the lives of children (Miles 2004). Children of emigrants are commonly provided with improved material conditions, but they overwhelmingly lack their parents' emotional support. Searching for an explanation for their situation, young children are prone to end up blaming themselves, as the following quote by one child in Ecuador conveys:

> I am guilty for the separation of my parents, he [my father] left in order to give me a better life but over there he had another woman and now my mother is alone. (quoted in Castillo et al. 2003: 71)

In Ecuador I visited a school where 40 percent of all pupils had at least one of their parents abroad. Wilson, the schoolmaster, told me that children of emigrants constituted a profound problem on a large scale:

> They tend to fare much worse in class and they often have to repeat years . . . they are also less disciplined and communicative and show higher rates of involvement in violent incidents, cases of drug abuse, and participation in street gangs.

Wilson told me that a widespread stigma regarding children of migrants consequently led many schoolmasters to refuse to enroll them in their schools. In his school Wilson chose to tackle the problem by employing a special psychologist for counseling children of migrants. The psychologist explained to me that three major factors affected these children: an emotional deficit, the lack of power and/or will of grandparents to discipline and guide their grandchildren, and children's outlook, which dominantly ties their expectations from life to immigration. The impact of this last factor was reaffirmed by extensive research of attitudes among children of migrants in another Ecuadorian school. Children were asked to write a fictional "future diary" describing their aspirations; of all twenty-one participants, only four mentioned Ecuador as the place where their future plans would be realized; the rest connected their ambitions to living in places outside Ecuador (Castillo et al. 2003: 137–39).

The Challenge of Children: Unexpected Rewards
for Practical National Belonging

Although challenging in more than one way, establishing one's family in Israel was extremely rewarding for Latinos who could first and foremost emotionally recover, at least partially, from their sense of displacement and loss. Moreover, many Latinos believed that their best chance for legalization of status in Israel rested on the fragile shoulders of their young children. It is important to note that Latinos believed in this idea years before it finally materialized in 2005. Indeed, early on, there were already some signs in the overall oppressive Israeli policy that Latinos could and did optimistically interpret.

Most tellingly, the Israeli police refrained from arresting and deporting undocumented mothers with children younger than eighteen. This more humane approach was imposed on the police by the High Court of Israel in response to an appeal by Israeli NGOs, which claimed it was traumatic for children, and inconsistent with Israel's commitment under the UN Convention for the Protection of Children's Rights. Yet the High Court of Israel did not oppose the deportation of the father in case both parents were in Israel. Indeed, in practice the police deported many fathers, and as a result an increasing number of mothers remained in Israel alone with their children, or "voluntarily" followed the husband back home (for more, see *Haaretz* 16.07.2004). The Israeli policy transformed children younger than eighteen into human shields for their mothers, who regularly took their children along whenever they went out to public places, such as automatic laundromats, calling centers, or supermarkets. Some Latinos, at least partly, were induced to form families or bring their children to Israel precisely for this unique advantage that it conferred on the survival strategies of undocumented migrants.

Another encouraging sign for undocumented migrants with respect to the special treatment of their children by the state of Israel was given in the case of births. Whenever Israeli employers of undocumented migrants paid social security tax for their workers (as was the case with some domestic workers and nannies), the latter enjoyed full coverage of delivery expenses at Israeli hospitals as well as the customary "birth bonus" (*ma'anak leida*) of around US$400 and "birth payments" (*dmei leida*) that roughly equaled the sum of two months' salary.[4] To receive such benefits undocumented migrants had to register with the Israeli Social Security Institution and provide their full details, including their residence in Israel. Such bureaucratic procedures deterred many pregnant undocumented migrants, who feared these details would be leaked to the police. However, the number of cases in which Latino mothers delivered in state hospitals and received state social benefits was taken by Latinos more generally as an indication of the responsibility and inclusiveness that Israel exercised with respect to their children.

In addition, children of undocumented migrants were allowed into Israel's national healthcare system. After a lengthy legal battle led by the Israeli NGO Physicians for Human Rights, Israel offered undocumented migrants the opportunity to insure their children in a similar way to the health insurance of Israeli children. The only difference was the higher monthly fee, of approximately US$35, which undocumented migrants needed to pay. Many Latinos actually chose not to purchase this insurance for their children because they found it to be too expensive, or again because they feared that the police would get access to an official registration that included their residential address. But here again, although not all children of Latinos were integrated into the national healthcare system, most Latinos saw it as a sign of Israel's openness and responsibility toward their children.

MESILA, the municipal flagship that dealt with Tel Aviv's undocumented migrant population, also focused much of its attention on alleviating the predicaments of children. MESILA organized recreational activities for children on its premises, and in the year 2000 it also offered to undocumented migrants who operated *guarderias* a free professional course for becoming kindergarten teachers. This was largely done in reaction to graphic media reports about the poor conditions in which some clandestine kindergartens of undocumented migrants operated, and the fact that operators mostly had no formal pedagogic education. One of my informants who operated a *guardería* and participated in MESILA's course, praised the initiative and clearly chose to see it as a vindication for her stubborn belief in a possible normalization of undocumented migrants' situation through their children. She once told me in a triumphant tone, "Israel will not remain indifferent to children who were born here or are being raised here, I knew it all along."

The Israeli media played an important role in highlighting the case of children of undocumented migrants. Many articles treated the issue with much empathy for children and a clear condemnation of the state for not regulating their position. I will cite here only a few lines from an extensive article, the first in a series of articles about undocumented migrants' children that appeared in one of Israel's daily newspaper. The article was titled "The Crime of Living in Israel," and in it the journalist, Nurit Wuhrgaft, elaborated on the case of two undocumented girls, one from Colombia and the other from Venezuela, who had lived in Israel most of their lives and now at the age of eighteen became deportable. After charging the state of Israel with creating this absurd situation, the journalist stated, "These children know Hebrew better than their mother tongue. They are the heroes of this series of articles which will describe their lives, so close to the Israeli experience, and nevertheless so far from it" (*Haaretz* 10.07.2002). In one of the following articles, another journalist, Aviv Lavi, wrote in his headline, "They look like Israelis, they act like Israelis, until at the age of 15 they get the first slap—no driving license. At 16 comes the second—no identity card, and at 18 the third—no army [recruitment]. From now on they are deportable" (*Haaretz* 16.05.2003).

Undocumented migrants were probably most encouraged about their future prospects in Israel when they learned that their children were legally accepted into the Israeli national education system. Israel's Compulsory Education Law stipulates that all children older than four who reside in Israel for more than three months must be enrolled in a recognized educational institution. The law did not specify the religion or nationality of children, and it therefore potentially allowed an opening for undocumented migrants' children into the Israeli educational system. Yet most undocumented migrants were first unaware of this law and the implications it had for them. They thus used to register their children in Christian Arab schools in Jaffa, or in Christian boarding schools in Jerusalem. After they learned about the possibility of enrolling their children in Israeli schools, most Latinos initially feared an official registration would lead the police to their doorsteps. MESILA and Israeli NGOs were actively informing and encouraging undocumented migrants about the benefits and safety of this option. The experiences of a few Latinos who dared to send their children to Israeli schools gradually reassured the rest about the safety of such registrations.

Yet undocumented migrants needed to pass a crucial hurdle before their children could safely step through the gates of the Israeli education system. Head teachers in Israel had a degree of discretion about the pupils whom they enrolled, based on criteria such as the school's capacity and children's qualifications. It was therefore easy for unwilling head teachers to decline the enrollment of undocumented migrants' children, using all sorts of pretexts. Under the general climate of state oppression of undocumented migrants, head teachers could rest assured that their refusal to enroll children of undocumented migrants would never be overruled by the state. Moreover, there was hardly a chance that undocumented migrants would come forward and protest such a refusal to the Ministry of Education or any other state institution.

Under these circumstances, the willingness of some head teachers to welcome children of undocumented migrants was crucial to the children's integration into the system. This willingness clearly illustrated the divergence between the general oppressive state policy and the more humane and ethical approach of many Israeli civil servants. Head teachers in south Tel Aviv were mostly committed to the non-discriminatory education of all children regardless of their parents' status in Israel. Consequently, schools such as Bialik, Rogouzin, and Nordeo received increasing numbers of children of undocumented migrants.

Bialik was the first elementary school in Tel Aviv to open its doors to children of undocumented migrants. Located in a very poor area in south Tel Aviv, the school was notorious for its harsh environment and the low achievements of its pupils. The school regularly dealt with a disadvantaged population of children. Besides Israeli pupils from poor backgrounds, there were also some Palestinian pupils—the children of former collaborators with the Israeli Defense Forces, who were relocated with their families from towns in the Occupied Territories to neighborhoods in south Tel Aviv. Furthermore, in the early 1990s some Jewish immigrants from the former Soviet Union were accommodated in this area, along with their children, who hardly spoke Hebrew. In 1990 an experienced and widely respected head teacher, Amira Yahalom, was put in charge of the school in what proved to be a successful attempt to rehabilitate it. Yet Amira became known publicly not for the miraculous regeneration of the school, but for leading a battle for the incorporation of undocumented migrants' children into the Israeli education system.

When I interviewed Amira in 2002, she expressed her deep rooted humanist approach as the motor that drove her to respond readily when in 1995 the first undocumented migrants in the area came to register their children to the school:

> I always believed that all of humans are born the same and we should all be given the chance to make it in life. We could have ignored this situation, leaving it for the government to take care of, but we saw it as our own responsibility because we were the ones who confronted parents and children. It became our mission to make sure that the Compulsory Education Law will be applied to every child here.

Amira was positioned, according to her own definition, "far on the left in Israel." She was born and raised in a kibbutz (a cooperative rural community) under an inclusive socialist system, with strong emphasis on communal and universalistic values whose influence on her standpoint she proudly acknowledged.

Since Israel never envisioned such a scenario, there were no official forms to register children whose parents did not have an Israeli identity card. Schools could thus not formally include enrolled children of undocumented migrants in their listings for the Ministry of Education. The ministry in turn refused to budget schools for undocumented pupils. Although compulsory education in Israel is entirely sponsored by the state, Amira also received discouraging messages from some politicians who came to visit the school in order to learn about the evolving "problem." For example, the chairman of Israel's Parliamentary Committee for Education, Zvulun Orlev (the leader of the National Religious Party), told Amira that budgets should never be diverted from the education of "our children to the children of foreign workers." Other politicians blamed Amira for her inclusive treatment of these children promoting the increasing settlement of undocumented migrants in Israel. Even more blunt was a member of the religious party Shas who told Amira, "You are dealing here with a cancer in the body of the nation." Despite such remarks, Amira accepted as many children of undocumented migrants as she could, pushing the school beyond its full capacity. The general political and institutional opposition she encountered never deterred her:

They tried to discourage me from registering them in the first place; they said, "Try not to enlist them," or "Why do you need all of this in your school." When I insisted, they avoided the problem by saying, "So there will be some unregistered pupils." Even when in 1997 they finally accepted it and budgeted the school accordingly, they still tried to hide it; they told me, "Do what you have to do but do it quietly; don't start with your grand ideologies."

However, Amira did not stop there; she supported and assisted the work of Israeli NGOs that concertedly fought for an official and full integration of undocumented migrants' children into the Israeli education system. In 2000 this goal was achieved when the Ministry of Education amended its procedures and allowed pupils without Israeli identity cards to complete the whole of the Israeli educational trajectory from the age of four to the age of eighteen. These pupils were also entitled to attend the matriculation exams (*bejinot bagrut*) and officially graduate.[5] Having won her battle against the Ministry of Education, and after heavily criticizing and openly fighting it, Amira expressed a positive viewpoint: "We managed to recruit the ministry to our own goal, it is now in the forefront of the incorporation process of foreign workers." She praised this achievement and proudly compared it to arrangements in other Western countries, before turning her critique toward some Israeli NGOs, which she blamed for being too radical and for souring relations with the state instead of trying to work with it constructively:

I disapprove of their methods; they always want contention, and they fail to see the positive side of the work that can be done together with different ministries. At every small failure of a ministry they immediately go out to the press and publicly denounce the government. It is not constructive; you don't always have to be right but sometimes just be smart, learn how to do the things in a way that practically helps you move forward.

When I suggested that the uncompromising line of some NGOs was driven by their will to see a fully fledged revision in Israel's definition as a Jewish state, Amira got agitated: "I know their radical agenda, but they should not promote it on the backs of poor foreign workers." I then asked Amira where she stood on this deeper ideological question. Amira responded:

It has nothing to do with religion. I don't belong to any religion; I am secular. This has to do with the fact that the Jewish nation decided that part of the solution to its problems would be to establish a homeland in Israel. I think that the real problem of Israel is that it is an immigration country which refuses to acknowledge it and instead calls itself an *Alia* country [solely refers to the immigration of Jews to Israel]. I am against the immigration of foreign workers to Israel; I believe that we should be able to sustain ourselves here without using another population as hewers of wood and drawers of water. It is morally wrong in my eyes. We still have serious problems as a nation with more than a million Palestinians who are citizens of this country, and with receiving and incorporating the Ethiopian and the Russian [Jewish] immigrants that came. We must first solve these internal problems before we can pretend to incorporate others into our nation.

Having said my personal opinion on the whole issue, I strongly believe that if foreign workers are brought here, we should do everything to incorporate them. We cannot create another exploited minority. They should get an equal chance and rights; we should do everything to help them.

It should be noted that Amira's opinion represents an ultra-secular and progressive understanding of the situation in Israel, which is shared by only a minority of Jewish Israelis.

Latinos reactively and proactively attempted to enhance the integration of their children into Israeli society, not least because parents believed that it would promote a normalization of their undocumented situation in Israel. Latinos, in comparison with other undocumented migrant groups, were more inclined to bring their children over to Israel and raise the ones who were born in Israel as Israelis. This tendency was almost opposite to the one adopted by African undocumented migrants. As Naana Holdbrook, one of the leaders of the African community, once explained, "We're not Zionist, and we haven't come here to change the demography of the state of Israel" (*Jerusalem Post* 14.01.2002). In the same article, another African leader, John Essian, reflected on his own personal dilemma regarding his two Israeli-born children:

The older will be entering kindergarten next year, so we're thinking of sending them home. We know that doing so will break up the family and deprive them from parental affection, but it is important to us that they have proper schooling and develop a strong sense of their African identity. We don't want them growing up confused about who they are—half African, half Israeli.

In another newspaper article (*Haaretz* 16.05.2003), Sigal Rozen, the head of Hotline for Migrant Workers in Detention, explained that most migrants from Africa, the Philippines, and other countries tended not to bring their children to Israel, and to send the ones who were born in Israel back home to be raised by relatives. She then made a clear distinction: "The exception to this rule is the Latinos. They, in most cases, have no intention to return back home [and therefore do not send their children to their countries of origin]."

Table 4.1. Latino Pupils in Bialik Elementary School

Year	Latino Pupils	Total Number of Pupils	Proportion of All Pupils
1995–1996	16	300	5%
1996–1997	32	273	11%
1997–1998	40	272	15%
1998–1999	50	240	21%
1999–2000	62	243	25%
2000–2001	70	275	25%
2001–2002	70	270	26%

Source: Bialik School, internal registration records, 2003.

With respect to education, Latinos were probably most enthusiastic, in comparison to other undocumented migrant groups, about sending their children to Israeli schools. This tendency is reflected in the overrepresentation of Latino children among pupils in Israeli schools. Table 4.1 illustrates the steady increase in the absolute number of Latino pupils as well as their relative proportion to the total population of pupils in Bialik.

Children of undocumented migrants were admitted to Bialik from all countries indiscriminately. Indeed, the school's record included children from the Philippines, Thailand, and several countries in Africa and in Eastern Europe. Nevertheless, for example in the year 2002, of all the children of undocumented migrants in Bialik, some 55 percent were Latinos. Moreover, in 2002 Latino pupils comprised one quarter of all pupils in the school. Amira, the head teacher of Bialik, told me that after it became widely known in Israel that children of undocumented migrants were studying at Bialik, she received phone calls from many Israeli employers who asked on behalf of their undocumented workers whether it was possible to enroll children there. Among Latinos this was largely the case, as mostly women who worked as nannies or domestic cleaners established good relationships with Israeli employers, who assisted them in enrolling their children in Israeli schools.

Latino pupils, like all other pupils, participated in all kinds of activities that were arranged by their school, for example, visits to museums or daytrips in the country. However, some private recreational courses, such as kayaking, basketball, and martial arts, were offered to pupils after school. Latino children obviously wanted to participate in such courses with their Israeli friends, but paying for them was often a serious economic challenge for parents. Nevertheless, Latinos were often disposed to dig deep into the household budget to pay for these courses. This was done not least because of Latinos' aspiration to further the integration of their children into Israeli society. Latino parents who sent their children to Israeli schools were extremely proud and positive about their experience. They often praised their children for their smooth integration and for having Israeli friends. The following is an anecdotal yet telling example of the way in which Latinos perceived their children's incorporation.

For their graduation from elementary school, it is a tradition in Israel to give pupils the Bible as a present.[6] For some Latino parents the gifting of the Bible to their children was a very moving experience. Knowing how religious identity in Israel was inextricably bonded to issues of citizenship and belonging, Latinos deeply appreciated this symbolic gesture. Claudia, a devoted evangelical, was very touched when her daughter Veronica returned from school with the Bible. She excitedly told me:

> You know, they gave all the children in school the Bible as a present, also to Veronica. When she showed it to me I had to cry . . . I was so touched. They really treat my daughter like an Israeli. Maybe I still have to become an Israeli, but Veronica is here from since she was five; she goes to an Israeli school and speaks perfect Hebrew. In the beginning I was worried that Israeli children and teachers would not treat her nice, but she has many friends and she loves the school. You know what she tells me? She says, "Mama, when I am eighteen I am going to serve in the army." Tell me, will she be able to serve in the army? She's a strong girl and she honestly loves this country.

Latinos often manifested their commitment and loyalty to Israel by expressing their willingness to serve in the Israeli army. Some Latino parents projected their sense of loyalty onto their children. Either intuitively internalizing their parents' outlook or independently developing an urge for belonging, most Latino children expressed a strong desire to remain in Israel. They held very positive opinions about Israel and hardly ever wanted to return to their country of origin or ancestry. Paula, a 9-year-old girl, was born in Chile and joined her parents in Israel when she was five. When I asked her if she wanted to return to Chile, she responded, "I would like to go back for a visit, to see my grandparents, but only for one week, then I want to come back." Children clearly conceived their "place" in a relational manner, and the fact that their parents, and often other relatives, were in Israel was decisive in shaping their sense of belonging.

Most Latino children spoke Hebrew among themselves. Although Latino parents almost always spoke Spanish with their children at home, they encouraged their children to speak Hebrew with their friends. Latino parents sometimes bought Israeli music, mostly at the request of their children. They played and enjoyed it at home with their children, who were often asked to translate from Hebrew to Spanish difficult words and sentences that their parents did not understand.

Yet children were often confused about their actual location in the matrix of nation-states, transnational families, and multiethnic schools. They often resorted to mother tongues as an indicative marker for their original place, as the following example illustrates. On one of my visits to the Bialik School I conversed in Hebrew with a group of pupils during the break between classes. Andres, who came to Israel from Peru when he was five, said something in Spanish, and to his surprise I responded to him in that language. Andres was visibly puzzled and asked me if I was "really" speaking Spanish. When I answered positively, Andres was still confused and asked, "But in which language were you born?" I explained that I was born in Israel and spoke Hebrew but later lived in Latin America and learned Spanish. Andres then explained to me his status: "I was born in Spanish, but now I live in Hebrew, and I even know how to swear in Russian."

Giving their Israeli-born children typical Israeli names was another indication of Latinos' inclination to advance the integration of their children into Israeli society. Many Latino parents decided to name their children after an Israeli employer they liked, or an Israeli friend they had, or simply an Israeli name that they came to like. Although Latinos knew that matters of citizenship in Israel were not decided upon the principle of *ius soli,* they still remained hopeful that enhanced cultural and social integrating of their children who were born in Israel, had Israeli names, spoke Hebrew, and went to Israeli schools would be legally recognized by the state of Israel in one way or another. I once visited Adriana after she had given birth to a daughter whom she named Sigal. After letting me hold Sigal, Adriana worriedly asked, "Do you think she can be an Israeli in the future?" Latino parents often stressed the Israeliness of their children. After a few months, when Sigal began to say some words, Adriana excitedly told me that the first word Sigal pronounced was *ima,* Hebrew for mother. She then enthusiastically added, "She is a real *tzabar,* isn't she?" *Tzabar* in Hebrew is a nickname for native-born Israeli Jews.

One of the most prominent initiatives of Latinos in Tel Aviv was the establishment in 2000 of La Escuelita, a supplementary educational program aimed to teach assimilated children of Latinos the Spanish language and provide them with knowledge about their (parents') countries of origin. The motor behind La Escuelita was Cristina Flores, a Colombian single mother in her mid-thirties, who had lived in south Tel Aviv with her 13-year-old son since the early 1990s. Given her energy, willingness to assist others, and organizational capacity, Cristina became a well-known figure among Latinos in Tel Aviv. She managed to establish good connections with Israeli NGOs, and she quickly learned the rights that undocumented migrants had in Israel. Cristina formed a support group for Latino women and established a Latino theater workshop with the help of Israeli counterparts. When MESILA was established in 1999, Cristina began to collaborate with it to improve the situation of Latinos in the city. La Escuelita, a joint venture of Latinos and MESILA, was a direct outcome of this collaboration.

Cristina recruited teachers from among her Colombian undocumented friends and advertised the program among the Latino community. For enrolling their children, parents were asked to pay a modest fee (US$7 per month), which was used to purchase educational material and to pay the teachers a modest wage. Around fifty children enrolled, and classes were initially held on Friday afternoon in one of the rooms in the office of MESILA. After three months, La Escuelita relocated its operations to classrooms in the Bialik School, where Amira gladly offered all the facilities of the school to the service of Cristina and her colleagues.

When I interviewed Cristina, she told me about her motivation in establishing La Escuelita:

> Children are the most vulnerable. They don't always understand their position in Israel and parents are often too busy here. It is therefore so important to have an institute where children can properly learn about their roots, so that when they'll return to Latin America they will be more prepared to deal with the situation.

However, what Cristina perhaps ignored was the fact that most Latinos enrolled their children in La Escuelita not to prepare them to return home. Instead, my impression from talks I had with parents was that Latinos saw La Escuelita mainly as an inexpensive recreational activity for their children. Some parents were particularly motivated to send their children to La Escuelita because of the broader activities that were organized there. For example, making use of her connections to Israeli NGOs and social activists, Cristina managed to organize summer camps for Latino children in Israeli kibbutzim, during the summer vacation when Israeli schools are closed for two months and undocumented migrants struggle to find and pay for an arrangement for their children. In addition, La Escuelita offered classes in Hebrew to Latino parents, and mothers regularly met to discuss and share their experiences of raising their children in Israel. Cristina's failure to establish a course for preparing migrants to set up small businesses upon their return back home was a telling sign of Latinos' increased focus on settlement in Israel rather than on their (undesired) return to their countries of origin. "I already made some arrangements for the course with a college, but I couldn't find enough people who wanted to participate in it," Cristina disappointedly told me.

In retrospect, Cristina was not only more responsible and sound than most other Latinos with respect to their future lives, she was also right. As the massive deportation campaign saw the forced return of most Latinos in Israel to their country of origin, a course to prepare them and their children for this day could not have been more useful. But in the early 2000s, most Latinos were unwilling to allow such a doom scenario to dissuade them from their plans for long-term settlement in Israel.

Chapter Five

Divisive Dynamics

The Absence of Political Community and the
Differentiations of the Recreational Scene

Non-cooperation is directed not against men but
against measures. It is not directed against the
Governors, but against the system they administer.
The roots of non-cooperation lie not in hatred but
in justice, if not in love.

—*Mohandas Gandhi*

After a period of several years, many undocumented migrants in Israel accommodated themselves economically, socially, and culturally to life in Israel. As the stakes were high for these undocumented but settled migrants, many of them became preoccupied with their future prospects, and particularly with the possibility of preventing their deportation and legalizing their status. One would therefore have expected concerned groups of undocumented migrants to politically mobilize their communities and attempt to negotiate their situation with the Israeli authorities. Indeed, several groups of undocumented migrants, including from different countries in Africa and the Philippines, organized and united under a political platform in order to pursue some basic demands regarding their status and conditions in Israel. Nevertheless, political mobilization among Latinos never succeeded, and the two main efforts to create a representative organization fractured and failed.

This is a surprising finding, as the Latino community of undocumented migrants was one of the largest in Israel, and its members experienced advanced stages of settlement and established a plethora of recreational and religious organizations. Moreover, the fact that all Latinos in Israel spoke the same language (Spanish), and shared certain migratory dispositions and goals, greatly enhanced their potential for creating a unifying political organization to advance their mutual interest vis-à-vis the state of Israel. Also, Latinos, like other groups of undocumented migrants, received encouragement and assistance from Israeli NGOs, academics, and journalists in politically mobilizing their communities.

Induced by all these factors, Latinos indeed attempted a political mobilization, but the Israeli police aggressively acted against the political leaders of all undocumented migrant groups. After the second failed attempt, Latinos by and large abandoned political organization as a strategy, while other undocumented migrant groups continued to pursue it. The failure of political mobilization among Latinos in Israel deserves a close examination. In trying to account for it, we should consider that Latinos essentially faced a zero-sum game in deploying the two main resources that were available to them: "invisibility" and political mobilization. Latinos thus strategically and consciously chose to shun political collective action, which turned them into a prime target for the repressive Israeli police, and instead preferred to follow as individuals the accumulation of practical national belonging that rendered them increasingly "invisible."

Consequently, a lack of political unifying organization exacerbated divisions in the rich recreational scene that they developed in Israel. My claim is that different national Latino groups developed a sense of competition instead of cooperation; each group looked to position itself best in the Israeli context and in particular among Israelis. As a result, the common and the unifying among Latinos in Israel gave way to a dynamic whereby they chose to highlight and reify the differences between them.

Political Mobilization among Undocumented Migrants in Israel

Political mobilization as means for getting recognition and entitlements from nation-states has been common among undocumented migrants in different migratory contexts (Miller 1989, Soysal 1994, 1997, Smith and Guarnizo 1998). Such political claims are regularly being framed within "repertoires of contention" that are meant to correspond to the political opportunity structures presented by the host society (McAdam, Tarrow, and Tilly 2001). Often in the case of migrant workers, demands for political, civil, and social rights are based on an emergent discourse of human rights (Jacobson 1996, Sassen 1999). Undocumented migrants, too, tend to articulate their demands for a legalization of status and an inclusion in public services by using this discourse. The United Nations has recently accredited undocumented migrants as a legal category and drafted conventions for their protection under the more immediate authority of all signatory member nation-states.

Israel is a signatory to a UN convention that safeguards the rights of undocumented migrants' children, as well as stipulates some of the working conditions of undocumented migrants. Nevertheless, the restrictive importation mechanism and strict control that was exercised over guest workers literally forestalled their ability to organize and articulate demands collectively (see Rosenhek 1999). In contrast, however, "the relative 'autonomy' enjoyed by the undocumented migrants allows them to establish communal associations that function as vehicles for claims-making" (ibid.: 576). In line with this pattern, different groups of undocumented migrants pursued political mobilization as an avenue for attempting to negotiate with the Israeli authorities regarding their status and situation in the country.

The most prominent example for a move in this direction was the establishment in 1997 of the African Workers Union (AWU), a pan-African organization of undocumented migrants. Similarly, in 1997, after a series of secret meetings among several Latinos who were committed to a formal improvement in their situation, a group of leaders took charge of mobilizing Latinos from different nationalities and cooperating on a pan–Latin American level. At the end of 1997, following the example of undocumented African migrants, Latinos established a similar political organization, the Latino Workers Union (Organización de Trabajadores Latinoamericanos), that was led by a group of leaders from Chile, Colombia, and Ecuador.

Both unions began drawing Israeli public attention to their unresolved situation in the country through articles published in the Israeli media. Leaders of these two unions also worked together with supportive Israeli NGOs, and in 1998 even managed to arrange a meeting with the chairman of the Israeli Parliamentary Committee for Foreign Workers, where they presented their proposals for the regulation of their status and improvement of their conditions in the country. Apparently, the political organizations of undocumented migrants successfully managed to enter into a constructive negotiation with the Israeli authorities, using on the one hand a global discourse of human rights, and on the other a more locally specific discourse that stressed compassion for foreigners, who, it was hoped, Jews could easily relate to, given their own history (see Kemp et al. 2000, Rosenhek 1999).

However, judging these attempts from a later point in time, it can be said that Israel never seriously cooperated with undocumented migrants' political initiatives. Despite the media coverage, and a series of talks between leaders of undocumented migrants and different Israeli delegates, none of the migrants' demands or propositions was accepted, not even a minor and temporary legalization program for undocumented migrants who entered Israel on tourist visas. In contrast, a more aggressive deportation campaign was championed as the sole solution, and although it was never officially acknowledged, the police specifically targeted reputed political leaders and organizations.

Only a few months after it began operations, the organized political platform of Latinos was brutally crushed by the Israeli police, who deliberately arrested and swiftly deported most of its active leaders. Gloria Mora, a Catholic nun from Chile, was one of the Latino leaders, and although in her capacity as a missionary she had a legal visa to stay in Israel, the police still broke into her apartment in the middle of the night and tried to arrest her. After she showed her visa and asked for an explanation for the raid, the policemen told her that they knew about her involvement in the political organization of Latinos and that her apartment was used as a meeting place for this purpose. After realizing that they could not arrest her, the policemen told her she was a troublemaker and pledged to make sure that her visa would not be extended (see *Halr* 16.4.1998).

The Latino Workers Union never recovered from the severe blow it suffered, and was subsequently disbanded. In comparison, while members of the African political organization also experienced similar arrests and deportations, their organization survived and resumed its activities in spite of the repeated police attempts to dissolve it. A team of four Israeli social scientists, who studied the political organization of undocumented migrants and particularly compared the Latino failure to the African insistence, reported, "Although persecution is a serious setback for both black African and Latino undocumented communities, in the case of the latter it endangered the survival of an already fragile and fragmentary organization" (Kemp et al. 2000: 107). In attempting to explain the unsuccessful Latino political effort, Kemp et al. quote active members in the Latino organization who blamed "personal enmities, gossip, intrigues, and power struggles" for undermining the mobilization attempts. In addition to this emic view of Latinos, Kemp et al. claim that "[t]he combination of lack of recognized leadership, lack of an integrated and coordinated organizational infrastructure, and lack of a ready-made participatory political culture imported from the country of origin, seems to account for the inability of Latinos to create a viable channel for claim-advancing into Israeli political public sphere" (ibid.). Engaging critically with this line of explanation, I believe that effects are being mistakenly confused here with causes. A lack of recognized leadership and an organizational infrastructure do not account for Latinos' failure to politically unite; instead, they are merely the outcome of this failure, its shattered reflection. When Latinos attempted a political organization, they did manage, within a relatively short period of time, to mobilize members, select recognized leaders, and establish an organizational body that coordinated joint efforts.

As for the claim that Latinos allegedly imported from their countries of origin an underdeveloped political culture, I argue that this rather Eurocentric view of Latino political culture is completely invalidated by the high proportion of participation in democratic elections across Latin America (especially in comparison with such rates in European countries and the United States). Furthermore, in recent years Latin America has seen some of the most prominent political mobilizations worldwide, with grassroots political organizations and trade unions particularly managing to massively mobilize the low-middle class and to effectively orchestrate protests, strikes, and petitions. These mobilizations from "below" led to major regime changes in countries such as Bolivia, Ecuador, Venezuela, and Argentina. In Mexico, the Zapatista movement has become a global model for a new kind of social movement that organizes against repressive states. These grassroots movements use innovative and powerful means, including digital technology, to reach out to the international community and to articulate their claims in a language that greatly appeals to a global discourse of human rights (see Tilly 1996).

I thus analyze the reasons that induced Latinos to evade political organization in Israel, in ways that do not point at Latinos' alleged deficient political culture and general tendency toward mistrust and chronic power struggles. I do not dispute the fact that such a tendency might have figured in the actions of some Latinos in Israel, just as it probably did among some African migrants. Indeed Sabar (2004: 418) reports on ethnic divisions, personal rivalries, and greed as factors that led to evident schisms among African migrants, and between their evangelical congregations in Tel Aviv. Thus, these factors can never explain the non-organizational pattern of Latinos, just as they do not explain why African migrants did remain committed to their organization.

Why Did Latinos Not Organize Politically?

In attempting to offer an alternative explanation for the difference in the political organizational patterns of Latinos and African migrants, I first stress the two dynamics that initially led to the political mobilization of undocumented migrants. Most clearly, political organization was a direct reaction to Israel's decision to implement its plan to deport undocumented migrants:

> The catalyst event that led to the politicization of the black African community and to the concomitant creation of the AWU was escalation in the deportation policy implemented by the Israeli authorities during 1997. . . . In a meeting with a group of Israeli parliament members, leaders of the black African community raised issues concerning the plight of migrant workers in general consequent to the deportation policy, and of black African migrants in particular, as they are more easily targeted by the police. (Kemp et al. 2000: 105–206)

As long as undocumented migrants were able to conduct their lives in Israel with relatively little interference from the police, they carried on without political organization, partly because they were aware of the Israeli authorities' sensitivity and strong opposition to any overt indications for the settlement of non-Jewish migrants, let alone political ones. Nevertheless, facing a deportation campaign, undocumented migrants had to readjust their survival strategies to the unfolding threatening situation.

The perception of many Israeli social activists and some academics was that un-documented migrants should enter the Israeli public sphere as political actors, to try to influence the government's policy. This involvement of Israeli activists in the political organization of undocumented migrants constituted the second most important dynamic behind this development, as Kemp et al. report: "The creation of the AWU was not only triggered by the demands articulated by the black African community itself, but also by the encounter with Israeli representatives and activists . . . and by their active sponsorship" (2000: 106). When discussing the Latino's similar political attempt, Kemp et al. clearly state: "The significant factor that led to the idea of founding a supranational organization was an encounter between members of the Latino community and Israeli social activists and academics who encouraged them to follow the black African example" (ibid.).

Thus, political efforts of undocumented migrants in Israel were by and large stimulated, facilitated, and formulated by a group of Israeli social activists. Some supportive Israeli journalists made it possible for undocumented migrants to voice their concerns and propositions in newspaper articles, while other social activists and academics practically assisted their organization and arranged for their leaders to meet with Israeli politicians.

While the motivations of counter-hegemonic Israeli activists undoubtedly sprang from a true desire to assist undocumented migrants in their disadvantaged battle with the state of Israel, the reactions of some academics to Latinos' failure to accomplish this type of organization suffer from myopia regarding Latinos' optimal life strategy in Israel. The assumption behind the push toward political organization was that mi-grants who faced a threatening deportation campaign had nothing to lose from this move and, potentially, something to gain.

However, as I suggest, unlike African migrants, Latinos did have something valu-able to lose from organizing themselves politically, namely, their accumulated "invis-ibility." Most clearly, Latinos carefully measured the possibility of improving their position through collective political mobilization against the price they had to pay in transforming themselves into a target group for the Israeli police. Black African migrants did not have the "invisibility" option, as their skin color plainly indicated for the police their undocumented status in Israel. There are of course black Ethiopian Jews in Israel, but only a handful of them reside in south Tel Aviv. Thus, since black African migrants were unwillingly visible in Israel, organizing politically had hardly any additional impact on their saliency both as an organized community and as individual undocumented migrants.

I therefore contend that once the police began to clamp down on the political organizations of undocumented migrants, Latinos quickly became reluctant to give up their relative invisibility to join a risky political organization. Indeed, Kemp et al. (2000: 107) report that from their interviews with Latinos it became clear that "members in the community believed that the escalation in the arrest and deportation policy was a direct reaction to the community's organizational activities." In contrast, African migrants, who also experienced an intensified deportation campaign, were actually motivated to step up their political efforts as the only viable way to counter this increasing threat.

In my interviews with Latinos who were involved in the political effort, I discovered that their attitudes were based on a careful calculation of their particular position and a subtle understanding of the Israeli context. Jason, an Ecuadorian migrant who took part in the Latino political attempt, explained to me his firm reluctance to ever again participate in such attempts:

> If you don't make noise and simply live your life here, there is a chance that the police will catch you, but this chance is not so big. After all, we don't stick out here. If I walk here in the streets nobody can immediately recognize that I am an illegal migrant. I live here for five years already and the police never stopped me. But if we organize and make demands and much noise, we turn ourselves into a clear target for the police.

When I brought up the possibility that political mobilization might improve the situation of undocumented Latinos in a more profound way, Jason quickly dismissed it in disbelief:

> If I thought that there was a real chance to gain something from it I might have taken the risk and stick to it. After all, I brought here my wife, my children, and my parents, and nobody wants to become legal in this country more than me. But you know, as well as I do, that these are useless efforts; Israel is the state of the Jews and only they can immigrate and become legal here. So there is no point in turning yourself into a target. On the other hand, Latinos have a good reputation among Israelis, and we can have a nice life here. That is why I say to my family and all my friends, "Just keep quiet, live your own lives quietly, and don't stick out."

Jason's claim with respect to the "good reputation" of Latinos is supported by a survey that was conducted among a sample of seventy Israeli residents in south Tel Aviv about their views of "foreigners." The survey showed that while on average only 20 percent of Israelis held a positive image of "foreigners," 66 percent held such an image with respect to Latinos. This approval rating of Latinos was substantially higher than any of the other migrant groups.

A New Attempt, an Old Pattern

After the breakdown of the Latino Workers Union in 1997, Latinos did not attempt again to unite politically. However, in the year 2000, MESILA, Tel Aviv's Aid and Information Center for the Foreign Community, sought to establish communication lines with undocumented migrants as part of the municipality's broader attempt to improve the migrants' lives, and more generally, the situation in the south of the city. In order to establish effective channels of communication, MESILA initiated a program for the cultivation of leaders from among the different communities of undocumented migrants. In October 2000, potential leaders from each community were asked to participate in a leadership course that was especially designed by MESILA and was delivered over three months in its facilities.

Three Latinos took part in the course and subsequently began to act as representatives of the Latino community vis-à-vis MESILA. Nevertheless, only three months after he successfully finished the leadership course, Patricio Diaz, a Chilean undocumented migrant, was arrested after the police broke into his apartment in the middle of the night. The arrest took place a week after Patricio Dias had published an open letter to the Israeli prime minister (Ariel Sharon), in which he charged the state of Israel with treating undocumented migrants unfairly. The letter was published online (12 March 2001) on a popular Israeli media Web site (www.walla.co.il) and received wide public attention. Less than two weeks later, a following article on the same Web site reported on the arrest of Patricio Dias. In the article, the manager of the Israeli NGO Hotline for Migrant Workers, was quoted: "In 1997 all the Latino leaders were arrested and it was made clear to them that this was a consequence of their attempt to organize. Since then we thought that the police came to recognize the importance of organizing these communities and having collaboration with them . . . but the arrest of Patricio proved that nothing has changed."

Another newspaper article, "First the Leaders" (*Haaretz* 03.08.2001), quoted Edna Alter, the head of MESILA, who wrote a letter to the interior ministry in which she demanded that Patricio not be deported, but instead be released and allowed to continue his work as a leader of the Latino community: "We worked hard and long to build a leadership among the Latino community, and this arrest might bring us a long way backwards . . . we are very sorry about his arrest and the more general feeling that every time such leadership develops it is being arrested." Indeed, in the following weeks more Latino leaders were arrested by the police; Juan Carlos, an undocumented migrant from Colombia who also participated in the leadership course, found himself behind bars, together with Oscar Revelion, who was the basketball coach of the Latino team that participated in the sport activities that MESILA sponsored. In a legal appeal for the release of the two leaders, Israeli NGOs claimed that their arrests represented a systematic violation of the freedom of association. The state of Israel defended its actions by maintaining that the two individuals were arrested on the basis of their illegal status in the country and regardless of their leadership positions. The court accepted the state's position, and opened the way for the deportation of most Latino leaders. These deportations brought about an abrupt and bitter end to the Latinos' second attempt to organize politically, after which no other one was registered.

The only Latino leader who came out of the MESILA training and survived deportation was Cristina Flores. Already before her participation in the course, Cristina was active in organizing educational and recreational activities for Latino children, and in forming support groups for female Latino migrants. After the damaging political saga, Cristina continued with her apolitical initiatives. In one of my conversations with her, she told me about her immediate reservations when the issue of political organization was firstly discussed:

> I warned Patricio [Dias] and the others that we were walking a thin line and that it was perhaps better not to adopt such a militant approach and promote a direct confrontation with the Israeli authorities. Don't get me wrong, I think that Israel should be ashamed about some of the policies it implements with respect to undocumented migrants, but we should be clever in the way we pursue our interests here.

Cristina then stated her more general view of the way forward for undocumented migrants in Israel:

> The state will never suddenly decide to legalize us; this change I hope will come through our children. But there are many Israelis in different organizations and functions that have abundant desire to improve our situation, and we should work with them to make the necessary changes on the ground, not by shouting in public that Israel is unfair. That will get us nowhere.

After the deportation of Juan Carlos, one of the Latino leaders, I conducted an interview with his closest friend, who was himself involved in the same political organization, but expressed his reservations:

> I told him [Juan Carlos] that they were running too fast with their political demands. He was giving interviews to newspapers, and even went to a meeting in the Israeli parliament. I told him that they had to be very careful and ask for changes very gradually and slowly, not aggressively. It is just like when you want to seduce a woman, you don't immediately grab her and say, "Let's go to bed." Israel is the Jewish state for centuries already; you can't try and change it in a few months.

In fact, at that time the Jewish state had existed for only five decades, but the perception of many Latinos that it was there "for centuries already" reflects the deep internalization of the hegemonic Jewish Israeli discourse in the country. Indeed, most Latinos were very skeptical about the prospects of political actions' improving their position. The harsh response of the Israeli authorities left most Latinos decisively unwilling to participate in such a line of action. Instead, many of them chose to make even greater use of their "invisibility," for example, by moving to live in neighborhoods outside south Tel Aviv and in nearby suburbs. Many Latinos also intensively increased their efforts to convert to Judaism (as will be explained in chapter 6), or marry an Israeli citizen.

To summarize, in devising the best life strategies under the Israeli circumstances, Latinos essentially faced a zero-sum game in deploying the two main resources that were available to them, "invisibility" and political mobilization. Despite the fact that undocumented migrants articulated their claims in compelling "repertoires," and received much assistance from counter-hegemonic Israeli actors, the task they faced was a formidable one. For non-Jewish undocumented migrants to enter the Israeli political sphere as legitimate actors, they needed to change nothing less than the very core ethno-religious logic under which the Jewish state operated. While this was not categorically unattainable, it required a lengthy battle and the kind of scarification that most Latinos were unwilling to undergo, not least because of their alternative life strategy of practical assimilation. Indeed, the harsh and sweeping reaction of the Israeli police against those involved in political organization clearly marked this undertaking as a risky one. In the absent of immediate and tangible advantages that political organization could yield to its members, most Latinos avoided it, and instead preferred to adhere to their invisibility as individual migrants.

And so it seems that the refusal of Latinos to accomplish political organization, which some Israeli activists envisioned for them, led some academics to unjustly explain this failure with a stereotypical view of Latinos' blemished political culture. Even though some Latinos may have pointed to their divisive political culture and spoiled habits as the reasons for their failure politically to unite, a different analysis suggests that Latinos preferred a non-organizational pattern due to their informed as well as informative reading of the Israeli context and their position in it.

The Divided and Dividing Recreational Arena

Recreational activities among Latinos in Israel were very developed, and they took on different forms. In the most spontaneous way, many Latinos began frequenting the beaches of Tel Aviv, which were at a convenient walking distance from their homes in the south of the city. A picnic at a park with friends and relatives also became a common recreational activity on weekends. In a more organized manner Latinos established and enjoyed clandestine restaurants, public football tournaments, and a rich nightlife scene of salsa clubs. While this type of an elaborated associational life could have potentially served to unify Latinos, it instead exacerbated further divisions between different national groups.

The factor that most shaped recreational activities of undocumented migrants in Israel was the strategic police decision not to allow any visible cultural representations of undocumented migrants' settlement. When, for example, a famous Nigerian singer, Shina Peters, was invited to perform in Israel, the Interior Ministry refused to issue him a visa, and a spokesman for the ministry claimed that "the show of the Nigerian singer is for illegal migrants and it thus gives a wrong signal . . . it is an attempt to establish the legitimacy of the illegal African community in Israel" (*Maariv* 20.08.2001). The decision was appealed by the Association for Civil Rights in Israel to the High Court, which then ordered the ministry to issue the Nigerian singer a visa for five days.

Repeated police raids rendered the public engagement in recreational activities dangerous, and thus led Latinos to develop and attend clandestine recreational institutions. Some Latinos decided to take part in public recreational activities despite the evident risk. Their insistence makes obvious the particular significance of this otherwise seemingly nonessential pastime in the Israeli context.

The importance of recreational activities for migrants transcends their sheer desire for fun and entertainment. Recreational activities enhanced social networks, offered entrepreneurial opportunities for some migrants, and formed one of the most prominent channels for integration between Latinos and Israelis. The opportunity to interact with Israelis outside the employer-employee context was valuable, for it provided undocumented migrants with a more humane and complete way to experience their place in Israeli society.

There were many similarities between Latinos and African migrants in their immigration patterns, socio-economic characteristics, and the rich social and cultural communitarian activities that the two groups developed. Nevertheless, as Kemp et al. report, there was also a marked difference: "While the black African community has developed a highly institutionalized organizational infrastructure, the Latino community consists of isolated and fleeting socio-cultural associations . . . [that] hinder their ability to engage in collective action and create a political platform" (2000: 101–102). Based on my ethnographic fieldwork, I certainly share the observation regarding the inharmonious character of Latino recreational life. It is also acknowledged that this fractured makeup encumbers a common identity formation, which is essential as a motivating factor in social mobilization (Marx 1996). Nevertheless, rather than concluding that a divided associational life hampered political organization among Latinos in Israel, I suggest that we should also consider the reverse, that the disunity in the recreational scene resulted from Latinos' lack of political unity. As Latinos strategically shunned the political pursuit of mutual goals, cooperation gave way to a competition between multiple Latino national communities. Within this framework of competition, in which each network separately looked to advance, Latinos moved to demarcate and extenuate national boundaries between them, instead of blurring them. This tendency became perhaps most evident within the divisive recreational scene.

The base for the segmented character of the Latino community primarily emanated from the fact that immigration from Latin America depended heavily on social networks, which were stretched between each country and Israel. These national networks not only facilitated international movement, but also largely eased adaptation to the Israeli context. Given the essentiality and functionality of separate national networks, there was initially little chance for Latinos in Israel to become embedded in a national network other than their own. Following this basic intra-national network structure, recreational activities of Latinos were initiated and established within groups of co-nationals. Nevertheless, some Latino recreational activities, such as football tournaments and bars, brought together migrants from different countries.[1] Yet, instead of inducing unity between national groups, these arenas actually brought to the fore the competition between rival Latino sides that lacked a common political bonding structure.

Private Initiatives, National Boundaries:
Latino Home Restaurants and Bars

An immigration process is typically a difficult one, as a sense of loss engulfs those who left their familiar environment. Although not necessarily first on the list of things immigrants long for, food often plays an important role in their lives abroad. This is probably because food, unlike emotional bonds or family atmosphere, can be relatively easily recreated in a foreign context. It would be, however, one-dimensional to claim that what immigrants miss is simply the taste and smell of their traditional dishes. Instead, we should consider food in a broader context, just as many Latinos in Israel perceived it, as a cultural element that readily managed, like music, to neatly capture and recreate a sense of community and shared culture (see Mennell, Murcott, and van Otterloo 1992).

Israel did have Spanish, Mexican, Argentinean, and Brazilian restaurants, which could potentially satisfy Latinos' desire for the taste of Latin American dishes. However, Israeli restaurants were trendy places that modified dishes to Israeli tastes, aiming to attract a bourgeois clientele under the guise of ethnic food. In accordance, the prices, fancy decor, and general ambiance of these restaurants deterred most Latinos from frequenting them. Consequently, most of the demand for traditional food among Latinos was supplied through the phenomenon of "home restaurants"; that is, different female immigrants began to cook customary dishes in their private kitchens and offered them for sale in their living rooms or roof terraces, which on weekends and holidays were temporarily transformed into makeshift restaurants. Going out to eat in home restaurants was a social event for most Latinos. Indulging in a favorite dish in the company of others was enjoyable. Latinos also benefited on those occasions from the valuable exchange of information, mainly regarding employment opportunities and accommodation, which regularly took place between the guests. Most home restaurants offered their clients a choice between two dishes, but a few proficient places cooked as many as five different dishes and also offered their guests a traditional desert. An average warm dish cost US$8–10, and was usually served on a plastic plate together with thick slices of white bread and a soft drink. The price of dishes was affordable for most Latinos, and successful home restaurants easily served more than fifty clients over a weekend.

In my visits to different home restaurants I clearly noticed the uniform national character of these institutions. Each home restaurant was almost exclusively frequented by co-nationals from the same country as that of the family who ran it. When I inquired about it with some of my informants, I was regularly told that each country in Latin America had its distinctive cuisine, and therefore each national group looked for a place that knew exactly how to prepare their particular dishes.

Eating out was a recreational activity that both functioned through and enhanced national social networks. The segmentation of the Latino culinary scene along national lines was triggered by the fact that information about home restaurants, their location and quality, commonly spread through social networks, which themselves were characteristically national in their makeup. An exchange of general impressions about home restaurants took place among friends and acquaintances whenever they met. For example, I was once walking with Alejandro on the street when he met a friend who hurriedly informed him:

> Last weekend I ate the best *guatita* I ever had in Israel at the apartment of Sandra; you must go there, she lives on *Alia* Street 26, on the roof floor. I have to run now, but if you'll be there on Saturday, I'll catch you then.

The Latino market of home cooking flourished in Tel Aviv, with some migrants trying to actually turn this business into their major source of income. Elsa and her sister-in-law, Clara, were very active in the Ecuadorian food niche; they served different traditional dishes every weekend to a steady clientele of Ecuadorian migrants. They expanded further by using the different networks in which they were each embedded. Elsa attended an evangelical church and thus advertised the home restaurant among her many "brothers" and "sisters." Javier, Clara's husband, used to play football with some Ecuadorian friends on Friday afternoons, where he encouraged his own teammates, as well as other players, to eat on Saturday at his wife's home restaurant. Elsa and Clara expanded their business even further by providing a take-away service; clients could call on their mobile phones to order meals, which Javier delivered on his bike to apartments in south Tel Aviv. Given that home restaurants became a business that competed for clientele, members in a certain national network almost always remained loyal to home restaurants that were run by their co-nationals.

Jeffrey, an Ecuadorian migrant, was very passionate about traditional food, and we often visited the home restaurant of Elsa and Clara, who became known for their mastery in preparing one favorite Ecuadorian dish: *encebollado* (fish in onion). One Saturday afternoon as we were sitting to eat *encebollado* together with many other clients in the living room, I asked Elsa how she prepared the dish. She patiently explained to me the whole process, and then stressed that the quality of the dish decisively lies in having the right fish. She then boasted of having the best fish due to her relationship with an Israeli shopkeeper in the fish market:

> The Israeli shopkeeper where I buy the fish knows me, so he keeps the best fish for me. In the beginning he once tried to trick me by selling me a poor-quality fish, but he didn't understand that Ecuadorians are very sensitive to the taste of the fish. When I prepared the *encebollado* with that fish all my clients were disappointed.

She looked around to see whether any of the clients that were present remembered the incident, and after a couple of men nodded their heads, Elsa continued:

> I went back to the Israeli shopkeeper and protested. He then saw that I understand much about fish, and he began to treat me with respect. Now we are good friends and that is my secret place. That is why my *encebollado* is so tasty. Even Ecuadorians who live outside Tel Aviv come to eat it.

I once asked Fernando, a Colombian migrant, if he would like to join me to eat *encebollado* at the home restaurant of Elsa and Clara. Fernando looked at me offended, and vehemently asked:

> Are you crazy? You want to take me to eat Ecuadorian food? No, no, no, I tell you what we'll do, I will take you to a proper Colombian lady and you will eat the tastiest Latino food, just like in Colombia, and then you will tell me which food is the best.

At a certain point in time Fernando got involved in a relationship with Daniela, an Ecuadorian woman, and the two regularly ate together at her place on weekends. One time the couple invited me to join them for dinner, for which Daniela prepared an *encebollado*. As we were eating, Fernando praised Daniela for her cooking skills and then asked me, "Isn't it delicious? She can really cook like a Colombian." Fernando's chauvinistic remarks neatly illustrate how imagined culinary national communities were socially constructed and reified by Latinos in Israel. Rather than a mere reflection of an objective difference between the national cuisines of countries in Latin America, these distinctions were arguably the product of a divided Latino community.

A variety of similar dishes are found across the Andean countries in South America. Differences in the type of dishes correspond much more to changes in geographic zones than to changes between countries. For example, along the coasts of most countries there is a high consumption of fish and seafood, while in the mountain areas cooked beef and fried pork are very popular. Since most countries in Latin America have both geographic zones, one often finds more variation in the cuisine of different regions within the same country than in similar geographic areas between different countries. Each country may still have different names for similar dishes or a slightly different way of cooking them, but by and large many of the traditional dishes contain similar ingredients and are prepared alike across countries.

Nevertheless, in Israel, differences between national cuisines were made more pronounced, despite the fact that Latinos mostly prepared their traditional food from the same products that they all bought at the same shop of *el Colombiano*. After he had married an Israeli woman and thus legalized his status in Israel, a Colombian migrant opened a shop in the popular Carmel market in south Tel Aviv. He imported all kinds of special Latino culinary groceries and even fresh vegetables such as plantain (*verde, platano*) and manioc (*yuka*). It was common for Latinos to complain about the high prices that *el Colombiano* charged for traditionally cheap ingredients, but it rarely prevented any of them from buying these products whenever they were available.

The divisiveness of the home restaurants scene cut even deeper than across national lines and into the fabric of national communities. As running a home restaurant was potentially a very profitable undertaking, competition often caused tension to rise between groups of friends and even extended families from the same country. In two cases I saw how a successful home restaurant was split into two competing establishments once differences in the division of labor and portioning out of income could no longer be agreed upon. In the first case this happen within an extended Ecuadorian family, and in the second between two Colombian friends. In both cases the splitting of the home restaurant also signaled the end of social contact between the vying parties. When I asked Adriana about the breaking up of the thriving home restaurant she had run together with her aunt for the last two years, she agitatedly responded:

Ask Marisa why we split. She should know better. [She paused for a second and looked at me with fiery eyes.] Some people are just disgraceful. When she arrived here I helped her to settle down; no, wait a minute, I even lent them [Marisa and her husband] money to come here, which also took them very long to repay. But I didn't say anything. I always thought, "they will pay it back when they can." I then also offered her to join me with the food [establishing a home restaurant]. But how did they repay me? By trying to take over the whole thing themselves and cutting me out. It's all right, God will pay them what they deserve, not me. I just don't want to hear from them ever again.

The Latino divisive tendency was also evident in the makeup of another private recreational institution—"home bars." Before going to Israeli public places at night became common among many Latinos, a series of Latino clandestine home bars offered alternative nightlife entertainment. As with home restaurants, some Latinos took the initiative to set up improvised bars in their apartments. Turning one's living room into an ad hoc bar was not a difficult task; one only needed a spacious living room, some plastic chairs, a CD player, and a large fridge. Home bars spontaneously developed from the prevalent Latino tradition of *reuniones*. Some of the people who more regularly hosted *reuniones* in their apartments decided, out of either convenience or entrepreneurial sense, to extend and commercialize these events. They thus modified the social custom of each guest bringing something to share, replacing it with modestly priced beers and liquors (*tragos*), which they provided to all guests.

The operation of home bars was kept as quiet as possible, both literally and figuratively. There was a pervasive fear among home bar owners that loud noise or a fight between drunken guests would lead an annoyed Israeli neighbor to complain to the police. Owners were also concerned that if their home bar became too popular, then a *sapo* (a migrant who worked for the Israeli police as a snitch) might also learn about it. The existence of most home bars was thus kept discreet; they were attended mainly by the owners' known and trustworthy circle of friends. Guests were also often warned not to bring with them just anyone, but only those relatives and friends whom they could completely trust.

The few times that I was invited to home bars by my close informants, my presence was first seen as a clear threat to all other guests and especially to the owner. However, after explanation from my side and strong support from my informants, I was usually warmly treated. On one occasion, when Jeffrey and I left an Ecuadorian home bar after a couple of hours, the owner kindly showed us to the door. He then invited us to visit again, but not before he extended a clear request:

Please don't tell or bring anyone with you when you come; you know how dangerous this could be. And never bring here a Colombian; you can't trust them, they are all *sapos*.

Groups of friends who met for *reuniones* were already regularly composed from migrants who came from the same country, and even the same region or town. As home bars were established around these nuclear groups, and were mainly extended by way of incorporating trustworthy friends in these groups, the national segregation of these institutions was largely maintained and even deepened. The protective measures taken by the owners of home bars enhanced the existing tendency of these institutions to be clearly formed along national lines.

Going Out, Getting In: Latino Public Bars

Home bars were mainly popular among Latinos before the establishment of public Latino bars, and during periods of harsh police enforcement that deterred many from going out to public places. However, in 2000 two public Latino bars were established in south Tel Aviv, and directly aimed at attracting a crowd of Latinos. The audacity of Latinos to attend public bars marked a new phase in the level of confidence that many Latinos experienced in Israel. Undocumented migrants, who were extremely sensitive to changes in police presence and enforcement efforts, gained much confidence in the period from the end of 1999 to early 2001, which was the calmest with respect to deportation of undocumented migrants in Israel. A left-wing government was in power, and Shlomo Ben-Ami, the internal security minister, adopted a more tolerant approach toward undocumented migrants, regarding their massive deportation as inappropriate.

The establishment of public Latino bars represented perhaps the most prominent sign of the settlement of Latinos in Tel Aviv, and the "Latinization" of the Israeli landscape. The two bars were both established by mixed Israeli-Latino couples, who tried to advertise the bars among Latinos as well as Israelis. Apart from obviously trying to broaden their clientele, the owners of these bars knew that Latinos greatly appreciated the presence of Israelis in the same venue. However, the location of the two bars in the rundown part of south Tel Aviv made them unattractive to most Israelis, besides those who already had a connection to Latinos and thus occasionally joined them on a night out. Moreover, some Latinos were suspicious of the Israelis who visited these bars, as I once learned all too well. After a visit to the restroom in the Cantina Andina one night, as I walked back through the narrow corridor which led to the saloon, a Bolivian man deliberately blocked my way. Looking angry, he lashed out at me in whispers: "Don't think that I don't know who you are." He was obviously implying that I worked for the police, as he then somewhat threateningly asked, "You think I'm afraid of you? Well you are wrong." Just when I feared that he would become violent, to my relief, someone came by on his way to the restroom. Immediately grasping the tense situation, he told the Bolivian man, "What are you doing? He's OK." He then grabbed him and signaled for me to walk away.

Although from an Israeli perspective the two Latino bars were similar, from a Latino perspective they reflected and reproduced perhaps in the most tangible way the strong internal divisions between different Latino groups. The Cantina Andina was established by Sigal, an Israeli woman, and Luis, her Bolivian husband, whom she met during a trip to Bolivia. The Cantina Andina (hereafter the Cantina) was very modestly decorated, and it resembled the kind of bars one commonly finds in Bolivia: a few simple shelves for a limited number of liquor bottles and some cheap white plastic chairs and tables scattered in one large space, for which a CD player provided the music. No great effort was made to conceal the fact that the bar was installed in an old building that formerly served as a wholesale shoe shop. The thick uninviting walls were heavily painted in a dark azure color in order to give the place an agreeable look. To add some character to the bar, the flags of different Latin American countries were hung on the walls. The only modern piece of equipment in the Cantina was an outsized transparent fridge where hundreds of beer bottles were horizontally lined to increase capacity.

Just a few weeks after the Cantina opened its doors, it enjoyed a steady clientele that formed the backbone of the place. During weekdays the bar was frequented by only a small number of regular clients who lived in nearby neighborhoods and stopped there for a beer on their way home after work. But on weekends the Cantina was packed with guests, and even Latinos who lived and worked outside Tel Aviv often visited it then. The Cantina had a license to operate until two o'clock at night, but the bar commonly applied a practice of "closed doors"; that is, the heavy metal flap was brought down more than halfway, giving the impression from the outside that the bar was closed, while many people were still "locked" inside, continuing to party and drink.

Prices at the Cantina were very affordable, and heavy drinking among groups of friends was the norm. Tables were often packed with dozens of empty beer bottles, a sign of the drunken state of the group that was seated around it. The general atmosphere was very casual, and the friendly manner in which Sigal and Luis ran the place added to the general homey ambiance. Almost everyone personally knew Sigal and Luis and used their names whenever ordering drinks. Many regular clients were even allowed to get beers directly from the fridge and only notify the owners. Guests could also request for certain music to be played, and some even brought their own cassettes and CDs with them. When a favorite song was on, it was not uncommon for guests to get up to dance in the limited spaces between the packed tables. Nevertheless, the homely atmosphere at the Cantina could not entirely prevent occasional scuffles that broke out between rival Latino groups. I was informed about several such violent incidents that took place in the Cantina. Twice, I also witnessed myself how a group of Peruvians fought with a group of Ecuadorians. Luis and some guests, who tried to stop the fighting, shouted at those involved that if they kept going the police would come to the bar and arrest everyone.

La Tita, the second Latino bar, was also run by a mixed couple: a Colombian former undocumented migrant who married an Israeli woman, whose chubby figure won her the nickname La Tita. Although located in a rundown building on the back road to the central bus station, La Tita was an upscale Latino bar that was chicly designed with pastel-colored lights illuminating its interior space. An expensive audio system played modern Latino music, and an elegant bar offered a variety of brand-name liquors, several types of beers, and all kinds of cocktails. Prices in La Tita were not cheap, almost double the prices at the Cantina. It was the regular custom for guests in La Tita to order for the table an entire bottle of expensive liquor in addition to imported beers. La Tita consisted of two floors; the ground floor had thick wooden tables, and served as the main sitting area, while the second floor was used as extra standing space where guests could also freely dance.

On weekends, La Tita had a bouncer at its entrance, mainly to enforce a minimal dress code and to keep out potential troublemakers who might start a fight in the bar. There was clearly an attempt to maintain a certain well-mannered ambiance and establish a respectable reputation. La Tita generally aimed at a higher segment of more "civilized" Latinos, but its owners had to manage carefully a compromise between keeping the reputation of the place and ensuring profitability by letting in as many customers as possible. That La Tita was run by a Colombian enhanced both its Colombian style and Latinos' perception of it as a Colombian bar. Indeed, as a rule, Colombians went out to La Tita, but hardly ever to the Cantina Andina. Some Colombians proudly praised the atmosphere at La Tita, drawing direct comparisons with the more stylish bars they were used to in Colombia, or as one guest put it, "we finally have a bar where we feel at home."

The fact that most Latinos saw La Tita as a Colombian stronghold did not prevent some who were not Colombian from attending it, mainly since the choice of Latino bars was restricted between the only two existing bars. But the fact that some non-Colombian migrants, mainly from Andean countries, were occasionally prevented from entering La Tita exacerbated further an already existing internal tension between Colombians and other Latinos.

One Friday night I went out with Jeffrey, an Ecuadorian migrant who worked as a cleaner in a repair shop for automobiles. When I went to pick up Jeffrey at around ten o'clock, he had just awakened after an evening nap, "to recharge for the night ahead" as he put it. Friday is not a working day for most businesses in Israel, but the garage where Jeffrey worked was open for half a day, and thus he usually finished working in the late afternoon, and then hurried back home to get some sleep before going out.

Jeffrey knew an Ecuadorian who was giving a birthday party in her apartment that night, but he suspected it would not be exciting and instead suggested that we pay a visit to the Cantina. When we reached the bar it was still quite early and the place was half empty. Jeffrey proposed that we go for a couple of drinks at La Tita and return a bit later. This was the first time that we went together to La Tita, and on our way there Jeffrey told me how he and some other Ecuadorians were often refused entry to the bar: "If they see that you look too indigenous, they immediately think you are inferior and they don't let you in. Colombians are quite racist, you know." I asked Jeffrey if he thought we would be allowed in at this time, and he quickly reassured me, "Don't worry, when they see you they'll let us in, no problem." Indeed whenever I went to La Tita with Latinos from all nationalities, we were always allowed in. This was a clear sign of the high value that all Latinos, including the owners and bouncers of La Tita, attributed to those who had Israeli friends. The presence of an Israeli in the company of Latinos was physical evidence for their advanced integration and acceptance into Israeli society, perhaps the merit most admired by Latinos.

Once inside La Tita, Jeffrey and I ordered half a bottle of whisky and two beers. We conversed leisurely for an hour before making our way back to the Cantina, which by then was packed with Latinos. Jeffrey saw at one table a group of Ecuadorians he knew and greeted them. In return, they signaled us to join them, making two chairs available at their table. It was on these occasions, when Latinos were drinking together with their friends, that they felt confident to express themselves with little reservation, and conversations were usually fluent and open.

When we told the group that we had just come from La Tita, Roberto immediately jumped in to say, "I don't go there anymore. After the last time when they didn't let me in, I decided to never go again to these damn Colombians." It seemed like the group just needed a spark to ignite a discussion about Colombians in Israel. Esteban followed up with his own view:

> They are very arrogant; they think that they are the best in everything, and that they know everything. I must admit they make it very well here in Israel, but they also immediately try to show off. They dress up in expensive clothes, and they act as if they are very important. At the end, most of them still clean offices just like the rest of us.

Antonio added his angle, indirectly making reference to my presence at the table:

> Colombians always boast about their Israeli friends. They pretend to be closer to Israelis than to other illegal Latinos. We also have Israeli friends but we don't go around saying, "You know, yesterday I went out with my Israeli friend."

Indeed, when I was in La Tita with my Colombian informants, they often expressed their fondness for the bar's exclusive character and praised the bouncers for "not allowing just anyone in."

Colombians commonly claimed that other Latinos' negative views of them stemmed from sheer jealousy of their success as migrants in Israel. However, while denouncing the use of stereotypes and prejudice against them, Colombians often independently engaged in a demarcating discourse about their distinctive character, using chauvinism of the worst kind against other Latinos. Here is a common example of how Colombians explained the rift with other Latinos:

> People from the Andean countries are mainly indigenous, you know; they feel inferior and that's why they envy us. We have very few indigenous people in Colombia; most of us look more like Europeans, like you. I don't say that there is something wrong with indigenous people, but most of them have a backward mentality; they are farmers, and for them to be here in a modern city in another country is overwhelming. We are more used to it; we come from a modern country, and we find our way here much better than the others. (Luis Alberto, 34, Colombian)

The presence of Israelis in La Tita clearly flattered Colombians, and many of them strongly encouraged me to bring along some of my Israeli friends to the bar. In order to convince me, one Colombian told me, "You see, this bar has style, just like Israeli bars, not like that filthy Cantina where all the drunken Latinos gather."

The Salsa Scene: Dancing for Identity

From the mid 1990s, Latinos could enjoy a night out in one of the several salsa clubs that operated in Tel Aviv, providing the kind of entertainment that greatly appealed to the taste of many Latinos. Salsa clubs became extremely popular in Israel as part of a larger global trend that saw Latino music and dances penetrating many Western countries, with world pop stars such as Ricky Martin and Shakira reaching the top of pop charts across Europe and the United States. This global Latino trend was particularly amplified in Israel due to the fact that different countries in Latin America became popular travel destinations for tens of thousands of young Israelis after their release from obligatory military service (see Noy and Cohen 2004). During these trips, which habitually lasted for several months, Israelis were directly exposed to Latino music, dances, carnivals, and general folklore. Upon their return to Israel, many of the travelers sought to relive the Latino experience in salsa clubs.

A typical salsa club had a wide dance floor, a large bar with a focus on Latino cocktails and liquors, and a sitting area where guests could enjoy a drink and observe the dancers in action. Salsa clubs regularly stayed open until the early morning hours, and diehard dancers usually made their way back home at sunrise. Dancing in salsa clubs was commonly done in couples, and it often involved passionate and sensual moves. The general atmosphere was charged with sexuality, as young energized people, often dressed in a provocative way, were drinking and dancing. Many guests attended salsa clubs together with their partners. However, it was also very popular for singles to frequent clubs in hope of meeting someone there. The rule was for men to invite women to dance, and if there was chemistry between the couple they could easily go on dancing together for the rest of the night.

Salsa clubs became very popular among Latinos who used to go out frequently in their countries of origin. For them, going out to salsa clubs in Israel was an attractive entertainment, as well as a way to regain some sense of normalcy in their undocumented lives in Israel. Yet salsa clubs had another undeniable appeal for many Latinos: these clubs were among the most integrative institutions for undocumented migrants in Israeli society. In most of their daily lives in Israel, Latinos were restricted to manual jobs in subordinated positions to Israelis, which not only located them at the lowest status, but also prevented them from demonstrating their skills and talents. In salsa clubs both Latinos and Israelis participated in a similar role as clubbers. Moreover, Latinos' supremacy on the dance floor and their familiarity with Latino music and style were well appreciated and even admired by many Israelis. It even became quite "cool" among some Israelis in the salsa scene to have a relationship with a Latino migrant, and accordingly many romantic relations developed in this environment.

Some young Latino males admitted to me that their main interest in salsa clubs was the possibility of meeting Israeli women, who "just love the way we move." Whenever a Latino man did start a relationship with an Israeli woman, he would often brag about it, and his status among his friends usually received a clear boost. Latino women were generally less vocal about their romantic desires; however, it was common for groups of Latino women to attend salsa clubs, making themselves available for invitations to dance with men. Latino women were, of course, often invited to dance with Latino men, but the way Maria-José once revealed to me her outlook was telling in this respect:

> Sometimes I am disappointed if I am asked to dance by a Latino guy. It is
> not that I don't like it; after all, some Israelis can't really dance so well. [She
> giggled.] But with Israelis it is different; they are so cute and gentle, they
> want to learn how to dance, and they let you lead them and treat you with
> respect. And it is always exciting because you don't know what will happen
> next, and if he would like to go on further after dancing.

Aurora, a 26-year-old Colombian, was more outspoken about her experience with Israeli men. She confessed that in her work as a waitress in a restaurant, she always hoped to develop a serious relationship with an Israeli man, but to no avail. It was only when she started going out to salsa clubs that Israelis showed serious interest in her, and she proudly celebrated it:

> It is so much fun; I tell you, all these Israelis try so hard to dance but they just can't move like us [Latinos]; they look at us with admiration when we dance. There are always some Israelis that come to me and ask me to dance or invite me for a drink. . . . I now have many Israeli friends who call me and want to come pick me up with their cars for the salsa. Many also invite me out for dinner in restaurants or cafés.

The integrative role of salsa clubs reached beyond the dynamic between the mixed crowds, and into the running of these nightlife institutions. As the presence of Latinos was taken by most Israelis to enhance the quality of salsa clubs, Israeli owners commonly paid some Latinos to advertise their club in the Latino community. Some of the DJs were also recruited from among Latinos, as in the case of Joni, a 22-year-old Colombian who used to be an amateur DJ in Cali before he came to Israel. In Israel Joni worked as an office cleaner, but one of his Colombian friends who was involved in the salsa scene recommended Joni to the Israeli owners of one club. After auditioning him, the owner then decided to offer Joni a job as DJ on Friday nights, and also helped him ship to Israel some two hundred CDs from Joni's collection in Colombia.

I accompanied Joni a few times to the club, and noticed the friendly relationship he had there with the Israeli staff (owners, bartenders, bouncers, and waiters). As a DJ, Joni was a popular figure, and he also enjoyed much attention from Israeli women, who occasionally approached him to request a favorite song or to inquire about a certain band or a recent album. After one Israeli woman, who remained talking to him for a long moment, left, Joni smiled at me and proudly said, "It is a pity I am a married man." Later that night, between mixing songs, Joni gazed at the dance floor and with a sense of self-reflexivity he somewhat sarcastically let slip, "If you didn't know me, you probably wouldn't have believed that just some hours ago I cleaned the toilets in an office, right?"

The popularity of salsa clubs with Latinos induced the Israeli police to target these institutions frequently. However, salsa clubs were legally established by Israeli businessmen, so the police could never simply close them down. Nevertheless, the police could, and did, regularly raid salsa clubs in order to arrest undocumented migrants. Some owners of clubs complained that the police were deliberately damaging their businesses, but the police claimed that they were simply fulfilling their duty to deport all undocumented migrants.

Despite the police insistence not to permit these establishments to operate peacefully, at least eight different salsa clubs operated in Tel Aviv between 1996 and 2002. No matter how pronounced was the risk for Latinos in salsa clubs, the temptation often superseded their fear. This was evident among most spontaneous migrants and some young economic migrants who did not have children to support back home. These migrants often conceived of their immigration to Israel not only as a crucial economic project, but also as an experience abroad, which they sought to enjoy as much as possible. Positively experiencing their cultural identity and enjoying an opportunity to interact with Israelis induced many Latinos to ignore the risk that was involved in going out to salsa clubs. Tamara, a 24-year-old single Ecuadorian migrant, put it in a somewhat romantic fashion:

> I don't mind sweeping the floors of my employer all week; what keeps me going are the weekends when I know I'll go out dancing all night. It's really *chevere* [cool]. I'll never give it up, and if they catch me one time then that's the end.

Hernán, a 22-year-old single Ecuadorian migrant, was also not willing to deprive himself of going out to salsa clubs with his friends, even after he personally experienced a police raid in a club:

> The police came in, stopped the music and opened all the lights in the club. They then ordered everyone who had an Israeli identity card to come to one side of the hall while the rest of us were gathered in another side. Then they started asking us for our passports and where we came from. At the end they arrested twenty Latinos and let the rest go free after telling us to leave the country. I was very lucky that they didn't have enough space in their vans to take all of us.

One Friday night I visited Vicente, who shared an apartment with Hernán. While Vicente and I planned to watch a movie at home, Hernán was getting ready to go out to a salsa club. He dressed up in fashionable clothes and sat down with us, waiting for his friends to come pick him up. I asked Hernán if he was not afraid, and he superciliously replied:

> They [the police] will not change my ways here. I came here to work but also to live and enjoy life. If they catch me then it is over, but till then I plan to have good time here. Don't worry about me, enjoy the movie. You never know, maybe I'll be back tonight with my future Israeli wife. [He laughed and winked at me.]

The integrative function of salsa clubs induced fierce competition for Israeli attention between different Latino groups that had invested much effort in positively distinguishing themselves. As I learned from speaking to Israelis in salsa clubs, stereotypes of Colombians and Chileans were particularly well known and recognizable to many of them. Colombians managed to establish their reputation as skillful dancers, and more generally as knowledgeable clubbers. Chileans were widely considered good-looking and more sophisticated than other Latinos. The two groups differentiated themselves from one another largely by adhering to a typical appearance. Colombians dressed up fancily, and they often wore golden ornaments such as rings, wristlets, and chains. Chileans dressed more casually, and many of them typically bound their long hair in a ponytail, and wore a small goatee beard.

The division between Colombians, Chileans, and other Latinos was not confined to the dance floor; it also fomented the kind of tension that sometimes erupted in violent clashes. Fights between Latinos often followed an exchange of verbal provocations and insults between two antagonistic groups or individuals. But with tension already heightened, sometimes the smallest reason was enough to start a scuffle between rival parties, for example, a long gaze at someone's girlfriend or an innocent stumble over someone's foot. The Israeli owners of salsa clubs did their best to prevent quarrels, not least because violent fights often necessitated police intervention, which instantly scared away all Latinos.

Latino groups often exchanged allegations about who was responsible for violence in salsa clubs. Most non-Colombian Latinos pointed to the bad temper of Colombians as the major reason for the recurrent fights. As we were leaving a salsa club one night after a very violent fight broke out, and it was clear that the police would arrive any minute, Carlos, a Venezuelan migrant, angrily remarked:

> Look at these idiots; if the police finally decide sometimes not to come and hassle us, then these Colombians with their stupid habits make sure that the police will come no matter what. They try to show that they are the strongest, that they rule the salsa. I just hope that you [Israelis] can see that they are actually just gangsters.

Martha, a Chilean migrant, also categorically blamed Colombians:

> They bring here their mentality from Colombia, and they give a bad reputation to all of the Latinos in Israel. The Israelis read in the paper that someone was stabbed in a salsa club, and they don't know that these are Colombians; they just think "oh, these Latinos again." I don't want to sound racist but the bad reputation of Colombians is real; everywhere they go they bring trouble. They are not pleasant people; I only have one Colombian friend, but she is really nice, not like most of them.

Stereotypical negative remarks about Colombians in Israel should be, at least partly, understood against the backdrop of a more ubiquitous unreceptive social categorization of Colombians in many migratory contexts. There is almost an automatic coupling between Colombians and drug trafficking, which stains their image as migrants all over the world. In the Netherlands, for example, Zaitch (2001: 105) reported how Colombians' need to cope with damaging stereotypes led one of his informants pessimistically to refer to a Colombian identity as a "cross on the forehead." Guarnizo and Diaz (1999: 403) also report "widespread stigmatization and discrimination against Colombians in the United States."

In Israel too, a few criminal incidents involving Colombians immediately made the headlines in the national media. For example, one headline in a newspaper warned that "Colombian assassinators settle down in Israel." The journalist cautioned that efforts by the police to combat professional Colombian assassins and drug traffickers were "a drop in the ocean," and therefore "Israel should get ready for the next explosion" (*Maariv* 26.02.1999). Police sources were also quoted in the article, saying that "Colombians in particular are considered problematic. They come to us directly from the world's drug barn."

Interestingly, however, most Colombians in Israel told me that they were positively surprised not to have experienced stigmatization in their interactions with Israelis. Colombians often even praised the general friendly attitude and lack of prejudice that Israelis demonstrated. They did, however, blame other Latinos for promoting hostile stereotypes and damaging preconceptions about Colombians. Fernando expressed his views of other Latinos in this respect:

All the other Latinos in Israel envy us. We are smart; we work hard and advance. Then the others think, "how come they made it and we didn't?" And so they always say that we deal drugs or have connections with the mafia. Believe me, I know almost all the Colombians here in Tel Aviv, not even one of us has a link to the mafia. On the contrary, many of us left Colombia precisely because we suffered there from the mafia or the paramilitaries.

The Football Scene: Pan-Latino Fever, Intra-Latino Competition

The Latino fever for football, by far the most popular sport across Latin America, drove many Latinos in Israel to gather on Saturday, the Jewish day of rest, for playing their favorite game on improvised pitches in public spaces. As early as 1992 some undocumented Chilean migrants formed an association (Chile Unido) that began to organize football tournaments at Yarkon Park, a large recreational area located in the north of Tel Aviv. Several teams were formed, and games were played from early morning until late afternoon. As more Latinos arrived in Israel, the event was extended in order to incorporate them. Teams were then formed along national lines, with players wearing uniforms in the national colors of their respective countries. The competition was named the Copa America (American Cup), emulating the yearly continental competition between the leading clubs from all countries in Latin America. Later, some more teams of undocumented migrants from other parts of the world (such as Ghana and Romania) were also incorporated into these tournaments, and the competition was renamed the Mundial (World Cup).

As I was told by some of my Chilean informants, around 1996 the Colombian team was discontent with the running of the tournament, and consequently decided to initiate a parallel football competition at Dolphinarium Park. This park, which is located along the beautiful Mediterranean coastline, borders the west side of south Tel Aviv. Unlike a trip to Yarkon Park, which involved a very long walk or a costly taxi ride (on Saturday there is no public transportation in Israel), the Dolphinarium was easily accessible to most Latinos who resided in its vicinity.

The Saturday football competition in the Dolphinarium became very popular with scores of Latinos who came to watch the games, cheer for their national team, and generally enjoy the entertaining event in the company of their friends. Many Latino families also frequented the Dolphinarium; while fathers closely followed the matches, mothers gathered to chat and children played in the nearby playground.

As the Latino football tradition attracted many players as well as spectators, some Latinos with an entrepreneurial sense began to make use of the event, wandering around with cool boxes selling cold drinks and beers. Subsequently, some Latino women began to sell traditional Latino food that they cooked and brought to the park in baskets tapped with towels to keep the dishes warm. With time the football scene turned into a weekly Latino gathering. In addition to these occasional vendors (*vendadores*), some big tents were installed around the pitch, selling drinks and different dishes that were prepared on small gas cookers or barbeques. Some tents had plastic chairs and tables where people could sit under the shade and watch the games while eating and drinking.

The Israeli media took positive notice of the Latino football scene, exposing it to the larger Israeli population through numerous colorful journalistic reports. Latinos who had Israeli friends regularly invited them to attend the event, while other Israelis, who visited the park regardless of its Latino football scene, occasionally became curious about the lively happening and joined it as spectators. At one point, a group of Israeli players joined the Latino football tournament and formed the "Israeli team." Latinos welcomed and appreciated the Israeli involvement in the event.

However, the supra-national harmonious image of a Latino community that united together to recreate was partly misleading. Closer inspection of the football event revealed national divisions, which further nourished animosities between groups. For one, the division into competing national teams on the pitch was mirrored in the grouping of fans. Tents that sold drinks and food to spectators displayed a pronounced national identity, and each group normally gathered around its own tent. This segmentation was especially epitomized by the marked opposition between the two biggest tents that dominated the scene: at one end of the pitch was the Chilean tent with a big Chilean flag adorning it, while at the other side the Colombian tent was easily recognizable by the merengue music coming out of two large loudspeakers.

At the football event as in the salsa clubs, Colombians and Chileans fought for a leading position among Latinos. Chileans mainly took their pride from claiming to be the pioneering Latino group in Israel. They often blamed Colombians for trying to disassociate themselves from other Latinos, and instead to assimilate as much as they could into Israeli society. One Chilean expressed this prevalent view as we were sitting in the shade of the Chilean tent:

> Colombians are egoistic; they only care about themselves, and that's why all other Latinos dislike them. We [Chileans] were, for example, the first to establish the football tradition, but when other Latinos came we always encouraged and welcomed their participation. But Colombians, they only call all the Israelis they know and beg them to come here and sit with them in their tent. They only want to associate with Israelis, not with other Latinos.

What also fuelled divisions among Latinos in the football scene was the tendency of some fans to invest in it nationalistic sentiments that were related to long-lasting conflicts between rival countries in Latin America. For example, Jose, an Ecuadorian with whom I went to the Dolphinarium one Saturday afternoon, warned me that "today we are playing Peru, it's going to be a very hot game." When I naively asked why, he reacted with amazement, "You don't know that we are at war with Peru?" He then exclaimed, "They still occupy Ecuadorian land." What I did know was that Peru and Ecuador settled their fight over land and signed an historic peace agreement in October 1998. However, for Latinos in Israel, in 2002, this was still a good reason for marking divisions.

Perhaps the ultimate indication of the underlying divided character of the seemingly inclusive Latino football scene was given when the whole event disintegrated under pressure from the Israeli police. Occasional police raids eroded participation in the event, until it eventually ceased to exist in late 2002. Many Latinos who were not ready to give up their desire for football established smaller-scale tournaments in pitches of schools across south Tel Aviv. Interestingly, almost all of these smaller tournaments, which consisted of around twenty players each, were organized by groups of migrants from the same country.

154 / PART 2

Mixed Marriages, Fixed Views: The Case of *Chilimbianos*

During my fieldwork I encountered a number of mixed marriages between Latinos from different countries of origin. It is, however, very difficult to estimate how prevalent this phenomenon actually was, since marriages between undocumented migrants in Israel were never registered in any official record. Notwithstanding the spread of such marriages, from my observational viewpoint, on an individual level many Latinos regularly developed constructive relationships, and even friendships, with Latinos from other national groups.

Relationships even developed between some Chileans and Colombians, who on a communitarian level appeared to be very antagonistic toward each other. When I once discussed this matter with Sergio, a veteran Chilean migrant who had already lived in Israel for more than a decade, he offered an interesting historical perspective:

> As you know, we [Chileans] were the first to come to Israel. And when the
> Colombians started to arrive it was mainly their women who came here
> first as cleaners. Then naturally many romantic relations developed
> between Chilean men and Colombian women, and that is why they are so
> many *Chilimbianos* now in Israel.

I asked Sergio if mixed relations and the birth of *Chilimbianos* did not help bridge the divide between the two groups. He clarified:

> When the Colombian men began to arrive, they were infuriated to discover
> that their women went with Chileans, and this is why we don't get along
> very well together with them.

Factually, Sergio's claim was not unfounded; Chilean men were among the first migrants to reach Israel, and the initial immigration from Colombia largely consisted of female domestic workers. Sergio obviously chose to articulate and treat the birth of *Chilimbianos* as a dividing dynamic that exacerbated animosities between the two groups rather than bringing them closer together. This case is a powerful demonstration of how the potential for unity between Latinos in Israel was consciously disregarded, and instead was socially constructed as ever dividing.

The divisive trends that I depict in the Latino recreational scene help to elucidate the discouraging effect that a political disunity had on an attempt to form a "Latino community." Attempts to unite politically were oppressed by the Israeli police, and left most Latinos disillusioned about the prospects of such mobilization in the Israeli context. While most Latinos perceived the potential of political organization to bring about changes in the Israeli policy to be slim, the risk involved was evidently high. Individual invisibility was therefore championed by most Latinos as the preferred strategy for combating the Israeli policy of deportation. Having lost motivation to join forces together, Latinos primarily formed a structure of parallel national Latino communities. This divisive structure largely followed that of parallel transnational migration networks that were independently stretched from each country in Latin America to Israel. Thus, most Latinos in Israel were embedded in social networks that were highly national in their composition, and in some cases directly led to the establishment of recreational activities along national lines, as in the case of home restaurants and bars. Nevertheless, in mixed recreational institutions such as salsa clubs and football competitions, and even in the case of mixed marriages, many Latinos invested much effort in socially constructing demarcations between national groups.

Chapter Six

The Religious Forms of Undocumented Lives

LATINO EVANGELICAL CHURCHES

> The Christian church is an encyclopaedia of prehistoric
> cults and conceptions of the most diverse origin, and
> that is why it is so capable of proselytizing: it always
> could, and it can still go wherever it pleases and it always
> found, and always finds something similar to itself to
> which it can adapt itself and gradually impose upon it a
> Christian meaning. It is not what is Christian in it, but
> the universal heathen character of its usages, which has
> favored the spread of this world-religion; its ideas . . .
> have from the first known how to raise themselves above
> national and racial niceties and exclusiveness as though
> these were merely prejudices.
>
> —*Friedrich Nietzsche*

Latinos in Israel were Christians to varying degrees of conviction; while some were deeply religious, others were secular and merely considered Christianity to be part of their cultural upbringing. Nevertheless, once in Israel, non-Jewish undocumented migrants were forcefully made aware of their religious identity, as it was precisely this component of their makeup as migrants that confined them to their undocumented status and officially defined them as the new Other in Israeli society.

Under Israel's democratic and legal commitment to freedom of religion, non-Jewish undocumented migrants were legally allowed to establish and operate their religious institutions. The Declaration of Independence (May 14, 1948) explicitly states, "The state of Israel will . . . guarantee freedom of religion, conscience, language, education and culture." Indeed, even at the height of deportation campaigns, the Israeli police tolerated the operation of Christian churches. There was one incident in which the police broke into a basement that was used as a church for undocumented migrants from Africa. The case was reported by a popular local newspaper (*Halr* 22.06.2001). A police spokesman publicly apologized and clarified that the agents raided the basement in search of undocumented migrants, and only once inside did the police notice that a small section of the basement was designated for holding religious ceremonies.

The protection that churches enjoyed rendered them sanctuaries from persecution for undocumented migrants, who considered attending them to be a safe activity.[1] With the police clamping down on all political and recreational organizations of undocumented migrants, it was religious institutions that, besides fulfilling migrants' need for spirituality, provided a framework for the cultivation of a sense of identity and the formation of communities. These multiple functions of religious institutions were evident in the lives of Latinos in Israel, and churches managed to attract hundreds of members also from among those who were initially disinterested in religion. Somewhat ironically then, the one most non-Jewish activity that migrants could engage in, namely, celebrating their religious Otherness in a highly organized and institutionalized fashion, was legally permitted under the Israeli Basic Laws (see Barak 1994).

Beginning in the mid-1990s, more than ten Latino evangelical churches were established in the basements of rundown buildings or in the lofts of industrial edifices in south Tel Aviv. Over the years, each evangelical congregation had dozens of permanent members and in addition many people who attended the church intermittently. It is therefore reasonable to assume that around 1,500 Latinos participated in the emerging evangelical scene in south Tel Aviv.[2] Latino evangelical churches formed part of a transnational religious network that assisted many of the religious migrants (see chapter 3) to reach and settle down in Israel. However, the success of evangelical churches in converting scores of Catholic Latinos in Tel Aviv emanated from the multifaceted roles that these churches played in the lives of their members. Efforts toward community building, individual empowerment, and identity making have all rendered membership in evangelical churches highly attractive and instrumental to Latinos in Israel.

Some Latinos, like other Catholic migrant workers, chose to attend one of the several Catholic churches in Jaffa (a district of Tel Aviv where Muslim and Christian Palestinians live). Since Sunday is a working day in Israel, Catholic churches in Jaffa began to hold weekly Mass on Saturday afternoon, to fit with the schedule of non-Jewish migrants. For example, at the Saint Peter Church in Jaffa tens of Latinos attended the Saturday service, which was conducted by a Chilean priest in Spanish. Given their time constraints, Catholic migrants from countries such as the Philippines, Poland, and Romania often also attended the same service although they hardly understood a word of Spanish.

Catholic churches offered migrants various services such as marriage ceremonies, baptism of children, and confessions. Some social activities were also organized by churches, for example, fundraising events for Catholic Palestinians in the Occupied Territories or for undocumented migrants under financial duress. While some Latinos formed a religious community that revolved around their Catholic church, from my observations, most Catholic Latinos only sporadically participated in other activities apart from the weekly Mass. While I would not pretend to judge the depths of Latinos' faith nor the effect of church attendance on their life, I contend that by and large the practice of Catholicism among Latinos in Israel did not amount, sociologically speaking, to the formation of a significant public sphere. Catholic churches fulfilled a social role in the lives of those who attended them, yet this role was rather limited in its scope when compared to the one performed by evangelical churches. One cannot discard the possibility that the success of evangelical churches in converting scores of Catholic Latinos had at least partly to do with the limited role the Catholic churches played in the lives of undocumented migrants in Israel.[3]

Thus, with their multifaceted functions, it was particularly evangelical churches that played a significant role in the lives of Latinos in Tel Aviv. As Levitt (2004) points out, flexible and decentralized religious organizations, such as evangelical churches, are more adaptable and responsive to the environment where they are being instituted and to the changing needs of their membership (see also Harding 2000). The spread and functions of evangelical churches among both documented and undocumented migrants worldwide certainly constitute a significant component in Appadurai's (1996) "ethnoscape," which reconfigures the globally shifting cultural landscape through immigration.

The approach of Latino evangelical pastors in Israel toward the Jewish state was underlined by a nuanced bipolarity. Pastors depicted evangelicals as subjected and committed to the cause of Jews and the Holy Land, but as simultaneously having an independent moral task that was endowed on them directly by God. This bipolarity rendered a compatible recognition of the complete sovereignty of Israel with a claim for the moral role and place of evangelical Latinos in it. Interesting in this respect is the unique meaning that the theological teachings of Christian Zionism assumed for evangelicals in Israel. Latino pastors preached to members to empathize and identify unconditionally with Jews and the Jewish state. Pastors blurred the distinctions between Jews and evangelical Christians, not least by demonizing and constituting Islam and Arabs as the common enemy of the Judeo-Christian tradition. In this and other ways, pastors significantly promoted a sense of belonging to Israel and facilitated Latinos' cultural assimilation. For example, they encouraged members to cultivate friendly relationships with Jews; they taught members the Hebrew language and Jewish customs and tradition; and they sometimes practiced a dress code that mimicked the Jewish orthodox one. More pronounced in this respect were the practices and theology that were adopted by a few Latino evangelical churches that embraced a messianic orientation. Pastors in these churches sometimes contemplated a conversion to Judaism. Although such conversion was unattainable for undocumented migrants in Israel, it ignited Latinos' imagination regarding the legalization of their status in Israel.

Evangelizing Tel Aviv: The Booming Latino Religious Scene

Unlike their Catholic counterparts, evangelical migrants had to establish their own churches, as Tel Aviv did not have even a single evangelical or Pentecostal church within its parameters prior to the arrival of non-Jewish migrants. Some evangelicals, mainly from northern Europe, had settled in Israel beginning in 1948, but mostly around Jerusalem. In Jaffa there are various Protestant churches, such as Anglican, Baptist, and Lutheran. The first Latino evangelical pastors, who aspired to establish a congregation in Tel Aviv, initially rented by the hour a hall in a Baptist or Anglican church in Jaffa. According to Pedro, a Peruvian co-founder of one of Tel Aviv's first Latino evangelical churches:

> There were sometimes three different services a day, each given by a
> different pastor to a different congregation. We had to finish our service
> precisely on time so that the hall would be available for another pastor who
> rented it.

After this initial phase, congregations with a substantial number of followers moved out of Jaffa to establish new churches in the basements of rundown buildings or in the lofts of industrial edifices in south Tel Aviv. The location of churches in the midst of the residential concentration of undocumented migrants permitted followers to frequent evangelical churches on a more regular basis. Dozens of evangelical and Pentecostal churches have been established in the city since the early 1990s by different groups of undocumented migrants.[4] After learning about their legal possibilities, clandestine congregations operated more openly, and the sound of religious singing coming from them could be heard in some streets in south Tel Aviv. Some congregations even registered in Israel as "non-profit associations," and accordingly received a reduction in the municipality property tax. In this sense, evangelical churches generated both visual and spiritual changes in the Israeli religious landscape.

The decentralized structure of the Protestant establishment facilitated the spread of evangelical churches in Tel Aviv. Unlike in Catholicism, where a central federated administration is responsible for erecting new churches and appointing new priests, the religious field of evangelicalism is more unrestricted and flexible. There exist hundreds of different evangelical ministries around the world that independently draft their theological vision, structural organization, and expansion strategies. In evangelicalism there is no strictly defined biblical education, no one standardized spiritual training, that a potential pastor must complete before being entitled to establish and lead a congregation. Accordingly, there is much more freedom for "religious entrepreneurs" who mobilize financial and religious resources for the establishment of "start-up congregations," as Peggy Levitt (2004) labels them.

Indeed, the variety of evangelical denominations that operated in Tel Aviv in the late 1990s reflects this pronounced openness that exists in evangelicalism. Some Latino evangelical congregations in Israel were established as chapters of globally recognized ministries. These included: King of Kings, Assemblies of God, the Light of the World, Prince of Peace, and Ambassadors of the King. Other Latino congregations emerged locally from the initiative of "religious entrepreneurs," who often came to Israel and worked as undocumented migrants. Religious entrepreneurs often maintained ties with the congregation that they attended in their hometown before going to Israel, and sometimes they also sought affiliation with a renowned ministry, with which they then established a theological rapport. Establishing such affiliations was not a difficult task, given that some prestigious ministries worldwide offer to provide congregations with a formal link via their Internet sites. Affiliations of evangelical churches in Tel Aviv to global ministries were of a very loose type. Congregations in Israel hardly ever received funds from aboard, and only occasionally were they instructed about theological teachings and mundane organization. Religious entrepreneurs in Israel sought global affiliations mainly in order to generate legitimacy for, and enhance the reputation of, their congregations. During my fieldwork I visited all Latino churches several times and talked with members as well as pastors. I also carried out a more extensive participant observation in two churches and developed close relationships with pastors there.

Relations between different evangelical churches in Tel Aviv ranged from cooperation to hostility. Pastors attempted to project brotherhood and teamwork. They established a Pastoral Center where they met for joint biblical studies as well as mundane discussions. As one of them put it, "We are all here to serve and adore God." Yet there existed a fierce competition between evangelical churches in Tel Aviv over members. Churches, even those that were affiliated with ministries abroad, could not rely on external resources for their operations. They were thus dependent for their subsistence on members' tithes and their additional voluntary donations. It was partly against this economic backdrop that some of the more veteran evangelical churches in Tel Aviv disapprovingly viewed the establishment of new congregations that aimed to get a share of the "religious market."

Antagonism toward new congregations was exacerbated when they were established by self-declared pastors who had first been members of other evangelical churches in the city. This tendency toward separation characterizes the non-hierarchal structure of evangelicalism, in which "[t]hose who get fed up with their spiritual mentors start their own churches" (Stoll 1990: 46). In Tel Aviv I came across three cases in which such "splinter congregations" were established. These congregations were sometimes condemned either for their spiritual orientation or for the qualifications of their pastors to lead them. For example, Raúl, a Colombian migrant, was a member of the Kad-Esh church for three years before he decided to withdraw and establish his own congregation. Raúl studied the Bible for many years but was never officially appointed as a pastor by any recognized evangelical institution. Nevertheless, building on his contacts with an evangelical messianic congregation in Europe, Raúl secured the necessary financial resources and theological material for starting his own congregation. Although Raúl was criticized by other pastors, he showed resilience and was not willing to bend under the pressure, as he once told me:

> I first used to go for meetings at the Pastoral Center, but I gradually received more and more critique from other pastors about my line of teaching, so I decided to stop attending these meetings altogether. It is sad, but there is much narrow-mindedness and even jealousy among pastors. I know that they don't approve of it, but I can't compromise my belief, of course.

Another telling example for the possibility of religious entrepreneurs to operate within the field of evangelicalism was the case of pastor Nestor. An undocumented migrant from Ecuador, Nestor worked as a cleaner and was a member of the Light of the World evangelical church. After one year, he decided to establish his own congregation. From my own interactions with Nestor it was clear to me that he was very charismatic, although his biblical knowledge was not solid. When we were first introduced at a social gathering at the apartment of one of my Ecuadorian informants, Nestor was very curious about my name. I was surprised he did not recognize it, and thus said, "As you surely know 'Barak' is a biblical name." I could clearly see that Nestor had no idea, and so, trying not to embarrass him in public, I quickly continued, "Barak ben Avinoam was not an important figure, he was the army general of the prophet Devorah, I think that the story is in the Book of Judges." Nestor tried to save face and said he simply wanted to know if my name carried any meaning in modern Hebrew. Nevertheless, being a true "religious entrepreneur," Nestor mobilized support for his initiative from his hometown evangelical church in Ecuador, where he had served as an assistant to the pastor. Nestor came from a region in Ecuador that saw many undocumented migrants leave for Israel, and he thus personally knew some of them, a fact that he used in his recruiting campaigns. In his attempt to win himself a crowd of followers from among Latinos in Tel Aviv, Nestor adopted a nationalistic line—an unusual strategy among Latino pastors in Israel. Nestor propagated his goal to have a prosperous Ecuadorian congregation in Tel Aviv, and he promoted it accordingly among Ecuadorians, exploiting their patriotic sentiments.

Nestor's congregation operated in Tel Aviv under his pastoral guidance for almost three years, during which it managed to attract dozens of Ecuadorian migrants. Nestor invested much attention and money in the aesthetics of his church. After one year he relocated the church from a rundown basement to a big hall in a new building. He bought an advanced sound system for the church and equipped his band with musical instruments that included an electric organ and a full set of drums. In 2002, to celebrate the second anniversary of his congregation, Nestor hired a fancy hall in a convention center at one of Tel Aviv's better hotels.

At the end of 2003 Nestor told his followers he had to attend an important pastoral convention in Spain, but he never returned to Israel. As I learned during my fieldwork in Spain, Nestor arrived there just before the institution of a new visa regime that required people from Latin America to apply for a tourist visa. In Spain, Nestor conducted "market research," as one informant told me; Nestor was calling all his acquaintances and ex-followers who were deported or left Israel and were now in Barcelona, to ask if they would leave their present congregations and join him if he established his own.

Converting to Evangelicalism: The Recruitment of New Members

Religious migrants constituted the backbone of evangelical churches in Tel Aviv. Many of them initially reached Israel through organized tours that were arranged by evangelical churches in migrants' countries of origin. Religious migrants were then introduced to one of the evangelical churches in Tel Aviv during the tour, and once they decided to stay in Israel, they joined it as members. What facilitated the incorporation of Latinos into evangelical churches in Israel was that "The 'model' for prayer and administration in certain denominations is similar around the world, [and] migrants know how to participate in any church wherever they are" (Levitt 2004: 6).

To increase their membership, evangelical churches sought to convert Catholic and secular Latinos. Evangelicalism is a very proactive missionary religious stream. Spreading the Word of God is a doctrinal tenet and a religious deed. Pastors in Tel Aviv were unequivocal and persistent in their demand for members in their congregations to evangelize and recruit their relatives, friends, co-workers, and even Latinos whom they met by chance in public places such as self-service laundries and calling centers. The immediate goal that Latino pastors set for their members was to get fellow Latinos to church. Pastors often explained that once someone was in church, he or she would be moved by the presence of God, and convincing would no longer be necessary.

One way to attract Latinos to visit churches was by celebrating non-religious festivities there. Churches regularly lent their venue for the celebration of members' birthdays, anniversaries, farewell parties, and other events. Usually, the hosts of these celebrations provided food and drinks for all guests, and they received a special religious blessing from the pastor. Members were happy to celebrate these festivities in church instead of in their own cramped apartments, which usually did not allow for a large celebration. Well-equipped and nicely decorated churches constituted an appealing setting for holding parties, which often involved loud music and singing. Rejoicing in church also freed participants from fear of a police raid. Pastors encouraged members to invite all their relatives and friends to these events. Visitors were then exposed to the church's facilities and communal atmosphere. Pastors always took to the stage at one point to offer a religious blessing to first-time-visitors and to cordially invite them to attend a forthcoming service.

Most pastors in Israel considered conversion to be an instant matter that simply required the acceptance of Jesus Christ as one's Savior and a declaration of intent to conform to the evangelical doctrine. Accordingly, pastors always accepted new members without much hassle, even when they required a certain training period in biblical studies before actually performing a formal conversion ceremony for new candidates. Individual conversion ceremonies were conducted in church, yet when churches had a cohort of new members they often organized a more spectacular baptism in the Jordan River at the place where, according to the New Testament, Jesus himself was baptized. Existing members were also offered this once-in-a-lifetime opportunity to be re-baptized at this unique location, and they commonly chose to join these trips together with new members. The whole event was very mystical; members wore a white piece of sheet around their bodies, and lying in the hands of the pastor they were lowered into the river water up to the top of their heads.

In practice, new visitors to an evangelical church always received a warm and personal welcome from the pastor. Visitors were given their own Bible and instructions for following the sermon. After their sermon, pastors approached visitors to inquire about their personal situation and spiritual state. Whenever pastors felt that visitors were "ready to receive Jesus into their heart," they initiated on the spot a collective prayer for the visitors to experience a Godly intervention. When visitors were hesitant about their intentions, pastors preached to them for a while about the value of submitting one's soul to Jesus, and then secured a follow-up visit by extending them a personal invitation.

Interestingly, in Latin America as in other places worldwide, evangelical pastors often denigrated Catholicism as part of their overall effort to convert Catholics to evangelicalism. In Israel, however, while some pastors negatively referred to Catholicism, this tendency was by and large avoided. This might be the case because evangelical pastors in Israel, in their attempt to identify with Jewish Israelis, chose to stress much more their hostility toward Islam and Arabs.[5] It might also be that since the Catholic Church in Israel was not very active among Latinos, it did not constitute a direct competition for evangelical churches.

Anniversaries to mark the founding of evangelical churches in Tel Aviv were always grandiosely celebrated, and members were encouraged to invite everyone they knew, including their Israeli friends and employers. For the fifth anniversary of the Prince of Peace church, I was invited by Antonio and Livia. This married couple from Colombia had been living in Israel for more than five years, but it was only recently that they converted to evangelicalism. Given that I had never been to the Prince of Peace before, I suggested that we meet and walk to church together, but Antonio and Livia explained that they would already be there a few hours before to help with preparations for the big event. I told them that it might look strange if I walked in alone, but Antonio brushed my worries aside, instructing me to say at the entrance that I was his friend.

Walking to the Prince of Peace on a Saturday afternoon, I could recognize on the nearby streets dozens of Latinos who were also heading toward the church. They were all elegantly dressed up for the occasion. Families with children, young couples, a group of four women—they all looked cheerful and energized. The church was located in a basement at the back of an old building, where a modest sign, with an arrow pointing downstairs, said "*Bienvenido Iglesia El Principe de Paz*" (Welcome to the Prince of Peace Church). Stepping into the church, I asked a man whether he knew where Antonio was; the man warmly greeted me and promised to fetch Antonio for me. Inside the church there was much commotion; some men were putting white plastic chairs in straight lines in front of a decorated platform, while two women were adorning the pulpit with bouquets of flowers. Paper strips with biblical verses printed on them were hanging all around, together with some white and blue balloons (white and blue are the colors of the Israeli flag and, as I was told, this was not a coincidence). Also glued on the walls were paintings that were drawn by children and portrayed different biblical scenes. On one side of the spacious basement, some women were busy receiving trays and pots of food from arriving guests and putting them into more decorative containers on tables. Notably, food that was prepared for consumption in evangelical churches was mostly Israeli in style. Only on rare occasions was a traditional Latino dish prepared.

As I waited at the entrance for Antonio I felt a tap on my back; it was Luisa, whom I had met in another evangelical church and who was very surprised to see me there. I explained to her that a friend had invited me, and she informed me that for church anniversaries all other evangelical members and pastors were also invited. She then sarcastically added, "but not all of them come," hinting at the tensions between some pastors.

A minute later Antonio appeared, smiling and cheerful; he gave me a fatherly hug and said that I honored him by coming. After politely greeting Luisa, Antonio grabbed me by the hand and took me to meet the pastor. He proudly introduced me as his Israeli friend to the pastor and some other members. Everyone warmly shook my hand and welcomed me to the festivity. The pastor said it was a great honor for his church that I participated in this special occasion. He began inquiring about my background, but people constantly interrupted our conversation, asking the pastor for instructions about the last arrangements for the ceremony. Finally the pastor excused himself and said he would be delighted to talk to me after the ceremony. Antonio too needed to help with some last arrangements, but before he left me he said, in a friendly but firm way, "You sit here with us in the first row."

The order of seating in evangelical churches normally reflected the importance and status of members. Front rows were typically reserved for pastors, their deputies, and other members who played a more prominent role in the church. As a rule, honored guests were also always seated in the first row. Some conservative evangelical churches kept a division between men and women in the setup of the church, but this was not the case in the Prince of Peace.

Waiting for the ceremony to start, I suddenly spotted Julio in the crowd. I excused myself and went to greet him. Knowing he was a Catholic, I was surprised to see him there, but before I could even ask him about it Julio somewhat apologetically explained, "My neighbor dragged me here, she said that I should come cause there will be a big dinner and I thought 'why not?'" He then asked, "Why did you come here?" After I told him, he asked if I wanted to come for a drink after it all finished. I said that I would probably have to stick around with my friends for a while but that I could meet him at the bar later.

The ceremony commenced with a theatrical reenactment of a biblical story that was put on by a group of children, the sons and daughters of members in the congregation. It was followed by a series of songs of praise (*alabanzas*), sung by two vocalists. An hour later, the crowd was animated, and the pastor went up to the pulpit. He first blessed all members and their guests and thanked them for coming to the celebration. Then, in an hour-long sermon, the pastor reviewed the history and achievements of the congregation in Tel Aviv, stressing that its success and determination were a testimony to the work God was performing with evangelicals in the Land of Israel. At the end of his sermon the pastor turned to a common recruiting technique, encouraging guests in the audience to step forward to the front of the platform, where he would bless them and ask Jesus to enter their hearts.

A woman in her late forties was the first to throw herself on the ground at the pastor's feet, weeping and crying out for God and Jesus to help her. Antonio whispered in my ear that she had come to Israel together with her son, who had never adjusted to life there; he did not want to go to school and was very violent, and his mother felt she had lost all hope. The pastor urged guests not to be afraid or ashamed, as this might be the crucial day that would change the course of their lives forever. Another woman stepped forward and then another one. The pastor kept on mobilizing and exciting the crowd; he then made a call to people who might have a problem with alcoholism or drugs to step forward. One man stepped to the front and collapsed. I looked to the place where Julio was, and he looked back at me. I could see he was struggling; his eyes were watery but he did not move although the pastor repeatedly made his call. At last, the pastor attended to those who stepped forward. He got down from the pulpit and moved between them, placing his hand on their heads, closing his eyes and very loudly praying for Jesus to enter their hearts. The crowd prayed along, with some members occasionally chanting "Holy Jesus" and "Glory to God." Finally, the pastor pulled the new members to their feet. He gave each of them a warm hug and then asked his deputy to escort them to the back office and take their details.

At the end of this climactic scene, the pastor thanked all members and their guests and invited everyone to enjoy a tasty dinner. Within seconds evangelical music came through speakers that hung from all corners in the spacious basement, and some energized members quickly put aside all the plastic chairs. Some women promptly took charge of the food tables and began to serve guests a variety of dishes. Guests started grouping and socializing. People slowly began to leave after an hour. Antonio and Livia had to stay longer to help out with the cleaning of the church, and so I thanked them for inviting me to this evening and hurried to the Cantina Andina to meet Julio. When I got there Julio seemed to be in a pretty bad shape; he was already a bit drunk and commented directly on the events in church:

> Did you see the pastor calling for alcoholics [to come forward]? It was
> meant for me, I know it. My neighbor told the pastor before the ceremony
> that she brought a friend who had problems with alcohol and asked him to
> help me. When he made this call I knew it was for me, but I don't believe in
> these religious rituals. I will never throw myself on the floor in front of
> everybody and cry like a baby. In the worst case I'll go to talk privately with
> the pastor, but not like that. I don't get these people who do it. Do you?

He then jokingly referred to his participation in the anniversary:

> I am only going to religious events when there are big festivities with free
> food. If they invite me to some boring regular ceremony on Saturday
> morning I never go.

Two months after the anniversary, Julio accepted his neighbor's suggestion to meet with the pastor in private. After that meeting, Julio eventually converted and joined the evangelical congregation as a member.

When I asked former Catholic Latinos such as Julio about their motivations for undergoing conversion, many of them played down their Catholic faith. They claimed that Catholicism had constituted a part of their cultural upbringing rather than a serious religious devotion. In contrast to their past religiosity that was based on tradition and inertia, converts often explained that their evangelical belief emanated from their own independent and deliberate conviction. This distinction was typically made within a more general narrative about a personal revelation and a deep inner experience whereby Jesus had appeared to converts, entered their hearts, and shown them "the way." Born-again Christians regularly considered their conversion as a life-changing event that gave a new meaning to everything around them. Many converts also stressed theological empowerment and the egalitarian character of evangelicalism:

> Do you know the first thing they do in an evangelical church? They give you
> a Bible in your hand. And every time the pastor preaches he tells you
> exactly which verses he refers to and you look them up, read them, and
> think about them. Also, if you don't understand or differ in your
> interpretation from that of the pastor, you are always invited to ask
> questions. Everyone is equal, you see, we're all trying to learn and
> understand together. I was a Catholic all my life and nobody ever asked my
> opinion in church. I always simply had to listen to the priest. (Alex, 38,
> Colombian)

Many Latino converts were attracted to evangelical churches by the many instrumental roles that churches played in the lives of their members. For example, Ángel, who at a certain point shared an apartment with two devoted evangelicals, finally accepted his roommates' recurring invitations to visit their church. He later became a member himself, although a very calculating and cautious one:

> I saw what the church did for them [Ángel's roommates], how many nice
> things were organized for them, and how they were always informed about
> everything that was happening in Israel. In the beginning I thought that
> these churches only tried to get money out of you, but then I decided to
> give it a chance. I first joined the church for couple of months as a listener
> [oyente], and I didn't have to pay a tithe. I then saw that you actually get a
> lot of support there and that learning the Bible could be very interesting. I
> became a member for now, but to be honest I can't tell you whether I'll
> always continue to be one.

In the following months Ángel experienced a drift in his religious belief and a growing sense of belonging to a community of churchgoers. His case neatly captures the way in which religion works its ways into becoming "real" for the people who follow it.

Despite his initial agnostic attitude, Ángel's participation in the congregation led to some positive changes in his everyday life. He associated these changes with membership in a religious community that stressed spiritually. It thus led Ángel to increasingly consider spirituality as a powerful resource.

The Social Role: Creating Communities

Worship services (*cultos*) in evangelical churches were regularly held on Saturdays and Wednesdays, with some churches scheduling a third service on Mondays or Fridays. Most members did their best to attend all services. While on weekends this was normally unproblematic, during the week some Latinos needed to return quickly back from work, freshen up, and rush to church. Members usually dressed up elegantly for the occasion; men would shave and women would put on makeup and carefully style their hair. Going to church was a special time in the routine of Latinos; as one congregant put it, it was a time for "nursing our souls." However marginalized their position was in the Israeli context, Latinos were made to feel important and special in their congregations. Members were always warmly welcomed by pastors who shared with them their hardship, and helped them to rise spiritually above their daily predicaments. Pastors were usually married, and their wives, who were called *pastoras,* regularly played an active role in the running of evangelical congregations. In addition to their work in church, pastors and *pastoras* often had to take on jobs similar to those all other undocumented migrants in Israel worked at.

A *culto* began with a collective singing of songs of praise (*alabanzas*) for God and Jesus that were meant to animate the crowd, or as evangelicals put it, "to bring into church the presence of *el Señor* [God]." Evangelical music was an integral part of every service. Most pastors tried to have a live band playing in their churches. Pastors bought musical instruments and encouraged talented members to form bands, come together after work to practice in church, and play on stage in services. When a band was not available, stereo equipment and CDs of evangelical Latino music provided a substitute. Members knew the words of *alabanzas* by heart and enthusiastically sang along, often standing up and raising their hands in excitement.

A short hour of singing allowed for all members to arrive in time for the official opening of the *culto,* with the pastor's sermon as its centerpiece. Sermons were preceded or followed by messages about upcoming events and special activities, or the provision of important information regarding the current situation in Israel. A service was usually paused two or three times for a round of donations. The pastor and his deputies asked members to make a contribution to the church, mentioning the high costs of running the church or the fact that donations were demonstrating members' adoration for God. Money was collected either by sending the assistants among members with trays or by asking members to step forward to place their contributions in a bowl that was located at the foot of the pulpit. The collection of money was performed in the open, creating social pressure on members to demonstrate their generosity and commitment to the church.

Beside regular *cultos,* evangelical churches organized various other religious ceremonies in accordance with the specific orientation of each denomination. It was thus possible for evangelicals in Tel Aviv to undergo healing sessions for curing their bodies from diseases or deliverance rituals to save their souls from the devil. Evangelical churches frequently held vigils (*vigilias*) in which followers prayed together in church for an entire night. Pastors also occasionally announced collective fasts (*ayunos*) whenever they found it necessary to elevate members' spirituality and strengthen their bonds with God. During fasting periods, which could last anywhere from three to forty days, frequent services were held to provide collective support to members' physical and spiritual efforts, and make the most out of the religious effervescence for communicating with God.

Studying the Bible was another regular activity in evangelical churches. Pastors offered Bible classes and courses in theology to members. In some churches, members were divided into groups of about ten affiliates (*celulas*) that met once a week, each time in the apartment of another member. In these meetings, members enjoyed a collective Bible class from the pastor or one of his deputies, followed by a meal for which the alternating host was responsible. Some churches also had a special *celula* for female members, which was usually headed by the *pastora* (pastor's wife). Female members studied the Bible with a special focus on teachings that concerned the role of women in maintaining a religious lifestyle. The group also served as a support group and a platform for discussing issues about which women felt uncomfortable consulting with the pastor.

Children of members in evangelical churches were given special attention. Volunteers, mostly women, supervised what was often called "the group of youngsters" (*grupo de jovenes*). This was a serious commitment that included a basic level of religious teaching, for which the supervisors were trained by the pastor. During *cultos* children were often gathered in a separate room or a corner and taught by their tutors. If children were too young, they were simply entertained so that their parents could concentrate on the religious service. Occasionally, children were directed to perform a special biblical play or a song, which they then staged for the pleasure of all members and proud parents.

Religious activities in evangelical churches involved a strong social element in their performance. While spiritual relief and sociality were closely intertwined in most religious ceremonies, evangelical churches also hosted activities that were in essence recreational. Pastors encouraged members to celebrate their birthdays and other life-cycle events in church. Some evangelical churches celebrated secular festivities such as Mother's Day (*Dia de la Madre*), or the supranational Americas' Day (*Dia de las Americas*). Every couple of months, evangelical churches organized tours to different places in Israel, from the single snowy mountain on the Syrian border of Israel to the southern holiday resort of Eilat. Pastors hired a chauffeured bus for an entire day, dividing costs among all those who registered for the trip. Churches usually bought food and drinks for a picnic that took place during lunchtime in a countrified spot along the way. Demand for these tours was very high not only among churchgoers but also among most other Latinos in Tel Aviv; exploring Israel in the company of friends was a treat for everyone. While these tours were recreational in essence, pastors, who commonly served as guides on them, never missed an opportunity to highlight the religious significance of visited sites and to connect them to a biblical story. The religious aspect was more straightforward on tours to Jerusalem, which were very popular and which many members joined more than once.

The ability of evangelical churches to instill individual spirituality with a strong sense of community fostered cohesion and unity among members. Relationships between churchgoers, who referred to one another as "brothers" and "sisters," were very friendly and warm. This unity led to the creation of tight networks, whose fabric was woven from both religious conviction and social dedication. Belonging to such a cohesive network provided practical advantages and was instrumental to the life strategies of undocumented migrants. Most obviously, information about jobs and accommodations was almost always first passed on to fellow members. Some churches had a message board where members could put up notices with this kind of information. Private business initiatives, such as hairdressing services, electrical work, or home restaurants, were more likely to succeed when taken by members of evangelical churches, as a loyal clientele from within one's church was usually guaranteed. Also, whenever a member of an evangelical church was in acute need, the congregation mobilized its resources to offer collective support, special spiritual service, and a fundraising event.

Some pastors used their special position to organize rotating credit schemes for members, thereby facilitating access to loans of up to US$10,000 with no interest. Typically, ten willing followers were selected by the pastor and each deposited with him a sum of US$500–1,000 every month. The exact amount was set according to the ability of participants, which in turn depended mainly on their "seniority" in Israel (veteran migrants were able to save more than newcomers). The total deposited sum was then given each month to another of the ten participants. The pastor usually drew a lottery to decide upon the order in which each participant would receive the total sum. Yet in some cases, with the active encouragement of the pastor, the group acknowledged the burning necessity of one participant, and he or she would be exempted from the lottery and given the first spot.

The money from rotating credit schemes allowed newcomers to repay the loan they had taken to finance their migration trip. Veteran migrants mainly used this capital to purchase a new house in their country of origin or to pay for a relative's migration trip to Israel. However, there were also migrants who simply saw in these schemes a sort of saving account. Their participation in it forced them to put aside a fixed amount each month. These migrants were relatively indifferent about their place in the order of recipients and sometimes even volunteered to have the very last spot. While undocumented migrants could legally open an account in Israeli banks, and were protected by banks' confidentiality regulations, they hardly ever did so out of fear that the Israeli police would access their personal details from the bank's database.

Since religious communities were the only organized platforms for Latinos in Tel Aviv, many NGOs chose to work closely with pastors, whose churches became crucial nodes for providing relevant information and services for undocumented migrants. The municipality of Tel Aviv also communicated its services for undocumented migrants through evangelical churches. For example, when MESILA offered free pedagogy courses for managing kindergartens or a workshop for facilitating leadership among undocumented communities, it always publicized its initiatives at evangelical churches and often asked the help of pastors in stimulating participation. In this way Israeli NGOs and MESILA enhanced the authority and power of evangelical pastors.

The wide array of activities and socially driven spiritual and economic support that evangelical churches provided their members broadened the function of these churches, and reinforced their place as an axis around which the lives of their members revolved. Accordingly, churches were open almost every day of the week, and members who frequented them for different motives usually developed a strong sense of commitment and belonging. The commitment of evangelicals to their church was evident in the monthly payment of tithe, which was normally around US$50–100 for a member, as well as in the widespread spirit of voluntarism that governed the running of their churches. Members willingly participated in maintaining the house of worship, decorating it according to changing themes and events, and cleaning it before and after every ceremony.

The Moral Role: Reforming the Self

Evangelical churches are normally very exacting in their strict disciplinary demands from members, who are expected to regularly participate in services, pay a tithe, and maintain a healthy lifestyle. The last demand often includes a complete abstinence from smoking and drinking alcohol and an enduring investment in the cultivation of one's relationship with his/her family, colleagues, and friends. The justifications for these requirements are always presented with a strong religious overtone that concerns the sanctity of the body and Jesus' legacy regarding respectful conduct. It has been argued with respect to the evangelical doctrine that in Latin America, and elsewhere in the world, "for people surviving on the margin of society, reforming one's day-to-day practices can offer immediate results" (Stoll 1990:46). So while such demands for adopting a healthy lifestyle are certainly constructive for everyone, they were perhaps even more crucial in the case of undocumented migrants, who often came from an unstable background and could easily weaken under the constant tension that they faced in Israel.

A doctrinal emphasis in some evangelical churches on achieving individual prosperity was also empowering for Latinos. Evangelicals were actively encouraged to strive for economic success, which was theologically conceived as the right of every believer to enjoy the wealth which Jesus had fought for and won (Gifford 2001: 62). This positive motivation was explicitly generated and transmitted to members in pastors' sermons. Pastors also always seized an opportunity to spotlight the personal achievements of thriving members as a sign that Jesus was working closely with their congregation, and that it was thus possible for all other members to reach economic prosperity.

This collective encouragement of members to excel was complemented by personal crisis management that was supervised by pastors. Pastors were authoritative and fatherly figures whom members trusted with their most intimate problems. Therefore, members who suffered from domestic violence, alcoholism, or depression could always consult their pastor, who personally counseled and motivated them. On a religious level, pastors provided spiritual leadership and guided troubled members to read certain biblical sources and invest in their communication with God. Among some denominations it was customary to arrange for a special ceremony to rescue members' souls from demonic possession. On a more practical level, pastors advised members about useful strategies for confronting their problems. They also never hesitated to directly intervene, for example, by visiting members at home and speaking to their family, or by using their network to find a new job for members who had problems in their workplace.

These elaborate collective and personal support systems that evangelical churches installed in the service of their members can be seen as equivalent to the kind of "mental coaching" that secular people often seek in support groups and psychological therapies. Membership in evangelical churches automatically entailed participation in such support systems, which moreover were proactive in detecting members' instabilities and attending to them without necessarily awaiting the initiative of a troubled member. The close nature of relationships between members in evangelical churches, and the residential concentration of followers in south Tel Aviv, promoted social control that ensured that the disciplinary requirements for members were practiced and that deviations were quickly detected and reported. It was indeed common for members to tell pastors about problematic situations in which fellow members found themselves.

Gossip was commonly used as means of informing pastors about inadequate conduct of members, as I personally experienced. I once went to a bar with a small group of members directly after a service in one church (this was their initiative, and I was invited to join them). It took only days until a rumor about our night out reached the pastor, who then reprimanded the involved members and voiced his concerns to me in a private meeting to which he promptly summoned me. In another congregation, a single female member had an affair with a married man who had immigrated to Israel alone. The man was one of my closest informants, and thus I knew of the affair and of the couple's best efforts to keep it confidential. Nevertheless, after a few weeks rumors about the affair circulated among members and reached the infuriated pastor, who immediately declared that the devil had taken over the woman. He then demanded, as a condition for her continued membership, that a deliverance ceremony be conducted. The man received a severe warning from the pastor and was lectured about the importance of controlling bodily desires that can weaken one's bond with his spouse and family.

Pastors sometimes threatened to expel disobedient members who did not follow the moral conduct that was expected from evangelicals. Nevertheless, throughout my fieldwork I never came across a case of expulsion from evangelical churches. Unruly or sinful members always repented their actions to the satisfaction of pastors, who often punished them but eventually always forgave them. While this marked tendency among pastors to forgive members for unmoral behavior is anchored in the spirit of evangelicalism, it might have also reflected, in the Israeli context of competition between evangelical churches, pastors' unwillingness to lose one of their members.

Given the strong emphasis on moral conduct in evangelical churches, it was rather striking that a few pastors in Israel were implicated in serious cases of adultery and theft. For example, one of the first and most prominent Latino pastors in Tel Aviv was blamed for having an affair with a woman who was thirty years younger than he. The pastor initially denied the allegations, only to later admit to them, divorce his wife, and leave Israel with his young lover. Another pastor was accused of stealing a large amount of his congregation's income; he was suspended by the head of the ministry, who especially came to Israel to mend the damages and to appoint a new pastor for the congregation. There was also a pastor who allegedly lost US$10,000. This sum of money was given in cash to the pastor by members in his church for whom he organized a rotating credit scheme. The pastor claimed that the money was robbed from a safe in his home, leaving disappointed members with little choice but to accept his version and forfeit their money.

From the outside one would expect the dishonest conduct of some pastors to seriously undermine their moral authority. Nevertheless, I hardly ever detected among evangelicals in Tel Aviv signs of doubt about the moral stature of their pastors. If pastors were not completely evicted from their congregation, they were either entirely acquitted or otherwise their ill conduct was explained away by references to a personal crisis and a test under which God put them. Moreover, immoral incidents involving pastors in Israel never led evangelicals to withdraw from their congregation (as has been found in other contexts, see Harding 2000). This unyielding loyalty of evangelicals to their congregations emanates not least from the entwined, largely indistinguishable, affinity that exists between members' deep religious convictions and the myriad mental, social, and practical services that congregations provided.

The Theological Role: Christian Zionism

Evangelicals typically viewed their empowerment as directly emanating from their relation with God and the religious teachings and morals that they followed. Evangelical churches taught their members to appreciate the Bible as a source for understanding both the internal and the external realities that they experienced. Biblical lessons and sermons were seen as part of a learning process that deepened members' spirituality, increased their knowledge, and enhanced their mental as well as practical faculties. Pastors never drew a direct line between membership in their church and instrumental benefits; instead, they always stressed that the formative changes that members experienced were the direct fruits of their theological observance and Jesus' positive intervention in their lives.

Pastors in Israel widely emphasized in their orientation and teachings the theological motif of Christian Zionism, which Paul Gifford (2001: 74) describes:

> The idea that God has never abandoned Israel: God works through two agents on earth, the church and Israel. Thus so many biblical references to Israel refer to precisely that—the modern state of Israel established in 1948. Since God will accomplish his end-time purposes through Israel, and Israel is a prerequisite of Christ's return, Israel must be defended by every means possible. This leads to unquestioning support, on supposedly biblical grounds, for everything the modern Israeli government wants or attempts.

Christian Zionism has been put into practice in different forms by numerous evangelical churches worldwide. It led evangelical ministries in some countries, for example, to support Israel unquestioningly in its lasting conflict with Arab countries in the Middle East. While this has been perhaps most evident among religious leaders and neo-conservative politicians in the United States, it has also played a role in countries such as Zambia, where the evangelical Fellowship of Zambia has declared, "The Bible is clear that God will bless those who bless Israel. This may imply that those who oppose Israel can only expect the wrath of God. Some of the difficulties experienced in our country can be attributed to a direct result of rejecting Israel" (quoted in Gifford 2001: 76). A more concrete illustration for the way in which Christian Zionism informed the actions of evangelical churches was given by the missionary reorientation of a Swedish-based church, Word of Life, toward the repatriation of Jews from the former Soviet Union to Israel. Strongly believing that Jews from all diasporas must come back to the Land of Israel to ensure the return of Christ, the Word of Life purchased a ship that it then used for the free transportation of Jews to Israel (ibid.).

It has been shown that while evangelicalism is quickly winning hearts across the world, it is doing so in highly diversified configurations (Corten and Marshall-Fratani 2001, Gifford 2001, Martin 1994, Poewe 1994, Stoll 1990). As Coleman (1991) illustrates, even in the case of the same church "its doctrine and forms of worship take on new symbolic resonances as they are transferred almost wholesale from one country to another" (Coleman 1991: 7). Moreover, Harding (2000) eloquently shows the remarkable discursive flexibility that fundamentalist Protestant leaders strategically employ to adapt their doctrine to changing circumstances. It is thus interesting to examine the particular influence of the evangelical theology of Christian Zionism on the perception and conduct of evangelicals in Israel.

In the exclusionary Israeli context and in proximity to Jews, the belief in Christian Zionism produced three closely interrelated outcomes. First, it helped evangelicals achieve a sense of belonging in Israel, despite their official rejection by the state. Second, it compromised Latinos' political ambitions and mitigated their grievances toward the Israeli repressive policy. Finally, it rendered evangelicals more docile and submissive in their interactions with Israelis, which in turn increased their chances to establish effective working relationships with their employers.

Fostering Belonging: "We Have Spiritual Passports"

Given Israel's official exclusion of undocumented migrants, pastors conscientiously tried to alleviate their members' sense of rejection. Some pastors whose congregations were affiliated with a larger ministry often stressed the global and transnational character of membership in their church. They sometimes played videos in which pastors from congregations elsewhere in the world addressed the members of the Israeli congregation with a message of brotherhood. Notwithstanding other methods, it was more widely the particular interpretation of Christian Zionism that pastors used in order to disseminate among their followers a sense of belonging to Israel.

The theological teachings of pastors with regard to the Jewish people and the state of Israel were characterized by an underlying bipolarity that carefully decoupled the territorial sovereignty over the land of Israel from the spiritual one. On the one hand, pastors taught their followers to recognize the righteousness and sovereignty of the state of Israel. According to pastors, Israel historically belonged to the Jewish people, who had the right to establish in it their national home. At the same time, pastors maintained that it was God who held ultimate sovereignty over Israel, and thus he directly authorized the presence of evangelicals there. Moreover, evangelicals had a unique moral mission in Israel, to bring salvation by helping to wake their Jewish "brothers" and "sisters" from their state of "blindness." Although pastors used different rhetorical strategies, they all preached that while salvation would come through the Jewish people, Jews were currently in a state of "spiritual blindness." This "blindness," according to pastors, accounted for the numerous Jews in Israel who still lived secular lives, as well as for the millions of Jews worldwide who "delayed" their return to Israel, as the prophecy prescribed.

Evangelicals' moral mission in Israel was not to convert Jews to Christianity, but to reconnect Jews to their own Jewish religiosity. This careful articulation of evangelicals' mission vis-à-vis Israelis was crucial to its underlying purpose. Obviously, an attempt to convert Jews to Christianity would have met much resistance among most Israelis as well as the state of Israel. It would thus have been detrimental to Latinos' survival chances and life strategies. Nevertheless, trying to enhance the religious zeal of Jewish Israelis was seen as worthy by many Israelis, or at worst as superfluous but harmless.

Pastors often mentioned that they were awaiting and hoping for a Godly intervention that would make Jews realize that Christians were their allies and award them legal status in the country. Nevertheless, the fact that Israel refused to legalize their status did not invalidate evangelicals' legitimacy at being in Israel. Here is how one pastor subtly imbued his members' presence in Israel with a higher spiritual authority:

> It is God who brought you here and you all have a special place and a
> mission in this land. Those of you who don't have a visa or a passport
> shouldn't worry, don't let that stop you from spreading the Word of God,
> don't let that stop you from reaching out to your fellow Jewish people.

The pastor's explicit remark about members' visas in Israel clearly touched a sensitive cord, and the air in the church was filled with tension. As the pastor finished the last sentence, one member shouted, "We have spiritual passports," driving everyone in the crowd to burst into a loud laughter. The pastor compassionately smiled and nodded his head in agreement. Given the context, the joking remark and the laughter that followed should probably be seen as expression of displacement, rather than a comic breach.

Another approach that pastors employed to accommodate the identity of their followers was to blur distinctions between Jews and evangelicals. Pastors often mentioned the fact that Jesus was a Jew. To enhance an ideational unity between evangelicals and Jews, pastors stressed that evangelicals also believed in the same holy book, the Torah (Old Testament). Furthermore, pastors repeatedly reminded their followers that Jews and Christians were intertwined in their faith, as salvation would come only through the work of the Jewish people. Attending different evangelical churches, I was often publicly asked by pastors whether I was aware of the similarities between Jews and Christians. For example, one pastor addressed me during his sermon to make this point for his followers. He rhetorically asked me from the pulpit, "Do you know that there is not much difference between you and us?" Without waiting for my response he continued, "We believe in the same God, only you still await the messiah and we know that Jesus is the true messiah, that is the only difference." He concluded to loud cries of "Amen" from members in the audience.

In their attempt to forge unity with Jews, pastors frequently used Islam as their scapegoat, depicting it as a threat to the Judeo-Christian tradition and faith. Pastors sometimes demonized Islam as the antipode of the values and morals that Jews and Christians jointly stood for. Pastors tended to use hard language, categorically referring to Muslims as "uneducated," "warmongers" and "aggressive." This anti-Islamic rhetoric was more concretely mentioned in respect to the conflict between Israel and Palestine. Pastors unambiguously praised what they considered to be the moral superiority of the Jewish people, in their righteous fight against Muslims over the land of Israel. The following statement by one pastor at the Light of the World church is representative of the way in which the issue was treated discursively:

Israel is surrounded by Arab countries yet it won all its wars against them, and Arab countries are so poor while Israel is so powerful and prosperous; why do you think it is so? Because God is with the Jewish people. The Arabs should recognize that too and understand that Israel is the land God gave to Moses and Abraham thousands of years ago. Let us now pray for the sake of Israeli soldiers and the defeat of Arabs. [The pastor then closed his eyes, raised his right hand up in the air, and continued.] Oh God, we pray to you that you lift up the arms of the Jewish people and help them win their war just like you did with Moses, who secured the victory of the Jewish people over the Egyptian army of Pharaoh. . . . We pray tonight that God will keep blessing the Jewish people in the land of Israel, and that this land will keep yielding milk and honey, and will provide prosperity for this chosen nation.

Dozens of followers in the audience also lifted their hands, closed their eyes and repeatedly chanted "Amen" and "Glory to God." This unconditional support for Israel, combined with an anti-Islamic attitude, was clearly reflected in the views evangelicals held regarding the Israeli-Palestinian conflict. Usually after a terror act occurred in Israel the conflict figured in my conversations with Latinos. Notably, nonevangelicals generally held a balanced view and tried to understand the motivations and agony of both sides. They were often worried that Israel was on the brink of a total war with Palestinians and other Arab countries. In contrast, evangelicals evinced their one-sided and extremist position against Muslims, often using very harsh language to display their contempt for Arabs. Evangelicals saw themselves standing actively alongside Israel in its fight, and some of them eagerly expressed their willingness to contribute to the military efforts of Israel. In a newspaper article that discussed non-Jewish migrants' views on Palestinian terror acts in Israel, an evangelical Latino pastor was quoted as saying, "The thing that really hurts us is the fact that our sons are not allowed to serve in the Israeli army. We are here due to our love for Israel and we won't leave because of the terror" (*Haaretz* 07.01.2003).

Recognizing the prominent role that patriotism in general, and military service in particular, played in the Israeli construction of citizenship, evangelicals often expressed their loyalty to Israel by stressing their desire to serve in the Israeli army and risk their lives in defending the land. One of my informants told me:

> Give me a gun and send me along with the Israeli soldiers; I wish to be
> given the chance to fight against the Arabs for the sake of Israel. I know
> they don't let us, but we would fight just as hard against the Palestinians if
> we could join the army. (Leonardo, 22, Venezuela)

Another of my informants was eager to put his military experience into the service of the Israeli army:

> Before I came here I served in the army in Ecuador for twenty-three years. I
> can fight, I can lead a platoon. I fought in wars against Colombia and Peru.
> If they [Israeli officials] want to allow me to join the army here, I will
> happily join. I'd be honored to. I know the Israeli army is one of the
> strongest in the world, but still, I think I can contribute. (Marcelo, 46,
> Ecuador)

This explicit identification with Israel was demonstrated in other ways as well, for example, in a ritual performed by one evangelical church to protect Tel Aviv from the devil. Members in this congregation conducted a spiritual ceremony in which bottles of olive oil were blessed by the pastor. Then one night they took these bottles and splashed "blessed oil" on the pavements and at the corners of some streets in south Tel Aviv. As the pastor proudly told me, a few weeks after his congregation carried out this ritual for the protection of Israelis, an Arab terrorist with explosives was caught by the police precisely at one of the oiled street corners before he could commit suicide among the crowd.

Some evangelical churches also fostered a sense of belonging in Israeli society by engaging their members in charity activities for the sake of marginalized Israelis. For example, one church regularly mobilized its members to buy food and prepare hot drinks for a group of drug addicts and prostitutes who gathered nightly at a certain deserted construction site in south Tel Aviv. Participants in this initiative told me the people they fed were very enthusiastic about these actions, and the church members greatly appreciated the warm reactions they received. Apparently, what members appreciated even more was the opportunity to feel themselves as active agents in Israeli society, assuming social tasks to help out Israelis in an organized way that they initiated and sponsored. Needless to say, seeing marginalized Israelis living in acute conditions out in the streets must have also helped Latinos to relativize their own marginality in Israel.

Compromising Political Ambitions: Creating an Apolitical Public Sphere

One of the major appeals of evangelicalism for marginalized people in Latin America has been that it "demystifies social inequalities and makes situations explicit by telling people to face up to their oppression, get organized and do something about it" (Stoll 1990: 45). In the Israeli context, however, it is in the opposite sense that the evangelical doctrine assumed a distinctive meaning. In Israel, pastors widely advocated reversion to a religious comprehension of Latinos' experiences and realities. Using Christian Zionism to justify and comprehend Israel's actions, evangelical churches neutralized the rebellious potential of their members by theologically dissolving it.

Latino evangelical churches in Tel Aviv markedly shied away from any direct political involvement. They occasionally cooperated with Israeli NGOs and MESILA, but only on civil issues that were mainly intended to enhance the provision of information and facilities to which undocumented migrants had the right. Pastors avoided turning their congregations into political platforms, largely fearing the consequences of such a move. While churches were exempt from police raids, pastors were not. Since most Latino pastors in Tel Aviv were undocumented migrants themselves, any political involvement on their side would have made them a prime target for the police. Moreover, pastors recognized that churches were cherished by many of their followers precisely because they were not targeted by the police; turning churchgoing into another risky activity would certainly have deterred many Latinos.

In private conversations, some pastors admitted to me their fear of political involvement; however, they never openly acknowledged it in front of their followers. Instead, the deliberate avoidance of political involvement was publicly explained by cultivating loyalty to, and absolute approval of, the state of Israel. Pastors pointed out that although the official line of Israel was adversarial, in practice the state accommodated thousands of Latinos and allowed evangelical churches to flourish. Pastors urged their followers to show resilience, reminding them that salvation was never going to be an easy task and that it would require a thorough battle from Jews as well as their Christian "brothers." Clinging to this belief, pastors and their followers reconciled the discrepancy between their deep love for Israel and Israel's formal hostile attitude toward them. Police arrests of Latinos, although never accepted, were always understood and explained away. Pastors interpreted the worst of all—a deportation—in a religious way that endowed the act with a mystified meaning and attributed the responsibility for it directly to God rather than to the state of Israel:

> If you are deported from Israel it is because God has other plans for you; you must recognize it and accept it as a test, as a sign from God that you should take a new direction in your life. That is precisely why you must make the most of your stay in Israel, because you can never know what plans God has for you for the future. (Pastor Vega, Light of the World church)

Pastors' overwhelmingly positive approach toward Israel trickled down to their congregants. It even led some evangelicals to appreciate what they perceived to be a strict enforcement of laws in Israel, as the following comment illustrates:

> I perfectly understand that this is a Jewish state and that it should remain so. I only wish and hope that there will be a way for us to become a part of it; after all, we only want to support the Jews and the land of Israel. I must admit that I respect the function of the Israeli police. In my country if they catch you doing something wrong, you can always pay the cops or find a way to arrange things outside court. In Israel all the cops are honest; you can never bribe a cop here, right? I tell you this is in big part the reason why this country is so successful. Our countries are corrupt and nothing functions there according to the laws. (William, 48, Colombia)

Some evangelicals chose to stress the humane way in which the police handled migrants:

> It is not true that policemen here are all bad; some are very compassionate. For example, my friend told me that two policemen entered her apartment and wanted to arrest her husband. Then they heard children crying in the other room and asked if they were hers. When my friend said "yes" the policemen decided not to arrest her husband and only warned them they had to leave the country. (Marisol, 26, Ecuador)

While such incidents of a humane attitude by an individual policeman toward undocumented migrants occurred, they were clearly non-representative of the overall brutal and uncompromising treatment that characterized the actions of the Immigration Police. To choose to describe things as Marisol did says much more about the speaker's subjective standpoint than the situation.

Facilitating Cooperation: Docile Bodies, Submissive Spirits

Fostering admiration for Jews and neutralizing resentment against Israel's official rejection of non-Jewish migrants, pastors promoted a mental structure that favored cooperation with Jews on an ideological as well as on a practical level. The following messages from two pastors are representative of this tendency:

> Jews are our brothers and sisters; we originated from the Jewish people. Nowadays Jews find themselves in a very difficult situation, but we know all about it because it was clearly stated in the prophecy. It is our mission to support Jews during this crucial stage; you are all blessed to be here in the land of Israel during this historic moment, and have this unique opportunity to support the efforts of the Jewish people. (Pastor Vega, Light of the World church)

> If anyone of you wants to get closer to God and understand better what our religion means, you should cultivate a friendship with an Israeli and then carefully observe your Jewish friend. Reach out to your Jewish brothers and sisters; even if they reject you, insist, and make them see that you are here to serve them. (Pastor Temudo, Ambassadors of the King church)

Evangelicals in Israel were spiritually directed to approximate Jews, and actively encouraged to serve them in all possible ways. Evangelicals conceived of their role as allies and benefactors of the Jewish people in their divine task, and accordingly saw the very opportunity to work in Israel as a blessing from God. Evangelicals often praised their employers and expressed gratitude for the opportunity to work in an Israeli house or business. This religiously based admiration of Jews and a theological disposition to be at their service certainly rendered evangelicals more docile and obedient as workers for Israeli employers. Hard-working discipline blended with docility enhanced evangelicals' chances to receive better treatment from their employers. It also facilitated the development of friendly relationships beyond economic lines. Indeed, from my experience, evangelicals often enjoyed a warmer relationship with their employers than did other Latino migrants, as the following example demonstrates. Sandra, an evangelical Bolivian migrant, was employed as a nanny for the two children of Dorit, an Israeli woman. Dorit was not aware of her employee's religious convictions, but in an interview with me she commented on Sandra:

> I trust her one hundred percent with what is the dearest for me—my children. She treats them with so much care and she is always so diligent with maintaining the house. She works for us for nearly two years, and in

that period she practically has become a part of our family. We also really care for her, and we try to help her whenever she has a problem. I can honestly tell you that I would never have found an Israeli woman who would be so devoted to the children and me as Sandra is.

Appreciation and gratitude were mutual, as Sandra conceived her work as means not only for economic provision but also for religious and emotional fulfillment:

I love this family; I am so happy to work for them, they give me such a warm feeling. You know that they even invited me to celebrate Passover with them, not as a worker but as a guest. Dorit told me, "This time I will cook and clean everything and you will sit and enjoy it." Dorit never talks to me like a boss; you know, she always asks everything in a very polite way. Actually, by now she hardly ever gives me instructions; I know exactly what she wants me to do.

Sandra's remarks about the children were particularly telling:

I treat the children as if they were my own, and I get from them so much love back. You know that I left my four children in Bolivia, and I am here alone, but being with Liron and Tal [Dorit's children] makes me so happy. It is an honor for me to raise Jewish children in Israel; I know that I will be proud of that for the rest of my life.

While female domestic workers were perhaps best positioned to demonstrate their care for their employers and work, male workers were also often able to distinguish themselves positively as devoted workers. Some Israeli employers recognized what they claimed to be the enhanced quality of evangelicals as dedicated workers. For example, an extensive report in an Israeli newspaper announced in its headline, "If you ran into a foreign worker who performs his job with enthusiasm and joy, it is most likely that he is a member in the Adventist Church" (*Haaretz* 07.03.2003). The article detailed the establishment of a flourishing Adventist church in south Tel Aviv, whose members comprised legal guest workers and undocumented migrants from different countries. The article stressed how Adventists see themselves as allies of Jews and elaborated on their expressions of love for Israel and Israelis. Interestingly, the article also contained an interview with an Israeli employer who had employed fourteen undocumented Adventist migrants until the police arrested them one day. The employer declared:

If it were up to me I would have instantly given citizenship to all 1,500 [members in Adventist churches in Israel according to the journalist], and not because of self-interest. I swear to you, these are the nicest people I have ever met in my life. These are hard, excellent workers. They are honest. No [need for] working hour cards; I trust them with closed eyes. If you worked with them one time, you can't work with anyone else after that. I am absolutely certain about it, I only look to employ Adventists.

Several times I came across Israeli employers who attended the weddings of their evangelical workers. While for evangelicals this was an extreme gesture that brought them much honor, for some curious Israelis it was an opportunity to show gratitude to their loyal workers, and have a glimpse into the "unknown world of foreign migrants," as one employer put it. At the wedding of one of my Colombian informants from the Prince of Peace church, I met Avner, his Israeli employer. Exchanging impressions about the occasion, Avner told me:

Carlos is a great person; he is the best worker I have. When he first invited me to his wedding I thought I would just give him a nice present, but later I quite liked the idea to meet his wife and friends and see how they live here in Israel. Did you see that they put me on the first row next to their priest [pastor]? They told me it was an honor for them to have me there.

When I asked Avner if he was not bothered by the fact that these were undocumented Christian migrants, he replied:

I know that they are all illegals, but if you ask me, these people are such hard workers and they love our country, why not give them a visa? Finally there are some people in this world that love Israel, and we are making their lives here so difficult. Give them a visa, that's what I say.

But not all Israeli employers were as responsive as Avner. An unfailing devotion to Jews sometimes bitterly clashed with the exploitation of Latinos by their employers. When I asked evangelicals about it, they usually tended to play down the whole issue, as the following self-effacing remark conveys:

If you behave and work well there are never any problems with Israelis. I have the most amazing bosses, they treat me like a family member. . . . I heard that some people had problems, but most of the brothers and sisters I know are very happy with their employers. (Alejandra, 34, Peru)

Evangelicals typically implied that when relations with Israelis turned sour it mostly had to do with the spoiled attitude of migrants. When I somewhat provocatively mentioned renowned cases of ill-treatment by Israeli employers, evangelicals often resorted to a reference about the generic character of employers, for example, as Antonio once brashly remarked, "You have bad people everywhere in the world, do you know how employers in Spain or in the USA behave towards migrants? Much worse!"

Messianic Evangelical Churches: Approximating Judaism

Theologically promoting identification with Israel and the Jewish people was taken a step further by evangelical churches with a messianic orientation that increasingly infused Judaism into their spiritual doctrine and religious practices. Messianic faith can be divided into the two main traditions from which it springs, namely, Jewish and Christian. Messianic Judaism concentrates on the idea that Jesus was a Jew whose intention was never to reject Judaism, but to restore it. Accordingly, Jews in Israel and in Diaspora should recognize Jesus, or Yeshua as he is called by this stream, as the Messiah. Focusing its spirituality and theology around the figure of Jesus, messianic Judaism breaks away from a traditional Jewish exclusionary definition of membership, and instead promotes an inclusive vision that considers as brothers in faith all those who share a belief in Jesus. One messianic Jewish leader, David Hargis, has phrased the view of this stream in the following way:

> Since He is God of all, Yeshua also came to allow anyone of the Gentiles who trust in Him as the Messiah of Israel to be grafted into Israel by way of that same new covenant in Him . . . since Christianity professes the Jewish Messiah as their Savior, Messianic Judaism deems all faithful Gentiles as its siblings. (Hargis 1998)

Some Jewish messianic ministries, for example the American based "Jews for Jesus," have declared their mission as the conversion of Jews to a belief in Jesus. Often, Jewish members in such ministries consider themselves to be Christians.

In its Christian version, messianic theology, mainly since the 1970s, has gained popularity among some evangelical circles, mostly in the United States and Eastern Europe. Yet it has figured also in Latin America as part of the religious diversification that the continent experienced in its move away from the "Catholic monopoly" (Bastian 1993). The degree of Jewish tradition that is being infused into evangelicalism widely varies across congregations; but in its strongest version evangelicals spiritually consider themselves Jews and strictly observe the Jewish religious laws (*mitzvoth*) as well as cultural practices and traditions. It is important to note that no Jewish authority has ever recognized messianic Christians as Jews; to the contrary, even the moderate Reformist Jewish stream strongly denounced efforts by messianic organizations to convert Christians to Judaism. Jewish authorities also are distressed by and oppose the conversion of Jews, whom they consider errant, to Christianity. It led the Israeli High Court to determine in 1989 that messianic Jews were not eligible to immigrate to Israel under the Law of Return since they were officially considered to have renounced their Jewishness and should thus legally be treated as non-Jews.

In the last decade different messianic congregations have become active in Israel, and some have directly targeted Latinos in Tel Aviv. La Granada was the first messianic church to attract Latinos in south Tel Aviv. It was established and guided by a married couple who were both born in Latin America and converted to messianism from opposing directions, that is, the *pastora* from Judaism and the pastor from Catholicism. La Granada offered Spanish-language services that attracted dozens of followers, if not hundreds as the couple claimed.

At the end of 1999, Raúl, a Colombian migrant and one of the devotees at La Granada, decided to split and establish his own congregation, together with his wife, Ramona . The congregation was named the Open Gate, and unlike La Granada it was not declared from the outset to be messianic. Israel was not the first migration destination of Raúl and Ramona. Some fifteen years prior, the couple had initially left Colombia for a European country, where Raúl obtained a scholarship for doctoral studies in physics. Although the couple were both raised in Catholic families, during their stay in Europe they experienced a spiritual revelation and subsequently converted to evangelicalism. After the couple attended an evangelical church for some years, Raúl had a vision in which God told him he had a mission on earth and he should actively look for it. Consequently, Raúl decided to apply for postdoctoral studies in eight different countries, believing that his destiny was lying where he would be accepted. It so happened that he received only one positive response, which came from the University of Tel Aviv. For Raúl this was a sign from God that his place was in the Holy Land. After three years in Israel, in which Raúl and Ramona attended La Granada, Raúl had another vision in which God called upon him to found his own congregation in Israel. Raúl then contacted his former European pastor and informed him about his vision. The pastor encouraged Raúl spiritually and also agreed to contribute financially to the fulfillment of his mission.

My first encounter with the Open Gate was when José, a member and one of my key informants, invited me to attend a *culto* in his church (José first asked Raúl for permission to invite me). On a Saturday morning I met José, and together we made our way to a rather shabby industrial building in south Tel Aviv. From the outside one could have never imagined that on the fourth floor of that building, just above an aluminum workshop, there was a sizable church. There were about twenty-five people in church, and José proudly introduced me to everyone as his Israeli friend. After members' initial surprise, they questioned me about my interests, status in Israel, fluency in Spanish, and so on. Raúl interrupted the informal conversation to ask everyone to take a seat. He took his place behind the pulpit and formally opened the *culto*. Raúl began by welcoming me, and said how fortunate they all were to have the presence of an Israeli in church. As the *culto* continued and I settled in, it struck me that nothing in the decoration of the sun-drenched loft indicated that this was a Christian church; not a single crucifix or an image of Maria was to be found. In fact, the place looked more like a synagogue, with a large flag of Israel hanging at the back of the pulpit, on which a silver menorah was prominently placed on a special wooden stall. On one of the walls, the word *Canaan* (the biblical name of Israel) was written inside a map of Israel that was colorfully drawn with biblical borders that included vast parts of what is nowadays the territory of Jordan.

The *culto* progressed with the singing of *alabanzas,* which to my surprise consisted partly of Jewish religious songs that were phonetically written in Roman script, and displayed on a large screen from an overhead projector, so that members could sing them in Hebrew. Whenever a Jewish song was played, members looked to see whether I recognized it and was singing along myself. When I did, I received nods of satisfaction from all around and a friendly slap on my shoulders from those sitting next to me. After a lengthy sermon (of almost a full hour) by Raúl and some administrative announcements by his deputy, lunch was prepared in the kitchen at the back of the church and served to all members. Before tucking into the food, Raúl offered a prayer. He literally translated the Jewish blessing to Spanish, and simply added a sentence to it at the end, which was loudly pronounced by all other members: "Amen, in the name of Adonai and Yeshua ha'Mashiach." Adonai is one of the many Jewish names for God, and Yeshua ha'Mashiach is Hebrew for "Jesus the messiah."

The *culto* lasted till the late afternoon, and was finished by practicing some Jewish folkloric dances to traditional Jewish music. Upon my departure Raúl warmly shook my hand and said, "This is your home Barak, consider it as such and come here whenever you feel like it." José, who stood next to the pastor, could not hide his satisfaction with the affectionate way in which his pastor treated me, and he directly followed it up by inviting me to the next Kabalat Shabbat (the traditional Jewish reception of Shabbat celebrated by Jews on Friday evening). José said it was his family's turn to prepare the Kabalat Shabbat and that they would be honored if I would attend it. He added, "It is probably just like what you are used to at home, you'll like it I am sure."

The following Friday I attended the Kabalat Shabbat, which was conducted according to strict Jewish tradition. First, Ramona, the *pastora,* with a veil covering her head, lit the Shabbat candles and said the corresponding blessing. Next, it was Raúl's turn to say Kiddush—the traditional Jewish blessing over bread and wine. Again, he translated literally these blessings from Hebrew into Spanish, with the rest of the members joining him in the repetition of the addition: "Amen, in the name of Adonai and Yeshua the messiah." Just before a three-course dinner was served, Raúl delivered a sermon from his place at the head of a very long table with a white tablecloth, around which all members were seated. Raúl talked about the holiness of Shabbat in opposition to the meaninglessness of Sunday as a sacred day. He further informed his followers that many Christian people all over the world were not celebrating Christmas any longer. "They don't even go to church on these days," he announced. "And they certainly don't celebrate it at home with all these pagan decorations and a fir tree," he asserted with reproach. Raúl went on to preach that most Christian festivities have their origin in the Jewish tradition and it was thus desirable for evangelicals to get to know the Jewish festivities and if possible celebrate them. Indeed, all Jewish festivities were celebrated; during Pesach a complete *Seder* (the ceremonial Jewish dinner) was organized; in Hanukka the *Hanukkia* (an eight-branched candelabrum) was lit daily in church; in Shavuot dairy dishes were prepared and consumed by members; and in Sukkot (the feast of Tabernacles) a symbolic hut (*Suka*) was built out of a few palm twigs. In addition to acting out Jewish traditions, Raúl also provided members with lengthy explanations about the history and motivations behind each festivity.

Although it was apparent to me from the outset that the Open Gate was a hybrid of an evangelical church and a messianic one, most members who joined the Open Gate believed it to be an evangelical church. The church was initially presented as such to new members. Raúl also played in church videotapes of sermons by famous American and Latino evangelical pastors. During the months I spent attending it I clearly noted a marked drift in its orientation and religious teachings toward messianic Judaism. For example, Raúl encouraged members to mimic the dress of Israelis in general and of Orthodox Jews in particular. He demonstrated for members how to wear a *Talit* (prayer shawl) and a *Kipa* (Jewish head covering) and gave confidence to male members to wear them during service as he himself regularly did. Growing a beard was also seen positively by Raúl, who himself had one. Female members were encouraged to wear a headscarf and skirts as Ramona habitually did.

Raúl, who spoke Hebrew well, encouraged members to practice their Hebrew in church, and he commonly wove Hebrew words into his sermons and personal interactions with members. He also insisted on members calling him *Ro'ae* (Hebrew for "shepherd") instead of "Pastor." At one point Raúl decided to initiate Hebrew classes in church, basing the need for it on his conviction that the holiest deed for Christians was to read the Bible in its original language, as he explained at one of his sermons:

> People all over the world read the Bible in Hebrew and you, who live here
> in the land of Israel, still read it in Spanish. I am going to read to you from
> now on every week a part of the Bible in Hebrew and we are going to make
> sure that soon all of you will understand it and will also be able to read it
> yourselves.

The move toward messianism was gradual, and it provoked mixed feelings among members. Some members found the more pronounced infusion of Jewishness into their familiar Christian identity problematic. Reservations about it arose especially among those who had assisted other evangelical churches in their countries of origin or in Israel. Sarah, for example, had already converted to evangelicalism in Peru and joined the Open Gate in Israel, thinking she could maintain her religious beliefs and remedy her loneliness (she emigrated alone, leaving behind three children). She became a devoted member and was energetically involved in the practicalities of running the church, cooking on Saturdays and cleaning the loft. Nevertheless, the strong Jewish orientation struck her as a disquieting element, and when we once talked about it in private she tellingly remarked:

> It is a lovely congregation, and I feel excellent here. The pastor and the
> *pastora* are wonderful people, but when the pastor starts with his sermons
> about how we should do everything the Jews are doing I am sometimes
> happy to be busy in the kitchen.

Norma, another regular member who emigrated from Chile, expressed to me similar misgivings toward the church's Jewish orientation: "I find it strange that they ask us to wear Jewish outfits; we are not Jews after all. We probably look ridiculous anyway when we do that, don't you think?'

Raúl encouraged his unmarried followers (mainly women) to look for a partner from among members of the same faith, or, preferably, to marry an Israeli Jew. In all evangelical churches social control was practiced on the conduct of single women, yet this tendency was pronounced in the Open Gate. Raúl scrutinized his members' personal relationships. For example, Claudia, a single Bolivian migrant, needed Raúl's approval to develop an intimate relationship with an undocumented migrant from Ghana, whom she met while waiting for the bus. Claudia had to bring her boyfriend to meet Raúl, who was very skeptical about the religious conviction of the Ghanaian man, although the latter was a member of an African Pentecostal church. Due largely to Raúl's disapproval, the relationship quickly ended, and Claudia grew bitter. She once spitefully asked me:

> How can I ever find someone? The pastor would like us to marry a Jew or a
> member of the Open Gate, but there are very few single men here, and with
> Jewish guys I hardly have any contact. I don't understand why they don't
> allow us to go with people who do not share their religious belief with us; I
> mean they tell us that we should spread the Word of Adonai, so if my
> partner has not accepted Yeshua I can maybe show him the way, no?

Given that members in evangelical churches were forbidden to go out to bars and clubs, the task of finding a partner was indeed not an easy one, and the restrictions that Raúl additionally placed on his members rendered it even more difficult. Martha, a single mother and a member of the Open Gate, also voiced to me in private her discontent with the tight control:

We are not small children; they [the pastors] don't have to tell me with whom I can or can't go out. Sometimes I find this church very strange and I think I am going to leave it . . . but it also has so many positive things in it. . . . I really don't know what I have to do. . . . You must introduce me to one of your friends; I must find a Jew to marry or otherwise I will leave the country, like that I can't go on any longer, I am hopeless.

Victor Turner (1969: 198) points out that within Christianity one finds "founders of religious orders and sects who came from the upper half of the social cone, yet preached the style of life-crisis liminality as the path of salvation." The Open Gate can indeed be seen as such a Christian sect and Raúl as such a founder. In a way Raúl independently initiated a conversion of his followers toward a liminal Jewish identity as a form for reaching salvation. Yet Raúl seriously considered a possible completion of conversion to Judaism and thus rejected liminality as a chosen persisting mode that generated anxiety. The ambivalence regarding a full conversion brought to the surface the manner in which spirituality and instrumentality were closely intertwined in the minds of some evangelical Latinos in Israel. With time I developed a very close relationship with Raúl, who in one of our private meetings told me the following:

I am seriously looking into it, and discussing it with some people. I am ready to undergo the whole procedure, including circumcision. Studying and practicing the Jewish religion and customs is something I cherish and do all the time, and my conviction about Adonai is unconditioned. What worries me is that I will be asked to denounce Yeshua . . . what do you think?

Raúl looked perplexed, and I asked him why he wanted to convert to Judaism, given the enormous difficulties that the Israeli authorities raised in this regard. Raúl first chose to address my question theologically, saying that one can religiously and spiritually reach the highest levels only as a Jew. When I suggested that one could probably fulfill his spiritual aspirations as a Jew without an official recognition from the state of Israel, Raúl looked concerned and muttered, "You know how it is here Barak . . . if you want to make your life in Israel you have to be a Jew."

While the growing Jewish orientation of the Open Gate and the self-assumption of a Jewish identity were upsetting for some members, others were enchanted by it. When Raúl began contemplating with members the idea of full conversion to Judaism, some of them grew enthusiastic about the possibility for the legalization of their status in Israel.

Edgar, an Ecuadorian migrant, had never been a religious person, as he admitted. In the initial period, when he was in Israel by himself, he did not attend church.

Although offers to assist evangelical churches were regularly made to him by other Latinos, he always declined them. Things changed only after his wife, Mireya, who had converted to evangelicalism in Ecuador, joined him in Israel. Mireya was extremely pleased to learn from Edgar's friends about the existence of evangelical churches in Tel Aviv. After attending a *culto* in the Open Gate, on an invitation by a friend, she decided to join the congregation as a member. Subsequently she also put pressure on Edgar, who finally gave in and joined the church as well. Although Edgar's initial participation was a gesture to his wife, he grew increasingly committed and ardently attended Hebrew classes and the studies of Jewish traditions and biblical history. He recognized, as he told me, the practical skills that members were taught as well as the potential with regard to conversion to Judaism and legalization of status.

Yet some members appreciated the study of Hebrew and Jewish tradition beyond its potential instrumentality in Israel. Omar and his wife, Fernanda, were in Israel for eight years, of which they spent the last three as devoted members of the Open Gate. Their first son, Ariel, was born in Israel, and Fernanda was now pregnant with their second child. The couple decided to return to Colombia for good, four months before the expected delivery. The traumatic experience of the first delivery had been too much for them, and Fernanda now insisted on giving birth surrounded by her family:

> I don't want to go back; seriously, I don't miss anything in Colombia. I
> would love to make Israel my home, raise my children here, and spend here
> the rest of my life. I feel spiritually connected to this place. The only thing I
> want is to be legal and that I can bring my family here, but that has been
> impossible.

The couple twice tried to bring their relatives over to Israel; nevertheless, both Fernanda's parents and Omar's mother were turned back at the airport in Tel Aviv, on suspicion that they were planning to overstay their tourist visas as undocumented migrants. These futile efforts cost a fortune and were emotionally devastating for the couple, who decided not to try it for a third time. Although they had already bought tickets and a farewell party was scheduled for them in church, Omar still diligently attended Hebrew and Jewish studies at the Open Gate. When I asked him about it, he replied fervently, "What we learn here is making you a better person, you take it with you for life no matter where you are."

The Unattainable Belonging: Conversion to Judaism

Converting to Judaism was highly desirable among some Latinos, not least because it constituted a way to legalize their status in Israel. This practical fascination with Judaism was salient among evangelicals who partially already practiced it and were disposed to assimilate to it. For example, some members of the Open Gate seriously pondered the idea of conversion to Judaism that Raúl discussed with them. However, after three years in the Open Gate, members grew frustrated, as they bitterly realized the formidable task they faced. One of them expressed his desperation to me:

> What do you think, can I ever become a Jew? I love this country, I know the history of the Jewish nation, and I strongly believe in Adonai . . . will they give me a chance? I am also willing to serve in the army, defend this country, and die for it if I have to. What more can I do to become a Jew?

Non-Jews can theoretically choose to convert to Judaism, but this practice is being discouraged by the state of Israel, and in particular by Orthodox conversion tribunals, which are in charge of conversion to Judaism. Orthodox rabbis strictly believe that being Jewish is a birthright, and they thus agree to convert Gentiles only in unique cases, usually when the Jewishness of an alleged Jewish migrant is doubtful or when the spouse of a Jewish-Israeli citizen expresses what is considered to be a genuine desire to become Jewish so that the couple can build a Jewish home. An indication of this reluctance to practice conversion to Judaism is given by the low number of cases in which the procedure was used. For example, in 2000 the total number of converts stood at 2,465, of which 1,989 were migrants from the former Soviet Union and Ethiopia, whose conversion was more of a formality since their Jewish origin was under question (Rabbinical Tribunals Board 2003, quoted in *Haaretz* 18.03.2003). Non-Jews can convert to Judaism abroad, under the supervision of more lenient "liberal" or "reformist" rabbis. However, the state of Israel does not always recognize conversions that were performed abroad. It sometimes demands that converts fulfill additional requirements in Israel, for example, passing an exam on Jewish tradition or living in a religious community for one year.

Conversion to Judaism was indeed not at all a viable option for undocumented migrants. Their illegality in Israel precluded their ability to contact the religious authorities who perform conversion to Judaism. Nevertheless, many Latinos were encouraged by the experience of a few Latinos, who had married an Israeli partner and legalized their status in Israel and then went on to convert to Judaism. Although most Latinos realized it was impossible to convert in Israel, it did not exhaust their attempts to become Jews. Some Latinos began to investigate their origins in hope of finding a Jewish ancestor. These explorations of Jewish bloodlines were often stimulated by pastors in evangelical churches. Pastors alerted their members to the possibility that their ancestors were Jews who had immigrated to Latin America long ago and possibly concealed their Jewish origin. Some pastors also informed their members about the Museum of Jewish Diaspora (Beit Hatefutsoth) in the north of Tel Aviv, which enabled guests from all over the world to search in a computerized database whether their family name was linked to a Jewish family in the Diaspora.

Several Latinos decided to visit the museum, although worrying that they might be asked by a guard to show an identity card at the entrance. When I accompanied some of my informants to the museum, Israeli workers explained to me that having one's family name in the museum's database carried no legal evidence for claiming Jewish descent. Although I communicated this fact to my informants, it never stopped them from attempting this search. Some Latinos also called their families back home to engage them in this quest for Jewish origins. The slightest hint of Jewish reminisces among their grandparents instantly animated Latinos, as Vicente once excitedly informed me:

> You know, my mother just told me on the phone that her late father, my grandfather, mentioned once the fact that his father came from a Jewish family. He came from Europe on a boat almost a century ago, and when he married my great-grandmother he asked her not to tell anyone that he was Jewish. So we were never told about it, but if you look at my family name— Yepez—it sounds Jewish doesn't it? I must look into it.

The other option a few Latinos as well as some other undocumented migrants explored was the possibility to forge one's conversion to Judaism. There were some stories about rabbis in Israel who awarded non-Jews with official conversion certificates for a hefty bribe. Nevertheless, these stories mainly regarded cases of immigrants from the former Soviet Union whose Jewishness was taken to be partial or doubtful. To the best of my knowledge this was never practiced in the case of non-Jewish undocumented migrants. However, I learned of three cases in which evangelical Latinos had bought their conversion certificates abroad from a rabbi (for a sum of around US$8,000 per conversion). They subsequently immigrated to Israel as Jews under the Law of Return, and received all the corresponding benefits and assistance from the state of Israel.

I came to know one of these Latinos who "bought" their Jewishness. He was introduced to me by one of my informants in an evangelical church. However, at the time, I did not know, and was not told, about his fake conversion to Judaism. This secret was carefully guarded by those who had known him back home as a Christian. It was revealed to me by one of my closest informants only two years later.

Among his friends, the Latino Jew was called the *Judio Chimbo* (*chimbo* in Spanish slang stands for "low quality" or "not original"). The *Judio Chimbo* was often teased by his friends, who, for example, asked him sarcastically to offer the Israeli perspective on any issue discussed. The *Judio Chimbo* naturally intrigued me as a unique hybrid case of a Jew who was more connected to non-Jewish Latinos than to Jewish Israelis (at that point it did not occur to me that his Jewish identity was bought). I tried my best to develop a friendly relationship with him and learn about his perspective and feelings, but he was generally reserved and clearly reluctant to share with me details about his immigration and association with Latinos. He simply told me that in Latin America he always used to have Christian friends and for that reason in Israel he felt very comfortable among Latinos.[6] The successful case of the *Judio Chimbo* influenced some other Latinos to contemplate a forged conversion via rabbis in Latin America. However, most Latinos were deterred by the need to leave Israel and travel back to Latin America to undergo this risky and costly process.

FIGURE 1. *I prefer speaking Hebrew, my Spanish isn't very good, and I like it that way. My friends? Israelis or not quite Israelis, they're all human beings to me.*

Photograph courtesy ActiveVision. From Identity Document, photo project with children of migrant workers, 2006.

FIGURE 2. *My state is the street. That's what I know, and that's why I want to stay here. In the streets of this country, despite the police, I feel safe. At five in the morning, I can fall asleep on a bench in the street, and feel at home.*

Photograph courtesy ActiveVision. From Identity Document,
photo project with children of migrant workers, 2006.

FIGURE 3. *I see my mother working 15 hours a day, 6 days a week, 12 months a year, all without national insurance, or any kind of support from the state. She has no opportunity to find other work or hope that tomorrow she will find something that won't sap her energies as much or where she will earn more, rest a bit. . . . She rises every morning for this, and her work is forgotten with the setting of the sun. The only thing I can think about in this context is a machine. Drop by drop of sweat . . . she is building me a future.*

Photograph courtesy ActiveVision. From Identity Document, photo project with children of migrant workers, 2006.

FIGURE 4. *My little brother doesn't really understand what's going on. He was born in Israel. Children can't understand. I'm no longer a child.*

Photograph courtesy ActiveVision. From Identity Document, photo project with children of migrant workers, 2006.

FIGURE 5. *To the Interior Ministry we all went, the whole family. I was very nervous. All your life is compacted into a pile of forms. You're responsible for an entire family, which is in the hands of strangers. Mom doesn't really understand what they say, and my brother sits to one side and draws the bureaucrat a picture to hang on the wall. I really have to watch out what I say. Maybe I'll say something that isn't very Israeli.*

Photograph courtesy ActiveVision. From Identity Document,
photo project with children of migrant workers, 2006.

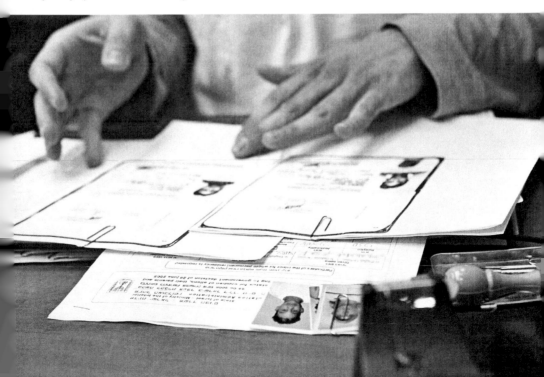

FIGURE 6. *Although I wasn't born here, this is where I want my children to be born, I don't have another country. Maybe at some point, I had another one, but now I don't know any other place.*

Photograph courtesy ActiveVision. From Identity Document, photo project with children of migrant workers, 2006.

PART THREE

Chapter Seven

Israeli Resolution, Latino Disillusion

FROM MASSIVE DEPORTATION TO SYMBOLIC LEGALIZATION

The true mystery of the world is the visible,
not the invisible.

—*Oscar Wilde*

Around midnight on a particularly cold night in January 2003, I returned together with couple of my Latino friends from a party, when all of a sudden we saw how two men in civilian clothes fell upon a pedestrian who appeared to be African, pushed his body and face against the wall and bent his arms behind his back. While I was baffled by what we witnessed, my Latino friends immediately recognized the aggressors to be undercover agents of the Immigration Police, and nodding me a quick goodbye, they walked away and disappeared into a nearby alley. Shocked by the violent incident and the cries of the apprehended person, I went up to the men and asked them what was going on. The two agents gauged me and one of them asked agitatedly, "Who are you?" and then before I could say something he added, "Move on, this is not your business, we are police." "But what are you doing to him?" I insisted. "It is an illegal worker, now move on," one of the agents grumbled at me. "But why do you beat him like that?" I complained, causing the agents to lose the little patience they had for me. "Get going now, do you hear? Or you will be in trouble as well." The agents handcuffed the man and then one of them pulled out a walkie-talkie and communicated their location to a patrol vehicle, which appeared at the scene within less than two minutes. "You are still here?" one of the agents muttered at me as they were pushing the apprehended man into the police car. "Go home, the show is over."

In July 2002 a special Parliamentary Committee for the assessment of the issue of non-Jewish migrants in Israel concluded that their presence constituted "a social and economic emergency situation" (*Yediot Aharonot* 22.07.2002). The government followed up on the committee's report and in August 2002 inaugurated a special Immigration Police whose task was to locate, arrest, and deport 50,000 undocumented migrants in its first year of operation. This decision marked a turning point in the government's approach, as it was followed by the allocation of a substantial budget for executing the task. Around seventy officers and more than four hundred agents were recruited to the ranks of the Immigration Police. The Immigration Police were given a great deal of authority, and all ministries and state institutions were directed to give their needs the highest priority. A central headquarters ensured the speedy processing of the deportation procedure. Two entire hotels were rented and converted by the state into detention centers to ensure that the process would not be obstructed by an overcapacity of detainees.[1]

Within just over one year the Immigration Police managed to deport around 25,000 migrants and to create a ripple effect of intimidation that induced an estimated 55,000 more undocumented migrants to exit the country independently (*Haaretz* 01.01.2004). For Latinos in Israel, as for many other undocumented migrants, the "success" of the Immigration Police meant the destruction of their lives as settled migrants. Many Latinos were deported after being captured in homes, work places, bus terminals, football pitches, salsa clubs, and all other places that the police targeted in their relentless effort to accomplish their task. In early 2005, more than two years into the operation of the Immigration Police, the presence of Latinos in Israel was almost completely obliterated. The custom of playing football on Saturdays died out. The two Latino bars in Tel Aviv closed down. A few salsa clubs shut down, while others continued operating without the presence of Latinos in them. Latino evangelical churches also closed their doors one after the other as the number of congregants dwindled away by the month. The Latino community in Israel was reduced mainly to mothers and their children who were exempted from the deportation policy of the Israeli state. As fathers were not exempted, many families were separated. Some mothers decided to follow their deported husbands back to their country of origin, while others remained in Israel either hoping that the father could rejoin them or fearing that a return of the whole family might spell complete devastation for their economic future as well as their children's emotional stability. As I discovered during my fieldwork in Ecuador among deportees, this fear was unfortunately well founded.

The effect of the new deportation policy was surprising for many in Israel, not least because similar actions by Immigration Police in other countries had failed to produce comparable results (cf. Gibney and Hansen 2003). During the years 1996–2002, which saw recurrent failure of Israeli deportation campaigns, a consensus began to emerge in Israel that a wholesale deportation of undocumented migrants who had settled down was not a realistic solution. For example, Professor Itzhak Schnell, who advised the government on the issue, asserted that "there is no doubt that massive deportation is an action a government in Israel could hardly realize" (Schnell 2001: 19); and a journalist who closely followed previous failures of Israel's deportation campaigns concluded, "Nobody in the world believes in a policy of entire population transfer, unless [states were to] adopt brutal and exotic methods" (*Haaretz* 17.05.2001).

Yet adopting "brutal and exotic methods" is precisely what the Israeli government resorted to in its attempt to eradicate settled undocumented migrants. Adopting certain methods by way of a political decision is, however, not sufficient; these methods must be carried out by people. To understand the efficiency of the Immigration Police we therefore need to take into account the particular Israeli "governmentality," to use Michel Foucault's term, which is based on the conversion of most political and civil issues into national security threats. In other words, we should consider the particularly Israeli way of managing a population and running a state, which is contingent on the cultivation of a particular subjectivity. This subjectivity of Jewish Israelis is conspicuously attuned to the need of the Jewish state to protect its territorial and ethno-religious borders from the perceived invasion of non-Jewish elements. The cultivation of this subjectivity among Jewish Israelis is largely predicated on the collective remembrance of the Jewish history of persecution and exclusion.

As economic circumstances changed in Israel, the presence of undocumented migrants was effectively construed as a national security risk by officials operating under the state-led and widely internalized governmentality. The plan for a massive deportation of undocumented migrants was then carried out with full conviction by the officers and field agents of the Immigration Police. Concomitantly, some Israeli civil society actors, who managed to escape the power of the Israeli governmentality, persistently fought to stop the deportation campaign and legalize the status of some undocumented migrants according to sensible criteria. These actors used Israel's democratic characteristics, which included freedom of association, freedom of speech, and the government's accountability to Israeli laws and international conventions.

Astutely, civil society actors compared the Jewish history of ethnic persecution with the situation of non-Jewish undocumented migrants in Israel. This dreadful contrast touched upon the sensitivity of many Israeli politicians, some of them the sons and daughters of Holocaust survivors. It consequently led many liberal politicians, as well as right-wing conservative ones, to consider empathetically the situation of undocumented migrants' children, who "became part of Israeli society" but were excluded legally from the Israeli state because of their belonging to a non-Jewish ethno-religious group. It is thus that the agonizing Jewish history of anti-Semitism has profoundly shaped the consciousness of Jewish Israeli citizens and political leaders in a way that could reconcile, on the one hand, the need to use all means toward the massive deportation of non-Jewish migrants and, on the other hand, the moral obligation to legalize the status of the children of undocumented migrants on universal humane grounds.

Massive Deportation and the Israeli
Governmentality of "Security Risks"

The Israeli migration regime of non-Jewish workers was bound to collapse, as it increasingly led to an unsustainable political constellation. To politically survive the increase in the number of undocumented migrants, it was crucial for governments in Israel publicly to appear to be fighting this development. But while successive Israeli governments used inflamed rhetoric against undocumented migrants and vowed to deport most of them, in practice, as I described in chapter 2, only a tiny fraction of the total undocumented migrants was deported each year prior to 2002. Increasingly, the Israeli government came under political fire for allowing the situation to get out of hand, as believed by many in Israel. The evident settlement of non-Jewish migrants rendered it unsustainable for the government to continue practicing a blind-eye policy and maintaining that the issue was controlled and contained.

In addition to this mounting political pressure, two factors were important in determining the timing of this move from a blind-eye policy to massive deportation. First, from around 2000, Israel needed fewer migrant workers. The strain in the construction sector eased after the housing predicament of Jewish immigrants from the former Soviet Union had been solved, and only small numbers of Jews had reached Israel during the late 1990s and early 2000s. The more acute predicament that the Israeli economy faced in the early twenty-first century was a persistently high unemployment rate among Israelis and a grave recession. The working assumption of Israeli policymakers was that if they toughened the conditions for welfare benefits and deported undocumented migrants, jobs would become available for long-term unemployed Israelis, who would now be willing to take them on (see *Jewish Week* 10.10.2003, *Haaretz* 15.06.2005). Thus, in 2002 the minister of finance, Benjamin Netanyahu, announced that "[t]he public in Israel must understand that foreign workers and Palestinians take the jobs of Israelis" (*Maariv* 23.07.2002). However misleading and economically false this assumption may have been, it was politically construed as being true, and the message resonated with the Israeli public. Deporting undocumented migrants thus became increasingly rewarding for an Israeli government that could portray itself as battling for the employment of Israeli workers.

The second factor that contributed to a change in the Israeli policy is that in 2001 Ariel Sharon, the hawkish chairman of the right-wing Likud party, was elected prime minister. Sharon has been nicknamed "the Bulldozer" for his determination as a politician in pursuing national projects and being able efficiently to mobilize resources.[2] It was thus that large-scale deportation, which was publicly advocated by former prime ministers but always contained by humane and practical prohibitions, was threatened to be realized under the Sharon administration.

With its establishment in August 2002, the Immigration Police engaged in new sets of methods to achieve its task. First, it aired a campaign to create a hostile environment vis-à-vis undocumented migrants, portraying them as a hazard to Israeli society. In radio and television messages, newspaper ads, public advertisements, and an Internet Web site, undocumented migrants were presented as people who were damaging the local economy by using the Israeli infrastructure while averting tax payments. Mixed marriages between non-Jewish migrants and Israelis were decried as hurting the "decency" of Israel and its Jewish character.

Second, the Immigration Police seriously targeted for the first time Israeli employers of undocumented migrants, punishing them with heavy fines and even bringing some of them to court. The penalties for employers were publicly advertised to enhance deterrence among Israelis. As it was now in the interest of the police for non-Jewish migrants to be in possession of their passports (so that they could be identified and if needed deported), within the first month of its operation the Immigration Police seized from Israeli employers and mediating agencies eight thousand unlawfully confiscated passports of migrants (*Haaretz* 10.10.2002). Although not all employers were impressed by the more aggressive attitude of the Immigration Police, in my interviews with some of them I heard concerns and a reported change in their habit of employing undocumented migrants. For example, Amit, who in the last six years had employed undocumented Chinese migrants in his small but profitable subcontract construction business, told me he now considered giving up his business and taking a "normal" job as a manager in one of the major Israeli construction companies:

I'm getting tired of it. All the time having someone [at the construction site] as a lookout for police agents. And there are many snitches who will give you in to the police for getting some immunity for themselves. It's becoming more and more impossible for small fish like me. [He paused to take a long puff on his cigarette.] I also hate the looks of people when I stop at the traffic light. They look at the Chinese in the back of my van and then they look at me as if I was a criminal. One time I stopped in red [light] and someone was giving me a very nasty look, then all of a sudden I realized that on the radio there was an advertisement against foreign workers, and he was probably listening to it too.

The third method practiced by the Immigration Police was the initiation of the so-called "depart on free will" campaign, aimed at getting undocumented migrants to "voluntarily" come forward and report themselves to the Immigration Police. Such migrants were then given up to three months to arrange their orderly exit from the country. The Immigration Police posted announcements in public spaces where undocumented migrants lived and in newspapers that they read that proclaimed: "We do not want to break your door, handcuff innocent people and separate families. We are offering a chance to all foreign communities to return to their homelands with preparation and dignity." The Immigration Police also financed one-way tickets for those who allegedly had no money for it. Driven by an atmosphere of intimidation, several thousand undocumented migrants took part in this campaign of "voluntary expulsion."

Finally, the Immigration Police deployed field units all across the country to apprehend suspected undocumented migrants in all places. In their quest to detain undocumented migrants the Immigration Police applied methods similar to those used by the Israeli army against suspected Palestinian terrorists. Once again it became clear that non-Jewish migrants substituted for Palestinian workers in the Israeli labor market as well as in the Israeli institutionalized invidious perspective. Terminologically, undocumented migrants, like non-Israeli Palestinians before them, were classified as *shabahim* (the acronym in Hebrew for "illegal stayer"). Operationally, the Immigration Police, with the help of the Israeli Internal Security Service (Shien Beit), offered some undocumented migrants the opportunity to cross the lines to work as undercover informants for the police in return for payment or a promise not to deport them in the near future. Israeli employers were also encouraged by the Immigration Police to report the living and working places of suspected undocumented migrants via a special information hotline service that promised anonymity. Some taxi drivers were offered money by the Immigration Police for reporting the address to which they brought suspected undocumented migrants (*Haaretz* 16.02.2004)

Intelligence units, with the help of informants, secretly marked suspected undocumented migrants' apartments with a special signature that was known to field units, which arrived there, usually in the middle of the night, to catch undocumented migrants by surprise. Agents of the Immigration Police forced their way into apartments, often without search warrants and sometimes by knocking down doors with heavy hammers in order to catch suspected undocumented migrants before they could escape the apartment through a back door or a window. Suspected undocumented migrants were literally pulled out of their beds, handcuffed, and loaded into vans of the Immigration Police as if they were dangerous criminals. Fathers were apprehended in front of their children. Many children were too young to be able to make sense of what they witnessed. Traumatized mothers were then left behind with the excruciating task of explaining the unexplainable to their dismayed children.

When Marisol called me on my mobile phone to tell me that Miguel, her husband, was arrested by the Immigration Police, she could hardly speak. From the broken sentences she managed to utter while crying agitatedly, I understood what happened. When I visited her later that day in her apartment, after she picked up her son and daughter from school, Marisol was surrounded by her aunt and two good friends, who came to support her and the children emotionally. Marisol asked me to follow her to the kitchen before she explained to me:

> Miguel called and said he doesn't want me to come with the children to visit him because he doesn't want the children to see him in jail. [She wiped her tears.] I'm afraid to go visit him without the children because they [Immigration Police] might arrest me too. You know how crazy they are. I wanted to ask you if you were willing to visit him, to see how he is doing and bring him some clothes and money.

Then just before we went back to the living room, Marisol pulled me back to the kitchen and whispered,

> The children don't know about it. I didn't tell them that their father was arrested. I just said he had to go urgently back to Ecuador to visit the family. So please don't say anything about it to them.

While 4-year-old Daniel was too young to understand the situation, I suspected that Laura, who was a very lively and bright 7-year-old, easily inferred from the weeping of her mother and the commotion in the house that her father was arrested. When I talked to children of undocumented migrants in the period of the massive deportation campaign, many of them complained that the number of their friends was dwindling quickly, as many families were deported or decided to leave. I have no doubt that Laura, who shared this feeling with other children, knew all too well that it was now her family's turn to go through this forsaking experience. Laura was playing that whole afternoon very dedicatedly with her small brother in a corner of the room, avoiding, rather on purpose, contact with any of the adults in the house.

Two days later, on Tuesday, the visiting day at the Maasiyahu jail where some undocumented migrants were detained, I went to visit Miguel. Marisol came with me but waited outside at a safe distance from the jail premises. The meeting with Miguel was very emotional. He first tried to appear to be in control. He smiled a lot and asked me in a casual way how everyone was doing. However, Miguel's emotional devastation became evident when he asked about Laura and Daniel. In response to my update, Miguel looked down to the floor, and mumbled, "I only hope that they will be all right. This is not right."

While the Immigration Police denied using any inhumane methods and claimed to always act according to the law, the many cases that were brought to court or reported by NGOs and the Israeli media presented a different picture. They presented a picture of brutal apprehensions with little consideration for the traumatic effects that an arrest could have on the individuals involved, especially for families with small children. Many newspaper articles provided graphic descriptions of police brutality in the apprehension of suspected undocumented migrants (see "Israel: Mean Streets," *Jerusalem Report* 21.05.2003). In several cases the Immigration Police who were arresting migrants paid no attention to the fact that small children were left behind all alone (*Haaretz* 24.02.2004). Reports by Israeli NGOs detailed the recurrent mismanagement of authority by the Immigration Police and the general trampling on migrants' rights throughout the deportation process (see Hotline for Migrant Workers and Kav La'Oved 2003, 2004, and also *Yediot Aharonot* 06.11.2003).[3] In addition to the violent arrest described above, during my fieldwork in Tel Aviv I witnessed several cases in which suspected undocumented migrants were detained by the Immigration Police in bus terminals, grocery shops, and salsa clubs. On one occasion I saw how teams of the Immigration Police arrived with two commercial buses, sealed off a whole street in south Tel Aviv, and indiscriminately arrested everyone they suspected to be an undocumented migrant.

The scars that the actions of the Immigration Police left on Latinos and other undocumented migrants should not be underestimated (see Willen 2007). The anxiety that engulfed Latinos was overwhelming, and it was manifested in erratic behavior, emotional breakdowns, sleepless nights, nightmares, and increasing tension among family members. Children of undocumented migrants were of course in the worst position to make sense of what was happening around them. Some years later, Natalia Leiber, the head of La Escuelita (the educational grassroots initiative of Latinos for their children in Israel), reflected on the hardship of children during the period of massive deportation:

> The children have undergone extremely difficult and traumatic experiences; the games they played became very violent. They saw the Immigration Police entering their homes, taking their fathers by force, and it was something we had to constantly deal with. Children who out of the blue start crying, who are scared of everything, who wet their beds at night when they are already adolescents. There was a very strong need among these children and their mothers not to appear to be Latinos. But to appear like Israelis.[4]

In an adverse reaction to the violence that they had witnessed, some children of undocumented migrants identified with the figure of the Israeli agents. On Purim, an Israeli annual festivity for which children traditionally wear costumes, many children of undocumented migrants chose to dress up as police agents. When I asked Naomi, an 8-year-old who witnessed how police agents arrested her father and later deported him to Colombia, why she chose a policeman outfit for Purim, the young girl answered, "Because I want to be powerful and decide who can stay and who can go." In a touching article, journalist Boaz Gaon (*Maariv* 26.12.2003) describes the shattered life of Galit, a 10-year-old girl whose father was arrested and was about to be deported to

Ghana. In her efforts to deal with her trauma, and with the naïveté of a young girl, Galit wrote a letter in Hebrew to the Israeli prime minister:

> My name is Galit. I am ten [years old] and I attend fourth grade at the Yarden school. You caught my father. Please release him . . . please, I beg you. If you take my father to Ghana I would prefer killing myself, because I have no one except my father and mother, so I am sad and cannot eat nor study. If you love your children and kiss them in the morning and in the evening when they go to bed, I also want my father to kiss me. I do not even know how to speak the language of people in Ghana. [The letter was signed, "Galit, the daughter of Philip."]

To grasp the militant ways in which the Immigration Police executed their task, we need to account for the particular Israeli governmentality that framed the issue of non-Jewish migrants as a national threat and prescribed a combative solution for it. Foucault (1991: 102) defined governmentality as "the ensemble formed by the institutions, procedures, analyses and reflections, the calculation and tactics that allow the exercise of this very specific albeit complex form of power, which has as its target population, as its principal form of knowledge political economy, and as its essential technical means apparatuses of security." Governmentality thus comprised both the "art of governance" as exercised by leaders who have access to the state apparatus and the saturation of society with a distinctive discourse that shapes the subjectivity of citizens and renders them governable in a particular way. Discourse should be understood here in the thick sense in which Foucault used it, that is, the power to construct reality and truth by applying specific knowledge that is produced precisely for that end by professional experts, institutions, and disciplines, and that is internalized by people and leads them toward a particular experiential understanding of the world.

Undoubtedly, the development of a particular Israeli governmentality that is rooted in managing national security threats has much to do with the daunting history of the Jewish people. Massive deportations, forced religious conversions, pogroms, the Holocaust, and numerous other manifestations of anti-Semitism worldwide have all contributed to a profound, prevailing consciousness among Jews about their hunted and beleaguered position in the world. It is against this backdrop that Israel has been established as the Jewish state, with its raison d'être to constitute a secure "home" for Jews and to protect them from external threats to their existence as individuals and as a nation. Nachman Ben-Yehuda (1995), for example, shows how the Israeli collective memory has turned the ancient story of Masada—a fortress in the Judean desert where a group of around one thousand Jews were put under siege by the Roman army and eventually committed suicide instead of surrendering—into a mythological cornerstone in the process of nation-building and the formation of a resilient Jewish identity.

In 1948, during its Independence War, Israel declared a "state of emergency," which has been maintained intact ever since by consecutive governments that still considered the security threat to Israel to be imminent. A state of emergency provides the government with the authority to bypass juridical institutions whenever there is, according to its own judgment, a credible threat to the security of its citizens. Although in the years after its independence Israel managed to built the strongest army in the Middle East, it has still kept perceiving, whether real or false, continuous threats to its national security. Israel practices an obligatory military service of three years for men and two years for women. Therefore, all Jewish citizens of Israel must contribute a significant part of their life to the army, where they are exposed to a military-infused perspective and they internalize the particular discourse on security risks.

Yet the identification of Israeli citizens with the military and the internalization of the feeling of eminent security threats is inculcated by various institutions, of which the army itself is only one. Other institutions that cultivate this subjectivity, and glorify service in the army, include schools, youth movements, a large part of the Israeli media, art, cultural production, and of course the political system. The political elite in Israel are saturated with retired military generals. Historically, most Israeli prime ministers had been top-rank generals in the military or other security institutions.[5] The military elite thus acquired an exclusive status in Israeli society and a direct connection to the power apparatus of the state. Former-generals-turned-politicians have tended to prioritize security-related issues and reduce many other political issues to their implications for national security. Here is, for example, how Shlomo Ben-Ami, the former Israeli foreign minister and a professor of history, describes the popular appeal of the former Israeli prime minister Menachem Begin: "He truly represented, but also knew how to exploit, the traditional Jewish paranoia and the structured pairing in the Jewish consciousness between the proven might of the eternal nation and the unceasing fear of disaster and annihilation" (Ben-Ami 2001: 19). Under the sway of Israeli generals-turned-politicians, questions about the management of water resources, the changing demographic composition of the nation, and the decision about founding new cities and settlements are all tightly linked up with and subordinated to national security considerations (for support for such link see Soffer 1988, 1999; for the critique thereof see Falah and Newman 1995, Kimmerling 1983, Newman 1998, Yiftachel 1992). A dominant discourse on the uncompromising need for security-above-all has produced a widespread consensus among Jewish citizens on issues of national security, and it has induced the formation of a particular Israeli governmentality of security risks. In the words of one observer:

> This [security] discourse is part of an agenda set by the dominant power—in this case Israel—focusing on the existential threat facing the country. . . . It is also an agenda around which the Israeli population (at least the 80 percent Jewish majority) are united in the social construction of the collective feelings of fear and threat emanating from the "other." (Newman 1998: 164)

Together with the external threat of a wholesale war by Arab countries, the biggest perceived danger for Israel is posed by attempts to undermine its Jewish character. Israel has outlawed political parties that call for the amendment of the state as a Jewish one. Israel is also most sensitive to maintaining a predominant Jewish majority within its population. Israel regularly produces statistics on the composition of the national population and the trends that influence the proportion of the Jewish majority in it. The high reproduction rate of Palestinian Israelis has always been considered a grave problem for Jewish Israeli officials and politicians (see DellaPergola 2001, Soffer 1988).[6] Immigration of Jews to Israel, within this framework of demographic concerns, is a first priority for the Jewish state, and reversely, the emigration of Jewish Israelis to other countries is a sensitive issue on which Israel refrains from producing transparent statistics, and which constitutes much of a taboo in Israeli public policy and debate (see Lustick 2004).[7]

Following the tenets of the Israeli governmentality of security risks, and against the backdrop of hypersensitivity for issues of immigration, the full meaning of a move by Israel to define undocumented non-Jewish migrants as an additional peril to its demographic threat becomes clear. The corresponding declaration by the police chief of staff that the massive deportation campaign would be conducted "like a military operation" is also lucid when we consider that undocumented migrants in Israel not only were blamed for undermining the sovereignty of the state, but were seen as threatening the single most important mission of Israel, that is, to serve as "home" for Jews and preserve its Jewish character. We are now in a better position to understand why the massive deportation campaign in Israel was assigned to the ministry of internal security, and why the Immigration Administration was headed not by an official from the interior ministry but by a major general who in his previous role was the chief commander of the army unit Border Guards (Mishmar Ha'Gvul), which is often assigned to deal with the Palestinian population in the Occupied Territories.

In fact, most of the field agents of the Immigration Police were also recruited from the Border Guards (*Yediot Aharonot* 02.09.2002). Agents hardly ever questioned the suitability of their methods for dealing with a civil population of workers; instead, they fully internalized the particular emotional orientation that follows from the Israeli governmentality, and thus became part of the "normalizing" force as they practiced, spread, and maintained this subjectivity. Here is how one agent justified the work of the Immigration Police when he was asked about it by a journalist:

> What troubled conscience? What are you talking about? What we are doing is a holy work. Every foreigner who is displaced to an airplane, makes space for an unemployed Israeli who can, god forbid, commit suicide because of the situation. That's why I fully identify with what I'm doing and I have no doubts as for the righteousness of our way. It is the right thing to do, it is proven on the ground. I'm certain of it. (*Haaretz* 05.06.2003)

In contrast, in an interview with the investigative TV program *Fact* (*Uvda*, broadcast on 04.06.2005), an unidentified agent from the Immigration Police, whose conscience was clearly troubled, recounted the following about the operations of his unit: "We became animals. It could be that the mission was too big, that the numbers were out of proportion. That is how they educated us in the army: forward-charge. Only later you begin to reflect on it. We acted like machines, we received a quota and we had to fill the buses accordingly." In a newspaper article that reported on this interview the following claim was made: "It appears that field units [of the Immigration Police] treat foreign workers as ticking bombs and act against them just like the Shien Beit [the Internal Security Service] acts against Palestinian terror" (*Haaretz* 05.06.2005). Although to this day there has not been a single terror incident of which non-Jewish migrants were the perpetrators,[8] their potential involvement in terrorist acts was labeled a "security risk" as early as 1998 by the Israeli Internal Security Service (*Yediot Aharonot* 09.07.1998), and the Immigration Police repeatedly adverted to the danger that Israel faced from a potential link between terrorists and non-Jewish migrants, who allegedly sought to make some "easy money" by assisting Palestinian radicals (see *Yediot Aharonot* 11.09.2002, *Maariv* 02.03.2004).

Shattered Lives: The Massive Deportation Campaign

Latinos were used to the fluctuations in Israeli deportation campaigns. Since 1996, almost every year at a certain point the state rhetoric regarding the need to exercise tough measures against undocumented migrants would peak. It would then be followed by a few weeks or even months of a more intense police effort to arrest undocumented migrants, before scaling back to the "normal" level of rather lax surveillance. Latinos had specific words to describe the full gamut of intensity in the fluctuating police inspection policy; from periods of "heat" (*caliente*) when the police were "acting crazy" (*locos*), to the more relaxed periods of tranquility (*tranquilo*) when anecdotes about running into the police with no fear of getting arrested were told by some Latinos (*no pasa nada*).

Latinos were trained in matching their vigilance to the fluctuations in the mood and mode of the Israeli police. As I learned through the many times I walked with them on the streets, went out at night, or relaxed on the beach during the day, Latinos' alertness to the surroundings was permanent. At first I failed to notice it, but later I understood that this was precisely the kind of competence that Latinos mastered, namely, being alert without appearing to be so. For example, when they were walking on the street, whenever Latinos detected a parked van of the Immigration Police, or spotted (undercover) policemen, they would change the course of their walk so as to avoid contact in a way that seemed very natural and did not reveal their nervousness. I remember very well the first time when I experienced this competence. I was walking with Antonio to buy some fish in Jaffa when all of a sudden, when we were only two hundred meters from the market, Antonio crossed the way to the opposite direction from where the market was, gently pulling my arm so that I would follow him, and then before I could even ask why, he said in the most calm way, "There are Immigration Police over there." It then dawned on me that many Latinos navigated the city with an embodied radar that was attuned to detect police endangerment and that they probably could not turn off even if they wanted to.

In early 2003 Latinos in Israel began to realize that something had changed in the familiar frequencies. "Is it true that they won't let go this time?" Vicente asked in evident desperation when I visited him in his house one evening. The intensity of the actions taken by the Immigration Police refused to mellow out; in fact, they became increasingly more persistent and indiscriminate. Latinos were confused and horrified, trying to make sense of the developing situation. I already noticed Vicente's agitation when he asked me, in an unusual manner, to identify by name when I rang the button of the intercom system in the apartment building where he resided with his wife, baby daughter, and three more Latino friends.

Some Latinos living together adopted a distinctive knock on the door or a particular ring of the intercom system as an identifying mechanism for members of a known and trusted group of friends. Whenever someone knocked on their door not in the distinctive way that they agreed on, the level of suspicion and alertness was raised immediately in the house. My best Latino friends, whom I was regularly visiting in their apartments, taught me the distinctive knock or ring that they were using. That is why I was surprised when Vicente asked me to identify before opening the door, although I had used the distinctive ring when buzzing his intercom system. When I asked him about it, he nervously explained:

> You can't trust anyone anymore. They [the Immigration Police] work with *sapos* [Latino snitches] all the time. You can't be sure that somebody you know, even know very well, is not working with the police. Do you remember the lady we met in the church the other day? You know, you were talking with her for a while and I was keeping a bit away. Well, I know that she's now a *sapo*. She gives people away to the police. She tells them exactly where they live. I try to avoid her now, but she knows where we live.

Vicente was tapping his foot nervously on the floor. An expression of distress covered his face in a way that I never saw with him before. When I asked Vicente why he thought this lady became a *sapo*, he answered in a language that was not typical for him,

> Why? Because she's a bitch that's why. The police promised her not to deport her family if she gives them the addresses of other Latinos in the

neighborhood. She made a deal with them. And now she still pretends to be friends with everyone, while she gives people away in cold blood. [He let out a bad curse.]

As we have seen, the tendency among Latinos to refrain from collective political mobilization led to a divisive Latino community in Israel. The limited trust that was there between different Latino groups received a final blow and was eroded completely with the widespread phenomenon of *sapos*.

The anxiety that Vicente and other Latinos experienced after 2003 resulted from the difficult realization that the rules of the game had changed drastically and probably for good. Latinos' physical and mental survival techniques appeared to be depleted when dealing with the invigorated assault of the Immigration Police. No doubt, other undocumented migrants such as Africans and Filipinos were even more helpless, since "evidence for [their] arrest is written on [their] body," as Willen (2007: 18) puts it. Nevertheless, the actions of the Immigration Police against almost everyone who lived in "suspicious zones," such as south Tel Aviv, circumscribed the bodily and embodied capital of Latinos as they tried to avoid police inspections. There were also clear signs that the Immigration Police singled out Latinos as one of its prime target groups precisely because of their advanced level of settlement in Israel.

As the deportation campaign continued, some Latinos relocated away from south Tel Aviv. Yet the Immigration Police, with the help of informers, followed undocumented migrants relentlessly and into cities that had previously been considered "safe zones." With every week that passed more Latinos were arrested and deported. The news about arrested relatives and friends spread quickly and augmented the fear of those who still managed to evade the Immigration Police. Fear pervaded and dissolved every remaining social fabric among Latinos. Groups of relatives and friends as well as evangelical congregants refrained from meeting in order to minimize the risk of being targeted by the Immigration Police.

Out of desperation, some Latinos adopted a fatalistic approach. They restored their public conduct, disregarding the new risks that such public presence entailed. They opted for some artificial normalcy by conducting their lives "as usual," believing that "if it is meant for me to be caught then it will happen anyhow." Other Latinos could not bear the emotionally racking situation and decided to return to their country of origin, often by making use of the Immigration Police program of "voluntary expulsion" that allowed undocumented migrants a couple of months to organize orderly exit. Some Latinos who realized that their time in Israel was running out tried to console themselves by rationalizing that a return home "after all, might not be such a bad idea." Latinos reminded themselves of the fact that they had not seen their parents and/or children for many years and that reuniting with them would be an advantage.

The economic capital that most Latinos managed to save was also mentioned as a reason to pick up life back home at a "different level."

Latino Deportees: Strangers at Home or Perpetual Undocumented Migrants

Most Latino deportees experienced their arrest as an abrupt end to a desired life in Israel. Although always in the back of their mind, when it happened, it caught them unprepared for a return back home. From my fieldwork among deportees in Ecuador, it appears that for many of them the return was an extremely difficult process that disrupted their expectations with respect to their position in the household, local society, and the market. Many parents had to come to terms with a lack of emotional bonding with their children. The children of Vicente and Blanca, for example, refused to grow out of their habit of calling their grandparents "Papi" and "Mami," while referring to their returned biological parents by their given names. Vicente tried to paint this painful experience in amusing colors: "They don't want to call me 'Papi,' so now we both call my father 'Papi' [laughing]." Yet the deeper emotional signification of this divergence caught up with Blanca, who at one point shouted at Genesis, her 10-year-old daughter, "Enough! I'm your mother, you should not call me by my name, I'm not the neighbor. I am your M-A-M-A." Blanca pronounced each syllable while fixing her burning eyes on her daughter's fragile face. Later the same day when I sat down with Vicente and Blanca for a drink in a local cantina, Blanca summarized the disillusion she experienced since her return: "You know Barak, sometimes I feel here like a stranger. It sounds incredible but it's like this. In Israel I felt more at home than I feel now here." Vicente lifted the bottle of beer to his mouth, and before gulping nodded his head in agreement with his wife.

A few returnees expressed to me their grievances about the lack of appreciation that their children showed for their efforts as migrants in Israel. As Pedro, who lived in Israel for four years before he was deported, puts it:

> If they only knew what I went through in order to provide for them. Every time it was difficult for me [in Israel] I was thinking of them . . . that I don't want them to have to live the life that I had. But now I see that they don't understand it. There is no gratitude. Only complaints. As if I did something bad to them.

Many children of emigrants in Ecuador suffered from severe difficulties in school and from problematic relations with guardians. These problems were often not resolved with the return of parents, and at times were even aggravated as children were kicking hard against their parents.

Deportees were also confronted with financial demands from close relatives who felt they were entitled to some help from successful returnees. This was causing much agitation, as expressed by Javier:

> They all think I became a millionaire or something, so everyone now asks
> me for help. They don't know how hard I worked for this money. And
> what? They think I have whatever quantity of money, but that's not true.

The bitter reality was that the money many Latinos saved in Israel was indeed not sufficient for upgrading their lives in a very significant way. Settled Latinos in Israel invested most of their income in their lives in Israel. At the point of deportation they tended to have very little money saved. The money many Latinos remitted regularly to families back home was also mostly used for financing an improved standard of living rather than for future investment. In fact many of the returnees I visited in Ecuador were living in their parents' house, not because extended households were still the norm in Ecuador, but because the returnees could not afford an independent household. Some returnees, who had a house built for them with the money they remitted in their first years in Israel, often could not or did not want to invest money in furnishing the house and connecting it to the electricity, sewage, and water system.

Returnees in Ecuador were not willing to take on the kind of jobs they had left before going to Israel. A salary of US$150 appeared unworthy of a month of hard labor for those who were accustomed to earn more than US$1,000 a month during their years in Israel. When I visited Pedro, he had all the time in the world to show me around in his hometown. Half a year since his return to Ecuador from Israel, Pedro still had no job. When I asked him about it, he dismissed the option of taking a "regular" job:

> Think about it, Barak. I'm now not working already for six months, but let's
> say I was working like a donkey all this time in a job that pays $150 per
> month. How much would I have earned by now? Less than $1,000. That's
> not what I'm going to do. It's better to take my time and think well about
> opportunities. I'm thinking of opening a restaurant with my brother, and
> I'm also checking the possibility of getting to the U.S.

In addition, social pressure also often prevented returnees from practicing the same job that they had occupied before their immigration, as this was considered an evidence of migrants' failure abroad. None of the returnees and deportees that I visited in Ecuador practiced his or her old occupation. In fact, most of them were either unemployed or involved in an entrepreneurial venture in an effort to reinvent themselves as businessmen.

Lacking knowledge and experience in the business world, some of the returnees who invested their money in entrepreneurial ventures often stood to lose most of their capital. Vicente was lured by a dubious cooperative to purchase a taxi and the permission to run it in Guayaquil. After two years he not only lost most of his savings but was now indebted to the taxi cooperative. In Loja, I met Ángel, who was convinced by his brother-in-law to invest the money he had saved in Israel in buying a bus and operating it in the city. The bus Ángel bought turned out to be in very bad shape, and the license for running it in the streets of Loja was much more expensive than he was initially told. But there was no turning back at that point for Ángel, who invested even more money in repairing the bus and then began to work as a chauffeur for more than twelve hours a day. When I accompanied Ángel one day on his bus routine, I asked him, when we paused for lunch after five hours of nonstop bumpy rides back and forth in the city, why he did not hire a professional chauffeur. Ángel, who was wiping his sweat with a small towel, answered in disillusion:

> I first hired a professional driver, but he was stealing from me [the drivers often also sell the tickets]. I then asked my two sons to help out and work as cashiers on the bus, but they don't like it. They say that all their friends look down on them if they do it. So now it's me and Lupe who are doing everything. I tell you, this is unjust. I'm 47 [years old]. I worked hard all my life, including as a cleaner in Israel. I did it in order to send my children to university. But now I still have to work around the clock, and my children are not used to work hard so they don't help me. This is no work for an old couple, but what can we do? Ah?

On the weekend, Ángel invited me for lunch in his house. He introduced me to his wife, two sons, and daughter, and before we sat down at the table, Ángel showed me the house. He explained which parts of the house were built and renovated with the money he had sent from Israel. He also pointed out a new oven in the kitchen and a large TV set in the common room. In the common room one of the walls was damp, and Ángel told me that after the investment in the bus turned out to be much more costly than he had expected, they had no money to finish the new tiling of the roof. As a result, on rainy days, such as this Saturday, water came in through cracks in the old roof tiles and into the wall. "I know that this moisture is bad for the health, but there's nothing we can do about it right now," he grimly concluded.

From my conversation with Ángel's children during lunch that day, it was clear that they all had their minds set on emigration. Paulina, the eldest, was about to finish her bachelor's degree in business studies and was applying for a scholarship to go study English abroad, in the United States, U.K., or Australia. Paulina asked me if I thought she could find a job if she got to any of these countries as a student. I told her that often students were allowed to work for a certain amount of time, and she reacted by saying, "I want to earn enough money so that my parents won't need to work in the bus anymore." The two sons of Ángel were listening closely, as they were both planning to try their luck abroad. Joaquin, who just started studying industrial engineering at the university, said he was dreaming about working abroad for a multinational company, perhaps an oil refinery, while Carlito, the youngest son, who was still in high school, said he would go to work in the United States, perhaps even before going to university.

In Quito, Alejandro, another of the deportees I met in Ecuador, invested in putting up a small grocery shop at the ground floor of his parents' house in a low-class neighborhood on the outskirts of the city. Although the family could get by from the income that the shop generated, Alejandro was unemployed and was frantically looking for schemes to emigrate again. When Alejandro invited me to visit his home, Rosa, his warm and affectionate mother, received me in their ground-floor grocery shop. We sat down around an improvised table to drink a soda. After an hour, Rosa invited me to stay for dinner and said she was going to prepare a traditional dish especially for me. I thanked her and politely explained that I could not stay too long, as buses stop running to the city center after a certain hour. In return, Rosa instantly decided to shut the shop and hurried us all upstairs to the family kitchen. At one point, Rosa asked Alejandro to fetch her onions from the shop, and while he was gone she turned to me and whisperingly implored:

> You are a gentleman, Barak. You know that Alejandro is not doing well. He can't find his place here; he has problems. The only thing he wants is to emigrate again. To the U.S. or somewhere else, it doesn't matter where. I think that this is the only solution for him. Please help him. Just see if you can do something to help him. Thank you, Barak.

The one life strategy that most returnees that I met in Ecuador seemed to favor was a new immigration plan that would again take them away from their families and to a place where they believed that more money could be made.

In fact, many Latinos avoided a return home after they had been deported from Israel. Most flights leaving Israel with Latino deportees on board headed first to Spain, where passengers had to transfer to another airplane that would take them to the their country of origin. In the airport in Madrid, many Latino deportees escaped the transfer flight and exited the terminal as visitors to Spain.[9] As I heard from some of my informants in Israel, knowledge about the way to escape the transfer flight in Madrid was disseminated to many potential deportees who already had a clear plan to remain in Spain if they were to be deported from Israel.

In Spain, Latino deportees were back to square one. They needed to start life as undocumented migrants all over again. Although speaking Spanish, and having a certain cultural familiarity with the Spanish context, Latinos had to start at rock-bottom jobs and suffered severe discrimination from Spanish employers and society at large (see Campaña 2002). Some of the deportees I met in Spain were toying with the idea of re-entering Israel at a point in the future, "when the Israeli police will stop acting so crazy." However, I know of only one case where such a plan was carried out. As a rule, Latino deportees became increasingly interested in the possibility of legalizing their status in Spain.

In an evangelical church in Barcelona I met a number of my informants who were all deported from Israel and had now regrouped in Spain. Seeing them praying to God with their eyes closed and their rugged hands holding their Bibles tight against their chests was an emotional and upsetting moment for me. Here were they, a group of perpetual undocumented migrants who were forced to endure astounding hardship. They had to maintain a household on the run with minimal stability, either leaving their children behind or dragging them from one place in the world to another. They worked in the most downtrodden menial jobs at the margin of rich societies, with no legal protection. And most distressful of all, they always had to overcome the paralyzing fright that tomorrow all their efforts to settle and gain some stability and normalcy could be brought to an abrupt end by the local police.

The New Children of Israel: Legalizing the Status of Some Undocumented Migrants

From the first day of the deportation campaign against undocumented migrants, there were many non-hegemonic voices in Israel calling for its immediate abolition. Israeli NGOs, numerous journalists, artists, social activists, and even some politicians adamantly demanded that the government must stop what they often called the "manhunt" against non-Jewish workers. All protests against the actions of the Immigration Police underscored the moral obligation of Jews, given their own suffering from persecution and discrimination on racial and ethno-religious grounds, to treat the Other with respect and dignity.

The Center for Jewish Pluralism addressed an official letter to the government and the police chief of staff, calling for the abandonment of the advertisements against undocumented migrants on the radio and in newspapers, on the ground of alleged racial incitement. One member of Parliament, Yossi Sarid, wrote an open letter to the prime minister in which he protested against what he called "A cruel and intolerable manhunt that reminds us of the hunting down of Jews under dictatorial anti-Semitic regimes" (*Galey-Tzahal* 30.08.2003). A prominent Israeli journalist, artist, and opinion maker, Adam Baruch, published in the weekend edition of one of the most widely read newspapers in Israel his opinion on the campaign against undocumented migrants. Under the title "The campaign of the Immigration Police against foreign workers develops into a cultural, humane, and political horror," Baruch wrote:

> The ads on television against the foreigners become more and more violent. Foreign workers are presented as "the enemy of the nation." Their humanity becomes transparent, nonexistent. The fact that Israelis brought them here and exploit them is denied. The campaign pits the unemployed against the foreigner. The campaign presents as a traitor those who employ a foreign worker. Substitute in this campaign the word "Jew" in place of "foreign worker" and you get anti-Semitism. (*Maariv* 22.11.2002)

If words were not enough to condemn the woeful arrest and deportation of undocumented migrants in Israel, the Israeli filmmaker Ori Bar-On made a documentary in which he followed with a camera in the footsteps of the field agents of the Immigration Police. The film is titled *52/50*, after the number plates of the vans used by the Immigration Police, which all started with 52 and ended with 50. The film documents violent encounters between police agents and suspected undocumented migrants, and it gives a face to the thousands of non-Jewish migrants who suffered persecution in Israel.

Israeli NGOs tenaciously pressured the government to modify its deportation policy by using legal means to derail and appeal the deportation order that was enacted against arrested undocumented migrants. However, the government modified and compacted the legal procedure that led to deportation, and special courts now operated within detention centers, ruled on cases of arrested migrants within twenty-four hours, and also dealt instantly with appeals from Israeli NGOs (*Yediot Aharonot* 20.12.2001).

Calls to stop or alter the massive deportation campaign seemed to fall on the deaf ears of a determined Israeli government and resolute Immigration Police. Importantly, many of those who called on the government to act humanely in its treatment of undocumented migrants fell short of endorsing the desire of those migrants for a regularization of their status in Israel. Notably, in many of the above-mentioned calls, the protesters used the word "foreigner" to speak about undocumented migrants. Thus, many critics of the Israeli deportation policy felt the need to condemn the brutal actions of the Immigration Police, but they never questioned the very paradigmatic Israeli way of thinking under which undocumented migrants were not considered as potential members of the Israeli state. It was only when the issue of the Israeli-born children of undocumented migrants was brought to the forefront of the public debate that a more comprehensive call emerged for the government to legalize the status of undocumented migrant families and recognize them for who they were, that is, the new members of Israeli society.

In 2003, the Association for Civil Rights in Israel appealed in court against the interior minister on behalf of four children of undocumented migrants who had reached the age of eighteen. These children, who were born in Israel or raised there for most of their lives, had no official status in the country and were thus deportable. The appeal demanded that the four be given permanent resident status so that they could conduct normal lives and earn a living legally. The interior minister from the religious party Shas, Eli Yishai, who had to respond to this appeal, left the government in February 2003 after a political crisis led to changes in the coalition government. The newly appointed minister, Avraham Poraz, a member of the liberal secular party Shinui, publicly clarified his disagreement with the views of his predecessor: "Leniency in citizenship matters should not be based on religion and conversion but rather on contribution to society, identification with the Zionist enterprise or humanitarian reasons" (*Jerusalem Post* 21.05.2003). Particularly on the issue of undocumented migrants' children, Poraz unequivocally announced, "Those older than 17 are Israelis in every sense. I do not intend to deport them. They are only familiar with the state of Israel; they study in Israeli schools, take exams, and live the Israeli reality. There is no reason why we should deport them" (*Yediot Aharonot* 04.05.2003).

The Israeli media also kept promoting the case of undocumented migrants' children. For example, one extensive newspaper article depicted the bitter reality of these children and explicitly called for legalization of their status: "They look like Israelis, they act like Israelis, until at the age of 15 they get the first slap—no driving license. At 16 comes the second—no identity card, and at 18 the third—no army [recruitment]. From now on they are deportable. The children of undocumented migrants are waiting for Poraz [the Israeli interior minister at that time]" (*Haaretz* 16.05.2003). In the same newspaper article Poraz, who was working on a proposal for a reform in the treatment of undocumented migrants, condemned the current deportation policy: "It is cruel, vicious and inhumane to deport children who were born and raised here when they reach the age of 18." He then went on to draw a comparison with the situation in which Jews found themselves under Nazi Germany: "When Hitler came to power he wanted Jews to leave but no other country was willing to receive them. It is decidedly wrong for the Jewish nation to treat in this way other people."

NGOs organized street demonstrations in support of undocumented migrants and against the actions of the Immigration Police. In one such demonstration in September 2003, hundreds of Israelis, including some prominent artists and politicians, gathered in south Tel Aviv. They protested against the police's campaign and the declared intention to begin deporting families with children. People in the crowd carried posters with slogans such as "We are all children of migrants" and "No person is illegal." The demonstration received wide media coverage, and a few famous artists were interviewed for television channels and newspapers. Hava Alberstein, a famous singer, proclaimed:

Manhunt and deportation remind me of dark days, not so far back in time. If in other countries undocumented Jewish migrants were hunted and deported, all the Jewish communities would cry out and turn the world upside down. And all this [deportation campaign] is done under a false argument about our need to preserve our economy and culture. (*Yediot Aharonot* 03.09.2003)

A popular actress, filmmaker, and national icon, Gila Almagor, was equally robust when offering her opinion on the situation:

Every child needs to have a home, and I'm afraid for the fate of these children [of undocumented migrants]. These children have no other language, home or culture, where do we want them to go? Can you imagine Israeli children being deported from Los Angeles, what an outcry there would be about anti-Semitism? I want to be able to look at myself straight in the mirror at the end of my life, and that is why I came to protest here today. (ibid.)

In another demonstration in June 2004, children of undocumented migrants and their parents protested in front of the Israeli Parliament in Jerusalem. Waving posters with slogans such as "I do not have another country" and "Let us live in peace in our country," they called on the government and in particular on the interior minister, Avraham Poraz, to legalize their status in Israel.

In fact, Poraz made great efforts to promote his reform for the legalization of status for undocumented migrants' children and their families. Nevertheless, his efforts were frustrated time and again by officials in his own ministry as well as in other ministries. These officials can be considered "traditional intellectuals," as Antonio Gramsci (1971) defined them, who are responsible for historical continuity in spite of changing ruling groups and political parties. Gramsci criticized "traditional intellectuals" for being a conservative force in society, as they support the status quo with all of the injustices that are built into it. Poraz seemed to understand this dynamic when upon his appointment he declared his ambitions but qualified them by saying that "[a] governmental ministry is like an aircraft carrier. Until it changes its course it takes much time, especially since the [interior] ministry was controlled by religious parties since the 1950s" (*Haaretz* 10.11.2004). Yet, more than a year after his appointment, a journalist's investigation into the inability of Poraz to enforce his reforms concluded that "[o]fficials have executed until now an independent agenda of their own, and whenever they wanted they did not follow orders from the minister and even refrained from implementing regulations which he drafted" (ibid.).

Following a political crisis in government, Poraz left the interior ministry in December 2004 before he was able to secure approval for his new policy. However, Poraz managed to step up the public debate on the issue and bring about an official re-evaluation of the modalities for incorporation in Israel. His successor in the interior ministry, Ophir Pines, a member of the Labor Party, followed Poraz's footsteps. With the approval of Prime Minister Sharon, he convened a Special Parliamentary Committee with a mandate to modify Israel's immigration regime. Pines echoed Poraz when he set the agenda for the committee's work: "In line with the humanist Jewish approach, we are obliged to grant a legal status to children who were born here, speak the Hebrew language, became part of us, of Israeli society, and will serve in the IDF" (*Haaretz* 20.03.2005).

The Special Parliamentary Committee eventually recommended the legalization of certain undocumented migrants and their children. After many delays, in June 2005 the government approved a one-time decision to grant legal status leading to citizenship to undocumented migrants' children who were born in Israel and were now ten years old or older, went to Israeli schools, spoke Hebrew, identified with the state, and expressed their will to serve in the Israeli army. The government decision also stipulated the granting of legal status to children's parents and siblings who were not born in Israel.

Reactions to this historic decision were mixed. On the one hand, conservative voices such as that of the former interior minister Eli Yishai proclaimed:

> We are dealing with an outrage that is comparable to a Trojan horse in the heart of the Jewish glow. Pines [the current interior minister] thought that under this law he can insert a pipe bomb against the identity of the Jewish nation without being exposed. The day will come when this decision will turn out to be a mega terror act, as the Jewish character of the state will be wiped out. (*Arutz 7* 26.05.2005)

On the other hand, Israeli NGOs protested the restrictive criteria for legalization and accused officials in the interior ministry of providing the government with inaccurate data, from which it appeared that less limiting criteria would lead around three thousand children to be eligible for legalization, and together with their families the total number of legalized undocumented migrants would stand at around ten thousand (*Haaretz* 28.11.2004). NGOs provided different data, based on the records of municipalities, schools, and family and health clinics, which indicated that under the current criteria only a few dozen children of undocumented migrants would be legalized. They thus demanded that the age of children who were entitled to legalization be lowered to six, and that legalization not be conditioned upon having been born in Israel because some children of undocumented migrants were brought to Israel as toddlers. To pursue their case NGOs decided to appeal the government criteria in court with the representative case of a 15-year-old who was born in Colombia but was brought to Israel as a 3-year-old child. NGOs brought the teenager to the court, and his presence and argumentation in fluent Hebrew apparently affected the judges, who ordered the government to explain the rationale behind its criteria. In the meantime the court ordered that children of undocumented migrants and their parents would not be deported.

In December 2005, Interior Minister Ophir Pines apparently realized that NGOs were correct in their claims, as only 150 children applied for legalization of status under the government's plan. The minister thus advised the prime minister to moderate the criteria and lower the minimum age from ten to six (see *Haaretz* 04.12.2005). It took another half a year and a new interior minister to amend the criteria in a way that would allow for the legalization of more children. One of the first decisions of Ronnie Bar-On, a member of the center party Kadima, who in 2006 became the new interior minister, was to bring before the government an updated proposal that would legalize the status of undocumented migrants' children who entered the country before they were fourteen and have been living there for at least the last six years.

In June 2006, the decision was passed in government by a majority vote of 18 to 5. Those who opposed the new criteria, such as Nissan Slomiansky, a member of Parliament from the Mafdal religious party, warned that "the government adds more and more gentiles in a move that undoubtedly will hurt the Jewish character of the state." Yet, Prime Minister Ehud Olmert dismissed these voices when he declared:

> I wonder how fanatic and without compassion we can be. I managed the policy of expelling foreign workers from Israel, and it was not always done gently. But the question of children constitutes a highly humanist issue, and that is how we should consider it. I, too, am concerned for the Jewish character of Israel, but these numbers [of undocumented migrants' children and their families] pose no danger to it. (*Maariv* 18.06.2006)

Arguably, Prime Minister Ehud Olmert realized what Etienne Balibar (1991: 60) argued when he discussed the counterintuitive outcome of racist nationalism: "By seeking to circumscribe the common essence of nationals, racism thus inevitably becomes involved in the obsessional quest for a 'core' of authenticity that cannot be found, shrinks the category of nationality and de-stabilizes the historical nation."

The government decision was this time applauded by Israeli NGOs, who stated that it would finally bring to a conclusion the situation of undocumented migrant families in Israel. Several newspaper articles celebrated the government decision by interviewing children of undocumented migrants who were now legalized under the new criteria. One such article, entitled "Finally I can feel Israeli," brought the story of Angelina Castigo, a 16-year-old who had arrived in Israel from Colombia ten years before. Angelina told about the fright that permeated the life of her family, as her parents were both arrested several times by the Immigration Police but were always eventually released because of Angelina and her 8-year-old brother. Angelina also told about the fear of visiting her grandparents in Colombia, knowing that they might never be able to re-enter Israel once they left it. "Now I feel that we will be free of all this." She celebrated her new status: "I want to thank the Interior Minister from the bottom of my heart, and the whole government that decided on this. I extend an enormous gratitude in my name and in the name of all the children" (*Maariv* 18.06.2006).

"The show is over," the agent of the Immigration Police told me in 2003 as I contemptuously remained watching how he and his colleague shoved a suspected undocumented migrant, whom they had just aggressively apprehended on the street, into a patrol car. In a way, in 2006, after the updated and celebrated decision of the government to legalize certain undocumented migrant families, the show was indeed over. In subsequent months and years the situation of non-Jewish undocumented migrants in Israel receded into the margins of the public debate, until it practically disappeared. In Israel, where public debate often fails to catch up with the intensity and quantity of events unfolding on the ground, many other issues took priority over this matter. A consensus prevailed that the case of undocumented migrants in Israel was by and large resolved. Even NGOs now prioritized, perhaps rightly so, the case of political refugees from Sudan who entered Israel from Egypt, and the trafficking of prostitutes into Israel from Eastern Europe.

Former undocumented migrants were left to enjoy their legal status and deal with the new reality—a reality that saw most of their relatives and friends deported, their communities dissolved, and their recreational and spiritual venues shut down. Traumatized parents and children were starting anew their life in Israel. Perhaps it was the incredible hardship that they had endured in Israel for many years that earned them their new identity as Israelis.

Chapter Eight

Conclusion

A New Assimilation?

Nur das ganze ist das wahre.
(Only the whole is the truth.)

—*Friedrich Hegel*

All access to the universal is through
the particular.

—*Philip Bock*

Thousands of Latinos who settled down in Israel in the mid-1990s can be said to have become Israelis. This is the case because Latinos championed the accumulation of practical national belonging as their primary life strategy in Israel. They strove for the kind of cultural assimilation that facilitated their de facto integration into Israeli society. A de facto integration into Israeli society meant better employment opportunities, prolonged settlement, formation of families, and a positive evaluation of children's embeddedness in Israeli society. The Israeli resolution that led to the legalization of selected undocumented migrant families with children, and that was passed by a clear majority vote in government, was based on a moral understanding that the state should incorporate as citizens those children who lived in Israel for more than six years, went to Israeli schools, spoke Hebrew, identified with the state, and expressed their will to serve in the Israeli army. According to these criteria, the majority of Latino children and their families would have been legalized. Nevertheless, only a few hundred Latinos eventually received the official recognition of the Israeli state and became Israeli citizens. Most Latinos were deported by the Immigration Police, or chose to leave Israel in the period of massive deportations that shattered their lives as undocumented migrants.

The desire of Latinos to root their lives in Israel illustrates the intensive way in which migratory trajectories could develop around very rudimentary connections.

The rapid expansion of undocumented migration between Latin America and Israel is explained partly by highlighting the migratory disposition of lower- and middle-class people in emigration regions in Latin America. These people experienced the powerful impact of different dynamics of migration on their physical and mental environment. As a result, they became not only conscious of, but also involuntarily disposed toward, international migration. Having acquired a migratory disposition, many Latinos were ready to emigrate even to a distant, unknown, and intimidating destination such as Israel.

Yet once they were in Israel, the efforts by Latinos to achieve an advanced degree of cultural assimilation precipitated positive feedback from Israelis and facilitated daily interactions between the two groups. Positive feedback from Israelis communicated a message of social acceptance that emotionally compounded Latinos' desire to belong. The evidence presented in this book indicates that debates focusing predominantly on the utilitarian character of migrants' life strategies are one-sided at best, deeply misleading at worst. We should not discount the effect that reception by members in the host society might have on migrants' emotional states and stamina. Migrants forcefully deal with the predicament of displacement, but this "deal with" is always already impacted fundamentally by the relational whole in which they find themselves. While hostility from the host society increases closure among migrant groups, openness and cooperation positively boost migrants' aspirations and efforts toward cultural incorporation. The accumulation of practical national belonging should thus also be considered from this relational and holistic perspective.

Latinos in Israel sought cultural assimilation both as an instrumental tactic and as a substantive resource. It made sense in terms of their economic futures and it felt right—on a pre-discursive, visceral level—in various everyday situations. We should thus conclude that Latinos both actively engaged in, and found themselves drifting toward, the accumulation of practical national belonging. This form of fellowship yielded significant economic, social, and emotional improvements for their position as undocumented migrants.

The tension that undocumented migrants constantly dealt with in managing their identity in different situations could become harmful. This led many Latinos in Israel to internalize their desire for belonging to such extent that it became "second nature" (Elias 1994 [1939]). Accumulating practical national belonging not only as a calculated and conscious strategy, but also as an embodied and intuitively desired state of being, significantly reduces the mental costs that are involved in the pursuit of this goal. In other words, Latinos' strategic choice to accumulate practical national belonging was reinforced and compounded by its subconscious embodiment. With time, and due to countless signals both sent and received, many Latinos started genuinely to feel that they belonged in Israel.

The fact that Latinos prioritized cultural assimilation more than other undocumented migrant groups in Israel is a configurational outcome of their interactions with Israelis. Latinos first became cognizant of the usefulness of this strategy when they learned that their phenotypical appearance did not cause them to stick out in an Israeli crowd. We should not discount the importance of phenotypical appearance in partly determining the socio-emotional interactions between migrants and dominant national groups. Latinos accumulated practical national belonging in order to further their "invisibility" as undocumented migrants and enhance the comfort of "passing" as Israelis. The accumulation of practical national belonging thus had a double impact on Latinos' positions and dispositions. On the one hand, it enhanced their phenotypical and cultural "invisibility" in public places. On the other hand, it rendered Latinos recognizable and sympathetic in the eyes of Israeli citizens who encountered them in particular settings. Israelis appreciated Latinos as workers, neighbors, clubbers, lovers, football players, and friends, and even as potential loyal citizens of Israel.

What's the Difference between Jewish and Undocumented Migrants?

In many ways the situation of Latinos in Israel is comparable to that of Jewish immigrants, especially Sephardic ones, who arrived in Israel in the 1950s and 1960s. These Jewish immigrants were assimilated into the Ashkenazi dominant national group via a forceful "melting pot" policy. They were given Israeli names, taught the Hebrew language, accommodated in poor neighborhoods, socialized into what was perceived to be distinctively Israeli "culture," and integrated into the national labor market in subordinated positions (see Elazar 1989).

Of course, the one crucial difference between Jewish immigrants and Latinos is their legal and social status in Israel. While the immigration of Jews was assisted and welcomed by Israel, the immigration of Latinos and other undocumented migrants was carried out independently of the state. Unlike the Jewish newcomers, non-Jewish migrant workers were defined as undesired outsiders if not as outright threats. Although this is a fundamental principle of division in the Jewish state, I would like to suspend it for a moment, and pursue four important similarities further. First, almost all Jewish immigrants suffered at least initially from social and to some degree institutional discrimination in Israel. Members of each new group of Jewish immigrants had to accommodate themselves in Israeli society, by overcoming stigmas and prejudice about their habits and "culture." The most recent reminder of this prevalent dynamic was given by the incorporation of Jewish immigrants from Ethiopia in the 1980s. Ethiopian Jews have suffered much discrimination in Israeli schools and hospitals, and they were sometimes objected to as fellow neighbors by veteran Israelis (Ojanuga 1993). In other words, being included as a member in the Jewish state provides no automatic immunity from social dynamics of exclusion and discrimination. At the same time, as in the case of Latinos, being excluded from the state does not necessarily deny migrants the opportunity to become socially accepted by the dominant national group.

Second, the fact that the Israeli state supported their immigration often helped Jewish newcomers very little in a practical sense of building their new lives in the country and becoming fully integrated into society. Similarly, but in a reversed way, the fact that the Israeli state rejected their immigration often meant very little for the ability of undocumented migrants to settle down, form families, and enjoy a de facto integration into Israeli society. In other words, it is almost a truism that the rhetoric of the state is not always accompanied by concrete policy measures that ensure its realization.

Third, both Jewish and Latino immigrants shun political mobilization to advance their narrow group interests in Israel. Although there were a few attempts to form political parties that would promote the interests of a group of Jewish immigrants from a specific country, these undertakings were always condemned for their separatist design, and they never succeeded in mobilizing supporters, not even from their "natural" constituencies, which always preferred to vote for one of the mainstream national parties. Latinos tried twice to organize politically, but their attempts were suppressed by the Israeli police. Fearing police action, most Latinos preferred the "quiet" accumulation of practical national belonging over the "noisy" mobilization of a political movement. Latinos were worried that their positive public image among many Jewish Israelis would be damaged if they were associated with a movement that confronted, and allegedly weakened, the state of Israel.

Finally, both Jewish and Latino immigrants desired a degree of cultural assimilation to what they perceived to be the dominant national group in Israel, albeit not in a totalizing fashion that obliterated any sign of the cultural characteristics with which they arrived in the country. But here we can no longer bracket the clear differences in the position of these two groups. Jewish migrants in Israel, like most legal migrants elsewhere in the world, often have to pass tests that prove their "belonging" to the nation-state. They are also offered, or indeed forced to accept, assistance from the state to facilitate their integration into different spheres, for example, linguistic, economic, and educational. In contrast, undocumented migrants are not expected to integrate into the society of their host state. On the contrary, undocumented migrants are discouraged and sometimes actively prevented by states from taking part in the social and civic life of the nation. Indeed, it is the express desire of states that undocumented migrants remain a distinctive, non-integrated Other who will eventually (be forced to) leave the country.

As a host state, Israel clearly discriminates immigrants according to ethno-religious criteria. Internationally recognized (UN Resolution 1947) and legally established (the Declaration of Independence 1948) as a Jewish state, Israel has as its declared purpose and aspiration to serve as a "home" for Jews worldwide. Israel unreservedly insists on what it defines to be its Jewish character. This is explicit at all the symbolic and institutional levels of the state, its laws, and its political and educational system. Both the state of Israel and the Jewish majority of its citizens associate national membership with partaking in a normative project.

Against the backdrop of an official rejection by the Jewish state, and despite their undocumented status, this study has highlighted the specifically constrained yet creative efforts of many Latinos to achieve a de facto socialization into Israeli society. Even among non-Jewish immigrants in Israel, a sense of belonging can grow organically from below through unmediated interactions, rather than be devised from above by the state. This indicates that bridging and binding transactions between natives and newcomers do not need to be either devised or condoned by the state. In fact, since undocumented migrants are condemned to an illegal status by states' modalities of incorporation, they often strive more intensely than legal migrants to accumulate practical national belonging. Latinos' persistent strivings to accumulate practical national belonging clearly highlight the importance of this practice for their life strategies. On the other hand, Jewish immigrants from the former Soviet Union, who enjoy an automatic legal status in Israel, have followed a communitarian tendency and often have insisted ardently on the preservation of their own "culture" (Siegel 1996).

We need, therefore, to do a bit of theoretical fine-tuning. The notion of practical national belonging has been conceived by Ghassen Hage (1998) and employed by other scholars to capture the underlying social dynamics that shape the situation of legal migrants, who are increasingly expected to integrate into their host societies. Yet, this notion is clearly also applicable to undocumented migrants. Excluded from the official domain of the nation-state, undocumented migrants are often also left outside the scope of theoretical debates about migrants' integration in host states. This is undeniably another powerful testimony for the pervasiveness of "methodological nationalism." While such methodological nationalism clearly serves the interests of nation-states, it is often detrimental to the pursuit of an overall understanding of migration-related processes. Most evidently, by independently settling down and establishing transnational networks, undocumented migrants subvert the integrality of the state. Whether successful or not in the final analysis, their coping strategies highlight the limits of the institutional and bureaucratic power of the state to determine, define, and control migrants' integration into another nation.

A critique of methodological nationalism should not be confused with an assumption that the role of the nation-state is necessarily declining when it comes to migration-related processes. This was evident in Israel, where most Jewish Israelis believe that Israel must vigilantly preserve its Jewish character. Accordingly, whatever undermines the perceived Jewish character of Israel is identified as a threat to its national security. This peculiarity helps explain Israel's ability to design and carry out massive deportation campaigns that managed to distance more than 150,000 undocumented migrants from the country.

The empirically based critique of "methodological nationalism" presented here should not draw our attention away from the specificities of the Israeli case. These particularities were and for the foreseeable future will continue to be critical for determining the position of all types of migrants in the Jewish state. The value of this critique lies in its ability to elucidate and treat the interdependent changes taking place inside and outside nation-states, inside and outside what are often constructed as disjunct populations. This critique implies a more balanced and holistic approach, that is, to the changing properties of nation-states and the subjectivities of people living in them.

Easing away from methodological nationalism and recrafting the notion of practical belonging as we have done implies more than just an epistemological shift. It also requires a moral reorientation. In making this shift we prioritize the lived realities of vulnerable people over both the letter of the law and the tidy-looking statistics found in droves of official reports. This at once cognitive and emotional reorientation comes along with openness to the following finding: undocumented migrants who live, work, and raise families for years in host societies are, in many cases, de facto members of those societies, and they should be treated analytically as such by social scientists. Academic fields are to some extent autonomous. Working together and challenging each other's bedrock assumptions, scholars are capable of at least a modicum of reflexivity. To a degree we can therefore resist the inclination to rely on and further legitimize states' (symbolically violent) schemes of classification even as we investigate the roles they play in migratory processes.

Non-Jewish undocumented migrants penetrated the bastion of Israel's exclusionary ethno-religious logic. Such penetration was inconceivable only a few years ago. When it occurred it was largely perceived in Israel as nothing less than a "revolution." Yet exceptional as our case may be, this move by the Israeli state is by no means unique. Several nation-states have launched amnesties and other programs for the legal incorporation of undocumented migrants who had been living in their territory for a lengthy period of time. But what motivated most states to move in this direction was a mixture of economic interests, a fear of an increase in criminality among undocumented migrants, and an external pressure to abide by an emerging global discourse of human rights. Israel has been partly influenced by similar considerations. The fact that undocumented migrants proved to be law-abiding and productive workers in Israel strengthened the secular idea that they merited inclusion. Yet, it was clearly the cultural assimilation of undocumented migrants that impacted Israeli politicians.

The Israeli criteria for legalization of status specifically referred to individuals "whose deportation from Israel would constitute a cultural expulsion." In other words, the Israeli resolution effectively benefited those undocumented migrants who had accumulated practical national belonging and thereby managed for years to avoid deportation. These were, we might say, the new Israelis who formed families and encouraged the integration of their children into Israeli society. The formal inclusion of non-Jewish migrants in the state of Israel clearly marks a move toward the incorporation of increased "cultural particularities" under the Jewish state. I do not claim that the accumulation of practical national belonging by undocumented migrants somehow inevitably forced Israel to legalize their status. Yet it occurred only because of a prevailing Israeli perception that members in the incorporated group of undocumented migrants had acquired—on a practical level—a significant identification with the state and increased "cultural" similarity to the dominant national group.

Since these changes in Israel are linked to dynamics well beyond any one nation-state, there may well be conclusions to be drawn from this case. These conclusions contribute directly to a wider understanding of undocumented migration processes, and the challenges posed by the accumulation of practical national belonging to the increasingly normative adumbrations of membership in nation-states.

The National Belonging of Undocumented Migrants: Inclusion through the Back Door

Elie Wiesel, a Jewish writer and political activist who survived the Nazi concentration camps, once said that "[t]he opposite of love is not hate, it's indifference." Paraphrasing Wiesel, who won the Nobel Peace Prize for his contribution to the advancement of human dignity in the world, I would like to suggest that in the relation between modern nation-states and immigrants, the opposite of exclusion is not inclusion, it's belonging. Take for example the Nuremberg Laws, which in 1935 stripped Jews of their citizenship under Nazi Germany. The Nuremberg Laws were based on the pseudoscientific understanding that Jews constituted a separate race that did not belong to, and contaminated, the German Aryan nation. It was not that the formal exclusion of Jews created anti-Semitic feelings among German citizens about the non-belonging of Jews; but rather it was the reverse: a heightened national sentiment of anti-Semitic rejection led to the formal exclusion of Jews. One can hardly believe, yet it stands to reason, that had Jews still enjoyed formal inclusion as citizens in Germany, they would have escaped atrocious executions even after they were dehumanized by Nazi propaganda as not belonging.

It is for this reason that the question of belonging, both formal and practical, is pivotal in any assessment of the position of migrant and other minority groups in the nation-state. Today there is a widespread dissatisfaction in liberal states with the implementation of multiculturalism. Conservative voices push back for the "cultural-ization" of citizenship and the re-ethnicization of the nation (Castles and Davidson 2000). In a backlash against perceived "failing" multicultural regimes of incorpora-tion, migrants are nowadays increasingly expected to integrate "culturally" into their host society. Yet unlike a political definition of membership, which can follow pure bureaucratic criteria, one's belonging to the nation is not only a highly subjective matter, but also one that is difficult for the state to quantify and control for.

A marked shift from multiculturalism to a more assimilative model of integration has been documented in the United States as well as in most European countries (e.g., Todd 1994, Alba and Nee 1997, Joppke 1999, Koopmans and Statham 2000, Brubaker 2001). What we witness, according to Brubaker (2001), is not a return to the organic form of assimilation, which implied full absorption and insensitively homogenizing state projects. Instead, there are increasing demands for a more abstract form of assimilation that stresses a "normative and analytical concern with the nature and extent of emerging similarities" (Brubaker 2001: 534). Thus, while in its old form, assimilation was "a matter of either/or," in its new form, the stress is on "becoming similar *in certain respects*" (ibid.; italics in the original). What Brubaker thus high-lights is the emergence of a firmer demand in host states for migrants to accumulate practical national belonging. The observable tilt toward this "new assimilation" leads many nation-states whose political regimes are allegedly predicated on universal lib-eral principles to define their national and "cultural" particularities with greater precision than before. Redrawing the boundaries for integration around cultural and emotional belonging rather than formal status is clearly meant to tackle the noncon-formist position of certain groups of legal migrants. This redrawing of the boundaries is often tied to an additional call for a more robust attempt to keep away and prevent the settlement of undocumented migrants.

Yet by defining belonging substantively, and essentially using cultural norms and values, nation-states might face an unintended consequence of opening a back door for the incorporation of certain undocumented migrants. Using a mixture of camou-flage, cultural mimicry, learning processes, and strategies to transform available capi-tals, undocumented migrants can accumulate practical national belonging to a degree that renders them de facto integrated into the society where they reside. This process is challenging for nation-states that wish to reject the legal inclusion of such embed-ded undocumented migrants. The case of undocumented migrants in Israel might indicate a reversal in the process of membership acquisition in nation-states, that is, that the accumulation of practical national belonging precedes, and possibly leads to, the acquisition of citizenship.

The same dynamics, which significantly shaped the settlement of undocumented migrants in Israel, are found in many other nation-states: an unofficial tolerance of the presence of undocumented migrants by both states' officials and many ordinary citizens; an "implementation deficit" that obstructs the effectiveness of repressive polices; and a growing commitment to, and accountability for, a regime of human rights. Already twenty years ago some scholars addressed the emergence of an "informal social contract" between host societies and undocumented migrants (Schuck and Smith 1985, Chavez 1992). More recently, attention has been given to undocumented migrants' "effective" citizenship, which points to the legal aspects of what allows undocumented migrants to claim recognition and rights by virtue of prolonged residence (Sassen 2002). Related to this tendency is the marked move by most liberal Western states to include in their migration regimes the notion of *ius domicili*, that is, a set of prerequisites that immigrants have to fulfill in order to receive some kind of a permanent status in their host country (Faist 2000).

Based on the Israeli experience, we can conjecture that the accumulation of practical national belonging will increasingly shape the popular and legal battles over naturalization, recognition, and the de facto socialization of undocumented migrants. Increasingly, the question will become how democratic Western states react to claims of recognition based on de facto integration into host societies and conformity with what is discussed in terms of the normative project of the state.

The state of Israel "gave in" and incorporated some undocumented non-Jewish migrants roughly a decade after they first arrived in its territory in the mid-1990s. Acknowledging the variety of factors that led Israeli politicians to grant some undocumented migrants a legal status, I wish to highlight another important element, usually left out of the analysis. By insisting on constructing culturally assimilated undocumented migrants as Others, the state of Israel increasingly ran the risk of unveiling the feeble nature of its ethno-religious makeup. The Israeli media increasingly began to question the refusal of the state to recognize undocumented migrants who, to paraphrase one newspaper headline, "look like Israelis, talk like Israelis, behave like Israelis, and have the same feeling of belonging to Israel." Such a development, as some Israeli politicians undoubtedly realized, could potentially be more detrimental to the foundations of the Jewish state than the inclusion of a few thousand undocumented migrants. In this sense, the case of Israel and its internationally recognized ethno-religious criteria of immigration and exclusion may offer the clearest indication of what is to come in normatively based nation-state projects around the world.

NOTES

1. Introduction

1. Keeping my promise to all my informants, I use pseudonyms throughout the book. This also applies to the names of children. However, I use only Israeli names for Latinos' children who were given typical Israeli names by their parents. It was a common practice among Latinos to give their Israeli-born children typical Israeli names.

2. I use the term "Latino" throughout this book to refer to undocumented migrants who reached Israel from different countries in Latin America. Although problematic, this term was commonly used during my fieldwork in Israel by undocumented migrants, officials in Israeli state institutions, academics, Israeli journalists, and the public. Jews who immigrate to Israel from Latin American countries are not called "Latinos"; instead they are referred to, according to their specific country of origin, for example, as "Jewish Argentineans" or simply as "Argentineans."

3. See for example Nurit Wurgaft's book *Open the Door, Police!* and her many journalistic reports in *Haaretz;* films such as *James' Journey to Jerusalem,* directed by Ra'anan Alexandrowicz, or *Paper Dolls,* directed by Tomer Heymann; the exhibition of photos taken by undocumented migrants' children, which was organized by the activist group ActiveVision.

4. I use "culture" in quotation marks to indicate that I do not refer to the term as a singular, static, immutable noun. Instead, like others (Portes and Zhou 1993, Favell 2000, Brubaker 2001), I conceptualize cultural assimilation by different individual migrants or groups as being determined by different perceived notions of the native "core culture."

5. My first and most extensive period of fieldwork among Latinos in Israel was from October 2001 to July 2002. In October 2002 and from December 2002 to January 2003, I conducted two more fieldtrips to Israel, each one month long. From May to July 2003 I spent two months in Ecuador visiting returnees (or better put, deportees) in four major cities: Quito, Cuenca, Guayaquil, and Loja. In November 2004, I spent one month in Spain among Latinos who settled down in Madrid and Barcelona after they had been deported from Israel. Being an Israeli migrant in the Netherlands, between March 2003 and September 2005 I visited Israel six times, each time for around two weeks. On all these visits I met with my informants (who were by that time friends), and discussed with them their developing situation and plans for the future.

6. My initial hesitation to associate myself with an Israeli institution was probably warranted. I later saw how most Latinos avoided contact even with the most supportive Israeli NGOs. Those who did ask for help from NGOs usually refused to disclose details

about their personal situation in Israel, or simply lied about them, as I witnessed when I accompanied some of them to these meetings on their request.

7. For a more comprehensive theoretical discussion of my position and positioning during fieldwork see Kalir 2006.

2. Unsettling Setting

1. This last sanction was never mentioned in contracts as it contradicted basic civil and human rights and could never withstand a legal appeal; nevertheless, it was informally mentioned to guest workers and enforced by employers and the government (see Pilovsky 1999).

2. Israel adheres to the principle of *ius sanguinis*, qualifying the incorporation of immigrants by an ethnic belonging to what Zionism has redefined as the Jewish nation. This redefinition is first and foremost religiously based on a matriarchal system, whereby one's Jewishness is exclusively determined by the Jewishness of one's mother. Nevertheless, Israel additionally grants citizenship to non-Jewish children and spouses of Jewish men. Under some circumstances, even non-Jewish grandchildren of Jewish men are legally allowed to immigrate to Israel.

3. After its independence in 1948, a massive immigration of Jews largely from countries in the Middle East and North Africa reached the newly formed state. This latter group of Jews became known as "Sephardim" (or "Mizrahim," which literally means "Orientals") in distinction from the majority groups of European Jews that are referred to as "Ashkenazim." In the newly created ethnic hierarchy of Israel, and for decades to come, Ashkenazim occupied most positions in the primary labor market, while Sephardim mainly filled jobs in the secondary labor market (Smooha 1978, Lewin-Epstein and Semyonov 1986, Ben-Rafael and Sharot 1991).

4. The "binding contract" was initially designed in the 1950s to regulate the employment of foreign experts, at a time when Israel desperately needed their assistance in developing its national infrastructure as well as its industrial and technological sectors. Since free market forces and economic opportunities, which might have naturally attracted foreign skilled labor, were paralyzed by the impossibility of non-Jewish immigration to Israel, it became crucial for Israel to create a mechanism for the importation of non-Jewish temporary employees. A restrictive scheme was devised in order to protect young local industries in their relation with foreign experts, whose badly needed human capital put them in a significant power position. Binding foreign experts to an exclusive Israeli employer was meant to curtail experts' power to negotiate better working conditions by using market competition between local companies and employers. However, this mechanism was never meant to regulate a massive influx of unskilled labor. Israeli employers faced a seemingly infinite supply of unskilled labor from abroad and were never dependent on a particular worker who could pressure them for higher salaries. Employers could easily replace unskilled guest workers, whose own resignation carried little harm.

5. In 2006, the law was amended to allow recruitment companies to charge guest workers a fee of up to US$700.

6. For more on the ill-treatment of seriously injured guest workers and the deficient coverage of their insurance policies, see Kav La'Oved, newsletters May 1998 and March 1999; also *Haaretz* 09.05.1997.

7. A survey by the Ministry of Labor (2001) found that many undocumented migrants took on the jobs of undocumented Palestinians: 28% of all undocumented migrants worked as domestic servants; 13% were employed in hotels, restaurants, and other tourism related jobs; and 5% worked in manufacturing. The other 48% were employed in the construction sector, but these were mainly former legal guest workers who continued working after becoming undocumented.

8. A growing elderly population, a lack of geriatric institutions, and the high costs of hospitalizing disabled people all induced the government to allow families to import a caregiver on their own account. In some cases the government also subsidized the expenses of needy families that could not pay for it (see Ministry of Labor 2002b).

9. Many of the smuggled migrants were women from Eastern Europe who were misled by criminal organizations, which promised them a legal permit to work in Israel as secretaries or cleaners, but instead forced them to work as prostitutes in Israeli sex clubs. Much has been written about this appalling phenomenon in the Israeli media, and official reports were also prepared by NGOs and government departments (see, for example, Hotline for Migrant Workers 2003).

10. An unofficial policy of permissible undocumented migration to ensure a ready supply of labor to sectors in the national economy was found among many Western countries (cf. Zolberg 1990, Jones-Correa 1998).

11. The new arrangement still contained serious shortcomings as was widely outlined in a special article in *Haaretz* 26.01.2004.

12. For an extensive article that scrutinizes the government's changes and their limitation see *Haaretz* 09.12.2002.

13. In Germany, for example, in 1971 after the importation of guest workers was in full swing, an opinion poll showed that "Gastarbeiter" came after "Drug addicts" in a ranking of "People you would not like as neighbors" (Kastoryano 2002: 66).

14. Since such marriages lead to the legalization of the spouse's status in Israel, we should acknowledge that there were possibly at least some fraudulent marriages performed for the purpose of gaining legal status.

3. Destiny and Destination

1. Obviously, there may have been more initial connections of which I am not aware. Yet the fact remains that all connections between Israel and countries in Latin America were embryonic and limited from an international migration perspective.

2. The term "evangelicalism" is broadly defined; it generally refers to "born-again" or "reborn" Christians, and it encompasses various Christian denominations, such as the Assemblies of God, the Church of Christ, Southern Baptists, the Methodist Episcopal Church, the Presbyterian Church in America, and some Pentecostal churches.

3. *Migration and Globalisation* was published in 2002 by three parties: the Ecuadorian Episcopal conference, the Department for Human Mobility, and the United Nations Refugee Agency.

4. In Ecuador it cost in 2003 around US$12,500 to contract the service of a *coyote* for getting to the United States. It is a high price in a country where the average monthly salary is around US$120.

4. Shifting Strategies

1. I choose not to reveal the name of the famous Israeli who employed Vicente in his house.

2. Subsequently, since 2004 roughly, videoconference via the Internet has replaced the exchange of videocassettes.

3. For security reasons, all residential buildings in Israel have underground cemented basements, spacious enough to house residents in times of war. In practice, most basements in Tel Aviv are crammed, decayed, and used mainly for storage of residents' old furniture.

4. In 2003, as part of its even harsher line against undocumented migrants, the state of Israel abolished undocumented migrants' right to these social benefits.

5. See *The Encompassment of the Compulsory Education Law on Children of Undocumented Migrants* (Ministry of Education 2000).

6. Interestingly, at Bialik, Amira, who believed in a multicultural form of integration, insisted that Muslim pupils would receive the Qur'an and Christian pupils the New Testament.

5. Divisive Dynamics

1. For an account of the Latino recreational scene in Israel narrated by a Venezuelan migrant, see Lovera 1997.

6. The Religious Forms of Undocumented Lives

1. Although Israeli authorities never officially acknowledged it, Israel might have been careful and tolerant in its treatment of Christian churches because of the implication for the larger political ties between powerful evangelical ministries (mainly in the U.S.) and the state of Israel.

2. Throughout the chapter I use the term "evangelical" as an encompassing category that includes also Pentecostalism. Latino churches in south Tel Aviv were defined as "evangelical" by the Latino pastors who led them. Moreover, members in Latino evangelical churches referred to one another, and were called by other Latinos, *evangelistas* (or also *Cristianos*—a popular Latino term for "evangelicals").

3. Given the historical tension between the state of Israel and the Catholic Church, and knowing the position of Israel on the issue of non-Jewish undocumented migrants, it could very well be that Catholic priests in Israel felt uncomfortable about playing a too prominent and visible role in the organization of undocumented migrants.

4. While Latinos established ten different evangelical churches, African migrants founded more than forty Pentecostal churches (Sabar 2004). Filipino migrants also instituted a few evangelical churches, and Romanian migrants set up an Adventist congregation (see *Haaretz* 14.04.2002 and 07.03.2003). In 1998 a Chinese evangelical church was established in Tel Aviv (Kalir 2009).

5. See Sabar 2004 for a discussion of similar expressions of hostility against Arabs among undocumented African migrants who attended evangelical churches in Israel.

6. I do not want to disclose the name of the specific country he came from.

7. Israeli Resolution, Latino Disillusion

1. Israel had previously imprisoned undocumented migrants in ordinary jails as if they were criminals. Only after the interventions of NGOs were alternative civil detention centers created for them.

2. The most recent example was Sharon's ability in 2005 to evacuate all Jewish settlers from the Gaza strip despite fierce ideological resistance and many logistical difficulties.

3. While police brutality against undocumented migrants had been practiced since the first deportation campaign was launched in 1996, the scale of operations by the Immigration Police from 2002 led to the intensification and exacerbation of these practices.

4. Interview with Natalia Leiber, available online at http://kedma-edu.org.il/main/site New/index.php?page=112&action=sidLink&stId=173 (visited on 30.04.2008)

5. Yitzhak Rabin and Ehud Barak served as the army chief of staff before stepping into politics and ending up at the highest post. Two other prime ministers, Menachem Begin and Yitzhak Shamir, were both top commanders in pre-state underground military organizations, which fought against the Arabs and the British mandate rule of Palestine for an independent state. Shimon Peres was the head of the Israeli Navy and later the director general of the ministry of defense. Benjamin Netanyahu served in an elite army unit of which his brother, Yonatan Netanyahu, was the legendary commander (he was killed during the famous Entebbe operation). For more on the military-society relations in Israel, see Levy 2003.

6. These demographic concerns compelled Israel never to agree to the "right of return" of Palestinians into the pre-1967 Israeli borders. More recently, in 2003 it led Israel to amend its Entrance Law to prevent family reunifications of Palestinian citizens of Israel who marry Palestinians from outside Israel, so that this could not serve to further increase the population of Palestinian Israelis.

7. While Jewish immigrants are called in Israel *Olim* (the biblical word for "ascenders"), Jewish Israeli emigrants are called *Yordin*, a term that literally means "descenders" and is not used in the Bible but is adopted in Israel to slander those who choose to "leave Israel behind."

8. There were numerous terror incidents in public places, mostly perpetrated by Palestinian suicide bombers, of which non-Jewish migrants were the fatal victims.

9. Until 2004 citizens of most Latin American countries were not required to hold a visa for entering Spain.

BIBLIOGRAPHY

Alba, R., and V. Nee. 1997. Rethinking Assimilation Theory for a New Era of Immigration. *International Migration Review* 31, 4: 826–74.

Alexander, M. 2003. Host-Stranger Relations in Rome, Tel Aviv, Paris and Amsterdam: A Comparison of Local Policies toward Labour Migrants. Ph.D. thesis, University of Amsterdam.

Al-Haj, M., and E. Leshem. 2000. *Immigrants from the Former Soviet Union in Israel*. University of Haifa: Centre for Multiculturalism and Education Research.

Al-Haj, M. and H. Rosenfeld. 1990. *Arab Local Government in Israel*. Boulder, Colo.: Westview Press.

Anderson, B. 1983. *Imagined Communities: Reflections on the Origin and Spread of Nationalism*. London: Verso.

Appadurai, A. 1996. *Modernity at Large: Cultural Dimensions of Globalization*. Minneapolis: University of Minnesota Press.

———. 2002. Disjuncture and Difference in the Global Cultural Economy. In *The Anthropology of Globalization*, ed. J. X. Inda and R. Rosaldo, 46–64. Oxford: Blackwell.

Association for Civil Rights in Israel. 1997. *Annual Report*. (Hebrew). Jerusalem.

Bade, J. K. 2004. Legal and Illegal Immigration into Europe: Experiences and Challenges. *European Review* 12: 339–375.

Bailey, T. 1987. *Immigrant and Native Workers: Contrasts and Competition*. Boulder, Colo.: Westview Press.

Balibar, E. 1991. Is There a "Neo-Racism"? In *Race, Nation, Class: Ambiguous Identities*, ed. E. Balibar and I. Wallerstein, 17–28. London: Verso.

Bank of Israel. 2000. Press Release. (Hebrew). December.

Barak, A. 1994. *Interpretation in Law*. Vol. 3: *Constitutional Interpretation*. Jerusalem: Nevo.

Bartram, D. 1998. Foreign Workers in Israel: History and Theory. *International Migration Review* 32, 2: 303–25.

Bar-Tzuri, R. 1996. Foreign Workers in Israel: Conditions, Attitudes and Policy Implications. In *The New World of Work in an Era of Economic Change*, ed. R. Nathanson, 13–34. (Hebrew). Tel-Aviv: Friedrich Ebert Foundation.

Basch, L., N. Glick Schiller, and C. Szanton Blanc. 1994. *Nations Unbound: Transnational Projects, Postcolonial Predicaments, and Deterritorialized Nation-States*. New York: Gordon and Breach.

Bastian, J. P. 1993. The Metamorphosis of Latin American Protestant Groups: A Socio-historical Perspective. *Latin American Research Review* 28, 2: 33–61.

Baumann, G. 1987. *National Integration and Local Integrity.* Oxford: Clarendon Press.

———. 1996. *Contesting Culture: Discourses of Identity in Multi-Ethnic London.* Cambridge: Cambridge University Press.

———. 1998. Body Politic or Bodies of Culture? How Nation-State Practices Turn Citizens into Religious Minorities. *Cultural Dynamics* 10, 3: 263–80.

Ben-Ami, S. 2001. Introduction: Israel as a Multicultural Society. In *Israel: From Mobilized to Civil Society?* ed. Y. Peled and A. Ophir, 18–23. (Hebrew). Jerusalem: Van Leer Institutte and Hakibutz Hameuchad.

Ben-Rabi, D., and T. Hasin. 2004. *Young Children of Foreign Workers in Tel Aviv-Yafo: Standard of Living, Needs and Policy Directions.* Jerusalem: Brookdale Institute.

Ben-Rafael, E. 2007. Mizrahi and Russian Challenges to Israel's Dominant Culture: Divergences and Convergences. *Israel Studies* 12, 3: 68–91.

Ben-Rafael, E., and S. Sharot. 1991. *Ethnicity, Religion and Class in Israeli Society.* Cambridge: Cambridge University Press.

Ben-Yehuda, N. 1995. *The Mesada Myth: Collective Memory and Mythmaking in Israel.* Madison: University of Wisconsin Press.

Berman, Y. 2007. *Binding Migrant Workers to Corporations.* Tel Aviv: Hotline for Migrant Workers and Kav La'oved.

Bhabha, H. K. 1994. *The Location of Culture.* London: Routledge.

Bolognani, M. 2007. The Myth of Return: Dismissal, Survival or Revival? A Bradford Example of Transnationalism as a Political Instrument. *Journal of Ethnic and Migration Studies* 33, 1: 59–76.

Borjas, G. J. 1987. Self-Selection and the Earnings of Immigrants. *American Economic Review* 77: 531–53.

———. 1990. *Friends or Strangers: The Impact of Immigrants on the U.S. Economy.* New York: Basic Books.

Bourdieu, P. 1977. *Outline of a Theory of Practice.* Cambridge: Cambridge University Press.

———. 1984. *Distinction: A Social Critique of the Judgement of Taste.* Cambridge: Harvard University Press.

———. 2001. *Masculine Domination.* Cambridge: Polity.

Bowles, S. 1970. Migration as Investment: Empirical Tests of the Human Investment Approach to Geographical Mobility. *Review of Economics and Statistics* 52: 356–362.

Brubaker, R. 2001. The Return of Assimilation? Changing Perspectives on Immigration and Its Sequels in France, Germany, and the United States. *Ethnic and Racial Studies* 24, 1: 531–48.

Calavita, K. 1992. *Inside the State: The Bracero Program, Immigration and the INS.* New York: Routledge.

Campaña, E. O. 2002. *Ecuador en España: La realidad de la migración.* (Spanish). Madrid: The Author.

Carruthers, A. 2002. The Accumulation of National Belonging in Transnational Fields: Ways of Being at Home in Vietnam. *Identities: Global Studies in Culture and Power* 9: 423–44.

Castells, M. 1989. *The Informational City: Information Technology, Economic Restructuring and the Urban-Regional Process.* Oxford: Basil Blackwell.

——. 1996. *The Rise of the Network Society.* Oxford: Blackwell.

Castillo, P. R., et al. 2003. *Incidencia de la migración en la construcción de la identidad y proyecto de vida de los Jóvenes.* (Spanish). Cuenca: University of Cuenca.

Castles, S., and A. Davidson. 2000. *Citizenship and Migration: Globalization and the Politics of Belonging.* Basingstoke: Macmillan.

Castles, S., and M. Miller. 1998. *The Age of Migration: International Population Movements in the Modern World.* New York: Palgrave.

Central Bureau of Statistics. 2000. *Statistical Abstract of Israel.* Jerusalem: CBS.

——. 2002. *Statistical Abstract of Israel.* Jerusalem: CBS.

Chavez, L. R. 1992. *Shadowed Lives: Undocumented Immigrants in American Society.* Fort Worth: Harcourt Brace College Publishers.

——. 1994. The Power of Imagined Community: The Settlement of Undocumented Mexicans and Central Americans in the United States. *American Anthropologist* 96, 1: 52–73.

Chiswick, B. R. 1978. The Effect of Americanization on the Earnings of Foreign-Born Men. *Journal of Political Economy* 86: 897–921.

Cohen, E. 1995. Israel as a Post-Zionist Society. In *The Shaping of Israeli Identity,* ed. R. Wistrich and D. Ohana, 203–14. London: Frank Cass.

Cohen, R., and G. Gold. 1996. Israelis in Toronto: The Myth of Return and the Development of a Distinct Ethnic Community. *Jewish Journal of Sociology* 38, 1: 17–26.

Coleman, S. 1991. "Faith Which Conquers the World": Swedish Fundamentalism and the Globalisation of Culture. *Ethnos* 56, 1: 6–18.

Cornelius, W. A., P. L. Martin, and J. F. Hollifield. 1994. *Controlling Immigration: A Global Perspective.* Stanford, Calif.: Stanford University Press.

Corten, A., and R. Marshall-Fratani. 2001. *Between Babel and Pentecost: Transnational Pentecostalism in Africa and Latin America.* London: Hurst.

Coutin, S. B. 1993. *The Culture of Protest: Religious Activism and the U.S. Sanctuary Movement.* Boulder, Colo.: Westview Press.

——. 2000. *Legalizing Moves: Salvadoran Immigrants' Struggle for U.S. Residency.* Ann Arbor: University of Michigan Press.

Davis, M. 1990. *Mexican Voices, American Dreams.* New York: Henry Holt.

De Genova, N. P. 2002. Migrant "Illegality" and Deportability in Everyday Life. *Annual Review of Anthropology* 31: 419–47.

DellaPergola, S. 1998. The Global Context of Migration from the Former Soviet Union to Israel. In *Immigration to Israel: Sociological Perspectives,* ed. E. Leshem and J. Shuval, 51–92. New Brunswick, N.J.: Transaction.

——. 2001. *Demography in Israel/Palestine: Trends, Prospects, Policy Implications.* Paper presented to the IUSSP XXIV General Population Conference, Salvador de Bahia, Brazil.

Dorr, S., and T. Faist. 1997. Institutional Conditions for the Integration of Immigrants in Welfare States: A Comparison of the Literature on Germany, France, Great Britain, and the Netherlands. *European Journal of Political Research* 31: 401–26.

Drori, I., and G. Kunda. 1999. *The Work Experience of Foreign Workers in Israel: The Case of*

Filipino Caregivers, Thais in Agriculture and Rumanians in Construction. Discussion Paper No. 100, Golda Meir Institute.

Dustmann, C. 1993. Earnings Adjustment of Temporary Migrants. *Journal of Population Economics* 6, 2: 153–68.

Ecuadorian National Institute of Statistics and Census. 2003. *Anuario Estadistico de Migracion Internacional.* (Spanish). Quito, Ecuador: INEC.

Eisenstadt, S. N. 1967. *Israeli Society.* New York: Basic Books.

Elazar, D. 1989. *The Other Jew.* New York: Basic Books.

Elias, N. 1994 [1939]. *The Civilizing Process.* Oxford: Blackwell.

Ellman, M., and S. Laacher. 2003. *Migrant Workers in Israel: A Contemporary Form of Slavery.* Copenhagen and Paris: the International Federation for Human Rights and the Euro-Mediterranean Human Rights Network.

Escobar-Latapi, A., et al. 1987. Migration, Labor Markets, and the International Economy: Jalisco, Mexico and the United States. In *Migrants, Workers, and the Social Order,* ed. J. Eades, 42–64. London: Tavistock.

Faist, T. 2000. Transnationalism in International Migration: Implications for the Study of Citizenship and Culture. *Ethnic and Racial Studies* 23, 2: 189–222.

——. 2004. Dual Citizenship as Overlapping Membership. In *International Migration in the New Millennium: Global Movement and Settlement,* ed. Danièle Joly, 210–32. Aldershot: Ashgate.

Falah, G., and D. Newman. 1995. The Spatial Manifestation of Threat: Israelis and Palestinians Seek a "Good" Boundary. *Political Geography* 14: 689–706.

Favell, A. 2000. Integration Policy and Integration Research in Europe: A Review and Critique. In *Citizenship: Comparisons and Perspectives,* ed. A. Aleinikoff and D. Klusmeyer, 249–99. Washington, D.C.: Brookings Institute.

Filc, D., and N. Davidovich. 2005. Health Care as a National Right? The Development of Health Care Services for Migrant Workers in Israel. *Social Theory and Health* 3: 1–15.

Foucault, M. 1991. Governmentality. In *The Foucault Effect: Studies in Governmentality,* ed. G. Burchell, C. Gordon, and P. Miller, 87–104. London: Harvester Wheatsheaf.

Freeman, G. 1986. Migration and Political Economy of the Welfare State. *Annals of the American Academy of Political and Social Sciences* 485: 51–63.

——. 1992. The Consequence of Immigration Policies for Immigrant Status: A British and French Comparison. In *Ethnic and Racial Minorities in Advanced Industrial Democracies,* ed. A. Messina et al., 17–32. New York: Greenwood Press.

Fuglerud, O. 2004. Constructing Exclusion: The Micro-sociology of an Immigration Department. *Social Anthropology* 12, 1: 25–40.

Geertz, C. 1976. Art as a Cultural System. *Modern Language Notes* 91, 6: 1473–99.

Ghanem, A. 1998. State and Minority in Israel: The Case of Ethnic State and the Predicament of Its Minority. *Ethnic and Racial Studies* 21, 3: 428–47.

Gibney, M., and R. Hansen. 2003. Deportation and the Liberal State: The Involuntary Return of Asylum Seekers and Unlawful Migrants in Canada, the UK, and Germany. *New Issues in Refugee Research.* Working Paper Series 77. Geneva: UNHCR.

Gifford, P. 2001. The Complex Governance of Some Elements of African Pentecostal Theology. In *Between Babel and Pentecost: Transnational Pentecostalism in Africa and Latin America,* ed. A. Corten and R. Marshall-Fratani, 62–79. London: Hurst.

Gilroy, P. 1987. *There Ain't No Black in the Union Jack: The Cultural Politics of Race and Nation.* Chicago: Chicago University Press.

Glick Schiller, N., L. Basch, and C. Blanc-Szanton. 1992. *Towards a Transnational Perspective on Migration: Race, Class, Ethnicity, and Nationalism Reconsidered.* New York: New York Academy of Sciences.

Goffman, E. 1963. *Stigma: Notes on the Management of Spoiled Identity.* New Jersey: Penguin Books.

Goldberg, D. T. 1994. Multicultural Conditions. In *Multiculturalism: A Critical Reader,* ed. D. T. Goldberg, 1–44. Oxford: Basil Blackwell.

Gramsci, A. 1971. *Selections from the Prison Notebooks.* New York: International Publishers.

Granovetter, M. 1973. The Strength of Weak Ties. *American Journal of Sociology* 78, 6: 1360–80.

Grasmuck, S., and P. R. Passer. 1991. *Between Two Islands: Dominican International Migration.* Berkley and Los Angeles: University of California Press.

Grinberg, L. 1991. *Split Corporatism in Israel.* Albany: State University of New York Press.

———. 1993. *The Histadrut above All.* (Hebrew). Jerusalem: Navo.

Guarnizo, L. E., and L. M. Diaz. 1999. Transnational Migration: A View from Colombia. *Ethnic and Racial Studies* 22, 2: 397–421.

Gupta, A., and J. Ferguson. 1992. Beyond "Culture": Space, Identity, and Politics of Difference. *Cultural Anthropology* 7: 6–23.

Gurak, D. T., and F. Caces. 1992. Migration Networks and the Shaping of Migration System. In *International Migration Systems: A Global Approach,* ed. M. Krintz, L. L. Lim, and H. Zlotnik, 150–76. Oxford: Clarendon Press.

Gustafson, P. 2005. International Migration and National Belonging in the Swedish Debate on Dual Citizenship. *Acta Sociologica* 48, 1: 5–19.

Hagan, J. M. 1994. *Deciding to be Legal: A Maya Community in Houston.* Philadelphia: Temple University Press.

Hage, G. 1998. *White Nation: Fantasies of White Supremacy in a Multicultural Society.* Annandale and West Wickham: Pluto Press/Comerford and Miller.

Hall, S. 1991. The Local and the Global: Globalization and Ethnicity. In *Culture, Globalization and the World System,* ed. A. King, 19–39. London: Macmillan.

Hannerz, U. 1996. *Transnational Connections: Culture, People, Places.* London: Routledge.

Harding, F. S. 2000. *The Book of Jerry Falwell: Fundamentalist Language and Politics.* Princeton, N.J.: Princeton University Press.

Hargis, D. M. 1998. *Basics of Messianic Judaism.* Messianic Bureau International. http://www.messianic.com/articles/basics.htm.

Harker, R., C. Mahar, and C. Wilkes. 1990. *An Introduction to the Work of Pierre Bourdieu.* London: Macmillan Press.

Harris, N. 1996. *The New Untouchables: Immigration and the New World Worker.* London: Penguin Books.

Harvey, D. 1990. *The Condition of Postmodernity: An Enquiry into the Origin of Cultural Change.* Cambridge: Blackwell.

Hodson, R., and R. L. Kaufman. 1982. Economic Dualism: A Critical View. *American Sociological Review* 47: 727–40.

Hondagneu-Sotelo, P. 1994. *Gendered Transitions: Mexican Experiences of Immigration.* Berkeley and Los Angeles: University of California Press.

Hotline for Migrant Workers. 2003. *For You Were Strangers: Modern Slavery and Trafficking in Human Beings in Israel.* http://www.hotline.org.il/english/pdf/For_you_were_strangers_2nd_edition_Eng.pdf.

Hotline for Migrant Workers and Kav La'Oved. 2003. *Immigration Administration or Expulsion Unit?* http://www.hotline.org.il/english/pdf/Hotline _and_Kav_Laoved_paper_on _Immigration_Police_May_2003_Eng.pdf.

Hotline for Migrant Workers and Kav La'Oved. 2004. *Immigration Police as Means for Employers to Exploit Their Workers.* (Hebrew). http://www.hotline.org.il/hebrew/pdf/Kav_Laoved _%2526_Hotline_report_A_tool_in_the_hands_of_employers_053104.pdf.

Hugo, G. J. 1981. Village Community Ties, Village Norms, and Ethnic and Social Networks: A Review of Evidence from the Third World. In *Migration Decision Making: Multidisciplinary Approach to Microlevel Studies in Developed and Developing Countries,* ed. F. D. Gordon and R. W. Gardner, 186–225. New York: Pergamon Press.

——. 1994. *Migration and the Family.* Occasional Papers Series no. 12. Vienna: United Nations.

Jacobson, D. 1996. *Rights across Borders: Immigration and the Decline of Citizenship.* Baltimore, Md.: Johns Hopkins University Press.

Jamal, A. 2007. Nationalizing States and the Constitution of "Hollow Citizenship": Israel and its Palestinians Citizens. *Ethnopolitics* 6, 4: 471–93.

Jokisch, B., and J. Pribilsky. 2002. The Panic to Leave: Economic Crisis and the "New Emigration" from Ecuador. *International Migration* 40, 4: 75–102.

Jones-Correa, M. 1998. *Between Two Nations: The Political Predicaments of Latinos in New York City.* Ithaca, N.Y.: Cornell University Press.

Joppke, C. 1998. *Challenge to the Nation State: Immigration in Western Europe and the United States.* Oxford: Oxford University Press.

——. 1999. *Immigration and the Nation-State: The United States, Germany, and Great Britain.* New York: Oxford University Press.

Kalir, B. 2005. The Development of a Migratory Disposition: Explaining a "New Emigration." *International Migration* 43, 4: 167–96.

——. 2006. The Field of Work and the Work of the Field: Conceptualising an Anthropological Research Engagement. *Social Anthropology* 14, 2: 235–46.

——. 2009. Finding Jesus in the Holy Land and Taking Him to China: Chinese Temporary Workers in Israel Converting to Evangelical Christianity. *Sociology of Religion* 70, 2: 130–156.

Kaplan, S., and H. Salamon. 2004. Ethiopian Jews in Israel: A Part of the People or Apart from the People? In *Jews in Israel: Contemporary Social and Cultural Patterns,* ed. U. Rebhun and C. I. Waxman, 118–48. Hanover: Brandeis University Press.

Kastoryano, R. 2002. *Negotiating Identities: States and Immigrants in France and Germany.* Princeton, N.J.: Princeton University Press.

Kav La'Oved. May 1998. Newsletter.

——. March 1999. Newsletter.

——. May 2000. Newsletter.

——. July 2000. Newsletter.

——. October 2000. Newsletter.

Kemp, A. 2004. Labor Migration and Radicalization: Labor Market Mechanisms and Labor Migration Control Policies in Israel. *Social Identities* 10, 2: 267–92.

Kemp, A., and R. Raijman. 2003. Christian Zionists in the Holy Land: Evangelical Churches, Labor Migrants, and the Jewish State. *Identities: Global Studies in Culture and Power* 10: 295–318.

Kemp, A., R. Raijman, J. Resnik, and S. Schammah-Gesser. 2000. Contesting the Limits of Political Participation: Latinos and Black African Migrant Workers in Israel. *Ethnic and Racial Studies* 23, 1: 94–119.

Kimmerling, B. 1983. Some Implications of Military Service and the Reserves System in Israel. *European Journal of Sociology* 5, 2: 252–76.

———. 1998. The New Israelis: Multiple Cultures with No Multiculturalism. *Alpayim* 16: 264–308. (Hebrew).

Koopmans, R., and P. Statham. 2000. *Challenging Immigration and Ethnic Relations Politics: Comparative European Perspectives*. Oxford: Oxford University Press.

Koslowski, R. 2000. *Migrants and Citizens: Demographic Change in the European State System*. Ithaca, N.Y.: Cornell University Press.

Kwong, P. 1997. *Forbidden Workers: Illegal Chinese Immigrants and American Labor*. New York: New Press.

Kyle, D. 2000. *Transnational Peasants: Migrations, Networks, and Ethnicity in Andean Ecuador*. Baltimore, Md.: Johns Hopkins University Press.

Kyle, D., and Z. Liang. 2001. *Migration Merchants: Human Smuggling from Ecuador and China*. Working Paper no. 43. San Diego: University of California.

Kymlicka, W. 1995. *Multicultural Citizenship: A Liberal Theory of Minority Rights*. Oxford: Clarendon Press.

———. 2003. Immigration, Citizenship, Multiculturalism: Exploring the Links. *Political Quarterly* 74, s1: 195–208.

Larrea, C. 1998. Structural Adjustment, Income Distribution, and Employment in Ecuador. In *Poverty, Economic Reform, and Income Distribution in Latin America*, ed. A. Berry, 179–204. Boulder, Colo.: Lynne Rienner.

Layton-Henry, Z., 1990. *The Political Rights of Migrant Workers in Western Europe*. London: Sage.

Levitt, P. 2004. Redefining the Boundaries of Belonging: The Institutional Character of Transnational Religious Life. *Sociology of Religion* 65: 1–18.

Levy, Y. 2003. Social Convertibility and Militarism: Evaluations of the Development of Military-Society Relations in Israel in the Early 2000s. *Journal of Political and Military Sociology* 31, 1: 71–96.

Lewin-Epstein, N., and M. Semyonov. 1986. Ethnic Group Mobility in the Israeli Labour Market. *American Sociological Review* 51: 342–51.

Lincango, L. 2001. *El colectivo ecuatoriano en Madrid*. Conference paper from Ciclos de Actualidad Sobre Inmigración, Escuela de Mediadores Sociales para la Inmigración, Madrid, 30 May. (Spanish).

Lissak, M., and E. Leshem. 1995. The Russian Intelligentsia in Israel between Ghettoization and Integration. *Israel Affairs* 2: 20–36.

Lovera, M. F. 1997. *Latinoamericanos en Israel*. (Spanish). Tel Aviv: Aurora.

Lustick, I. S. 2004. *Recent Trends in Emigration from Israel: The Impact of Palestinian Violence.* Paper presented at the annual meeting of the Association for Israel Studies, Jerusalem, Israel, June 14–16.

Mahler, S. 1995. *American Dreaming: Immigrant Life of the Margin.* Princeton, N.J.: Princeton University Press.

Marshall, T. H. 1964. *Class, Citizenship and Social Development.* Garden City, N.Y.: Doubleday.

Martin, D. 1990. *Tongues of Fire: The Explosion of Protestantism in Latin America.* Cambridge: Basil Blackwell.

———. 1994. Evangelical and Charismatic Christianity in Latin America. In *Charismatic Christianity as a Global Culture,* ed. K. Poewe, 73–86. Columbia: University of South Carolina Press.

Marx, A. W. 1996. Contested Citizenship: The Dynamics of Racial Identity and Social Movement. In *Citizenship, Identity and Social History,* ed. C. Tilly, *International Review of Social History,* supplement 3: 159–84. Cambridge: Cambridge University Press.

Massey, D. 1987. Do Undocumented Immigrants Earn Lower Wages than Legal Migrants? Evidence from Mexico. *International Migration Review* 21, 2: 236–74.

———. 1990a. Social Structure, Household Strategies, and the Cumulative Causation of Migration. *Population Index* 56: 3–26.

———. 1990b. The Social and Economic Origins of Migration. *Annals of the American Academy of Political and Social Science,* 510: 60–72.

Massey, D., and K. E. Espinosa. 1997. What's Driving Mexico-U.S. Migration? A Theoretical, Empirical, and Policy Analysis. *American Journal of Sociology* 102, 4: 939–99.

Massey, D., and F. Garcia-España. 1987. The Social Process of International Migration. *Science* 237: 733–38.

Massey, D., L. Goldring, and J. Durand. 1994. Continuities in Transnational Migration: An Analysis of Nineteen Mexican Communities. *American Journal of Sociology* 99, 6: 1492–1533.

Massey, D., J. Arango, G. Hugo, A. Kouaouci, A. Pellegrino, and J. E. Taylor. 1993. Theories of International Migration: A Review and Appraisal. *Population and Development Review* 19, 3: 431–66.

———. 1994. An Evaluation of International Migration Theory: The North American Case. *Population and Development Review* 20: 699–752.

———. 1998. *Worlds in Motion: Understanding International Migration at the End of the Millennium.* Oxford: Clarendon Press.

Massey, D., et al. 1987. *Return to Aztlán: The Social Process of International Migration from Western Mexico.* Berkeley and Los Angeles: University of California Press.

Mauss, M. 1990 [1954]. *The Gift.* London: Routledge.

McAdam, D., T. Sidney, and C. Tilly. 2001. *Dynamics of Contention.* Cambridge: Cambridge University Press.

Mennell, S., A. Murcott, and A. H. van Otterloo. 1992. *The Sociology of Food: Eating, Diet and Culture.* London: Sage Publications.

Miles, A., 2004. *From Cuenca to Queens: An Anthropological Story of Transnational Migration.* Austin: University of Texas Press.

Miller, D. 1995. *On Nationality.* Oxford: Oxford University Press.

Miller, M. J. 1989. Political Participation and Representation of Noncitizens. In *Immigration and the Politics of Citizenship in Europe and North America,* ed. R. Brubaker. 129–44. London: University Press of America.

Mincer, J. 1978. Family Migration Decisions. *Journal of Political Economy* 86, 5: 749–73.

Mines, R. 1984. Network Migration and Mexican Rural Development: A Case Study. In *Patterns of Undocumented Migration: Mexico and the United States,* ed. R. C. Jones, 136–58. Totowa, N.J.: Rowman and Allanheld.

Ministry of Education (Israel). 2000. *The Encompassment of the Compulsory Education Law on Children of Undocumented Migrants.* (Hebrew). Chief Executive's Circular 10 (a).

Ministry of Labor (Israel). 2000. *Foreign Workers Deported from Israel 1995–1999.* (Hebrew). Jerusalem: Manpower Planning Authority.

———. 2001. *Foreign Workers without Work Permits in Israel: 1999.* Discussion Paper no. 5.01. (Hebrew). Jerusalem: Manpower Planning Authority.

———. 2002a. *Foreign Workers without Work Permits Deported from Israel in 2001.* (Hebrew). Jerusalem: Manpower Planning Authority.

———. 2002b. *Female Foreign Workers Who Entered Israel with a Work Permit during the Last Years.* (Hebrew). Jerusalem: Manpower Planning Authority.

Nathanson, R., and R. Bar-Tzuri. 1999. A Survey of Public Opinion towards Workers from Foreign Countries. In *The New Workers: Wage Earners from Foreign Countries in Israel,* ed. R. Nathanson and L. Achdut, 90–118. (Hebrew). Tel-Aviv: Hakibbutz Hameuchad.

Newman, D. 1998. Population as Security: The Arab-Israeli Struggle for Demographic Hegemony. In *Redefining Security: Population Movements and National Security,* ed. N. Poku and D. T. Graham, 163–86. London: Praeger Publishers.

Noy, Ch., and E. Cohen. 2004. *Israeli Backpackers and Their Society: A View from Afar,* New York: State University of New York Press.

Ojanuga, D. 1993. The Ethiopian Jewish Experience as Blacks in Israel. *Journal of Black Studies* 24, 2: 147–58.

Ong, A., 1995. Making the Biopolitical Subject: Khmer Immigrants, Refugee Medicine, and Cultural Citizenship in California. *Social Science and Medicine* 40: 1243–57.

———. 1996. Cultural Citizenship as Subject-Making: Immigrants Negotiate Racial and Cultural Boundaries in the United States. *Current Anthropology* 37, 5: 737–62.

———. 1999. *Flexible Citizenship: The Cultural Logics of Transnationality.* London: Duke University Press.

Peled, Y. 1992. Ethnic Democracy and the Legal Construction of Citizenship: Arab Citizens of the Jewish State. *American Political Science Review* 86, 2: 432–48.

Pilovsky, L. 1999. The Role of Manpower Agencies in the Treatment of Foreign Workers in Israel, and Their Connections with Government Institutions. In *The New Workers: Wage Earners from Foreign Countries in Israel,* ed. R. Nathanson and L. Achdut, 41–89. (Hebrew). Tel-Aviv: Hakibbutz Hameuchad.

Piore, M. J. 1979. *Birds of Passage: Migrant Labor in Industrial Societies.* Cambridge: Cambridge University Press.

Poewe, K. 1994. *Charismatic Christianity as a Global Culture.* Columbia: University of South Carolina Press.

Portes, A. 1995 *The Economic Sociology of Immigration: Essays on Networks, Ethnicity and Entrepreneurship*, New York: Russell Sage Foundation.

———. 1999. Conclusion: Towards a New World: The Origins and Effects of Transnational Activities. *Ethnic and Racial Studies* 22, 2: 463–77.

Portes, A., and R. L. Basch. 1985. *Latin Journey: Cuban and Mexican Immigrants in the United States*. Berkeley and Los Angeles: University of California Press.

Portes, A., L. E. Guarnizo, and P. Landolt. 1999. The Study of Transnationalism: Pitfalls and Promise of an Emergent Research Field. *Ethnic and Racial Studies* 22, 2: 217–41.

Portes, A., and R. G. Rumbaut. 1996. *Immigrant America: A Portrait*. Berkeley and Los Angeles: University of California Press.

Portes, A., and J. Walton. 1981. *Labour, Class, and the International System*. New York: Academic Press.

Portes, A., and M. Zhou. 1993. The New Second Generation: Segmented Assimilation and Its Variants. *Annals of the American Academy of Political and Social Science* 530: 74–96.

Rabinowitz, D. 1997. *Overlooking Nazareth: The Ethnography of Exclusion in Galilee*. Cambridge: Cambridge University Press.

———. 1998. National Identity on the Frontier: Palestinians in the Israeli Education System. In *Border Identities: Nation and State at International Frontiers*, ed. H. Donnan and T. Wilson, 142–61, Cambridge: Cambridge University Press.

Reichert, J. S. 1982. A Town Divided: Economic Stratification and Social Relations in a Mexican Migrant Community. *Social Problems* 29, 4: 411–23.

Rodriguez Garcia, D. 2006. Mixed Marriages and Transnational Families in the Intercultural Context: A Case Study of African-Spanish Couples in Catalonia. *Journal of Ethnic and Migration Studies* 32, 3: 403–33.

Rosaldo, R. 1984. Cultural Citizenship and Educational Democracy. *Cultural Anthropology* 9, 3: 402–11.

Rosaldo, R., and W. V. Flores. 1993. *Identity, Conflict, and Evolving Latino Communities: Cultural Citizenship in San Jose, California*. Research Report G5–90–5. Washington, D.C.: National Institute for Dispute Resolution.

Rosenhek, Z. 1999. The Politics of Claims-Making by Labour Migrants in Israel. *Journal of Ethnic and Migration Studies* 25, 4: 575–95.

———. 2000. Migration Regimes, Intra-state Conflicts, and the Politics of Exclusion and Inclusion: Migrant Workers in the Israeli Welfare State. *Social Problems* 47, 1: 49–67.

Rouhana, N. 1997. *Palestinian Citizens in an Ethnic Jewish State: Identities in Conflict*. New Haven, Conn.: Yale University Press.

Sabar, G. 2004. African Christianity in the Jewish State: Adaptation, Accommodation and Legitimization of Migrant Workers' Churches, 1990–2003. *Journal of Religion in Africa* 34, 4: 407–37.

Sassen, S. 1988. *The Mobility of Labour and Capital: A Study in International Investment and Labour Flow*. Cambridge: Cambridge University Press.

———. 1991. *The Global City: New York, London, Tokyo*. Princeton: Princeton University Press.

———. 1996. *Losing Control? Sovereignty in an Age of Globalization*. New York: Columbia University Press.

——. 1999. *Guests and Aliens,* New York: New York Press.

——. 2002. The Responsibility of Citizenship: Emergent Subjects and Spaces for Politics. *Berkeley Journal of Sociology* 46: 4–25.

Sayad, A. 1999. *La Double Absence: Des illusions de l'emigré aux souffrances de l'immigré.* (French). Paris: Seuil Editions.

Schnell, I. 1999. *Guidelines for Policy Making towards Foreign Workers in Israel.* (Hebrew). Jerusalem: The Israeli Centre for Political and Social Research.

——. 2001. *Foreign Workers in Southern Tel Aviv–Yafo.* (Hebrew). Jerusalem: Floersheimer Institute for Policy Studies.

Schuck, P. 1987. The Status and Rights of Undocumented Aliens in the United States. *International Migration* 25: 125–38.

——. 1998. *Citizens, Strangers, and In-Betweens: Essays on Immigration and Citizenship.* Boulder, Colo.: Westview Press.

Schuck, P., and R. Smith. 1985. *Citizenship without Consent: Illegal Aliens in the American Polity.* New Haven, Conn.: Yale University Press.

Semyonov, M., and N. Lewin-Epstein. 1987. *Hewers of Wood and Drawers of Water: Non-citizen Arabs in the Israeli Labour Market.* New York: ILR Press.

Semyonov, M., R. Raijman, and A. Yom-Tov. 2002. Labour Market Competition, Perceived Threat, and Endorsement of Economic Discrimination against Foreign Workers in Israel. *Social Problems* 49, 3: 416–31.

Shafir, G. 1998. *The Citizenship Debates: A Reader,* Minneapolis: University of Minnesota Press.

Shenhav, Y., Hever, C., and P. Mutzafi. 2002. *Mizrahim in Israel: Renewed Consideration.* (Hebrew). Jerusalem: Van Leer Institute.

Shohat, E. 1992. Notes on the Post Colonial. *Social Text* 31/32: 99–113.

Shuval, J., and E. Leshem. 1998. The Sociology of Migration in Israel: A Critical View. In *Immigration to Israel: Sociological Perspectives,* ed. E. Leshem and J. Shuval, 30–50. Studies of Israeli Society, vol. 8. New Brunswick, N.J.: Transaction Publishers.

Siegel, D. 1996. *The Great Immigration: An Anthropological Study of Russian Jews in Israel.* Amsterdam: Free University Press.

Sjaastad, L. A. 1962. The Costs and Returns of Human Migration. *Journal of Political Economy* 70: 80–93.

Smith, M. P., and L. E. Guarnizo. 1998. *Transnationalism from Below.* New Brunswick, N.J.: Transaction Publishers.

Smooha, S. 1978 *Israel: Pluralism and Conflict.* London: Routledge and Kegan Paul.

——. 1990. Minority Status in an Ethnic Democracy: The Status of the Arab Minority in Israel. *Ethnic and Racial Studies* 13, 3: 389–413.

——. 1994. Outline of the Discussion of the Impact of the Mass Soviet Immigration on Israeli society. *Newsletter of the Israel Sociological Association* 13 (March): 6–7. (Hebrew).

——. 2005. Jewish-Arab Relations Index. *Duet* 5: 4–5. (Hebrew).

Soffer, A. 1988. *The Demographic and Geographic Situation in the Land of Israel: Is it the End of the Zionist Vision?* Haifa: University Press.

——. 1999. *Rivers of Fire: The Conflict of Water in the Middle East.* Lanham Md.: Rowman and Littlefield.

Soysal, Y. N. 1994. *Limits of Citizenship: Migrants and Postnational Membership in Europe.* Chicago: Chicago University Press.

———. 1996. Changing Citizenship in Europe: Remarks on Postnational Membership in Europe and the National State. In *Citizenship, Nationality and Migration in Europe,* ed. D. Cesarani and M. Fulbrook, 17–29. London: Routledge.

———. 1997. Changing Parameters of Citizenship and Claims-Making: Organized Islam in European Public Spheres. *Theory and Society* 26, 4, 509–27.

Spivak, G. C. 1996. Diasporas Old and New: Women in the Transnational World. *Textual Practice* 10, 2: 245–69.

Stark, O. 1984. Rural-to-Urban Migration in LDCs: A Relative Deprivation Approach. *Migration Review* 32: 303–25.

———. 1991. *The Migration of Labour.* Cambridge: Basil Blackwell.

Stark, O., and D. E. Bloom. 1985. The New Economics of Labour Migration. *American Economic Review* 75, 2: 173–78.

Stark, O., and J. E. Taylor. 1989. Relative Deprivation and International Migration. *Demography* 26, 1: 1–14.

———. 1991. Migration Incentives, Migration Types: The Role of Relative Deprivation. *Economic Journal* 101, 408: 1163–78.

State Comptroller. 1990. *Annual Report* no. 40. Jerusalem. (Hebrew).

———. 1996. *Annual Report* no. 46. Jerusalem. (Hebrew).

———. 1997. *Annual Report* no. 47. Jerusalem. (Hebrew).

———. 2003. *Annual Report* no. 53. Jerusalem. (Hebrew).

Stolcke, V. 1995. Talking Culture: New Boundaries, New Rhetorics of Exclusion in Europe. *Current Anthropology* 36, 1: 1–24.

Stoll, D. 1990. *Is Latin America Turning Protestant? The Politics of Evangelical Growth.* Berkeley and Los Angeles: University of California Press.

Taylor, C. 1994. The Politics of Recognition. In ed. *Multiculturalism: Examining the Politics of Recognition,* ed. A. Gutmann and C. Taylor, 25–74. Princeton: Princeton University Press.

Teitelbaum, M. S., and M. Weiner. 1995. *Threatened Borders: World Migration and United States Policy.* New York: Norton.

Tilly, C., ed. 1996. *Citizenship, Identity and Social History. International Review of Social History,* supplement 3. Cambridge: Cambridge University Press.

Todaro, M. P. 1969. A Model of Labour Migration and Urban Unemployment in Less Developed Countries. *American Economic Review* 59, 1: 138–48.

———. 1976. *Internal Migration in Developing Countries: A Review of Theory, Evidence, Methodology and Research Priorities.* Geneva: International Labor Organization.

Todd, E. 1994. *Le destin des immigrés: assimilation et ségrégation dans les démocraties occidentales.* (French). Paris: Seuil.

Turner, T. 1993. Anthropology and Multiculturalism: What Is Anthropology That Multiculturalists Should Be Mindful of It? *Cultural Anthropology* 8, 4: 411–29.

Turner, V. 1969. *The Ritual Process.* London: Routledge and Kegan Paul.

Van der Leun, J. 2003. *Looking for Loopholes: Processes of Incorporation of Illegal Immigrants in the Netherlands.* Amsterdam: Amsterdam University Press.

Vertovec, S. 1999. Conceiving and Researching Transnationalism. *Ethnic and Racial Studies* 22, 2: 447–62.

Wacquant, L. J. D. 1996. Forward. In P. Bourdieu, *The State Nobility: Elite Schools in the Field of Power*, ix–xxii. Cambridge: Polity.

Wallerstein, I. 2003. Citizens All? Citizens Some! The Making of the Citizen. *Comparative Studies in Society and History* 15, 4: 650–79.

Wamsley, E. 2001. Transformando los pueblos: la migración internacional y el impacto social el nivel comunitario. *Ecuador Debate* 54: 155–74. (Spanish).

Wiest, R. E. 1984. External Dependency and the Perpetuation of Temporary Migration to the United States. In *Patterns of Undocumented Migration: Mexico and the United States*, ed. R. C. Jones, 110–35. Totowa, N.J.: Rowman and Allanheld.

Wieviorka, M. 2001. *La Différence*. (French). Paris: Éditions Balland.

Willen, S. 2007. Towards a Critical Phenomenology of "Illegality": State Power, Criminalization, and Abjectivity among Undocumented Migrant Workers in Tel Aviv, Israel. *International Migration* 45, 3: 8–36.

Wolf, D. L. 1990. Daughters, Decisions, and Domination: An Empirical and Conceptual Critique of Household Strategies. *Development and Change* 21: 43–74.

Yanay, U., and A. Borowosky. 1998. Foreign Workers in Israel: Rights and Access to Welfare Services. *Social Security* 53: 59–78. (Hebrew).

Yiftachel, O. 1992. *Planning a Mixed Region in Israel: The Political Geography of Arab-Jewish Relations in the Galilee*. Avebury: Aldershot.

——. 1997. Israeli Society and Jewish-Palestine Reconciliation: Ethnocracy and Its Territorial Contradictions. *Middle East Journal* 51, 4: 505–19.

Zaitch, D. 2001. Traquetos: Colombians Involved in the Cocaine Business in the Netherlands. Ph.D. thesis, University of Amsterdam.

Zolberg, A. R. 1990. Reforming the Back Door: The Immigration Reform and Control Act of 1986 in Historical Perspective. In *Immigration Reconsidered: History, Sociology and Politics*, ed. V. Yans-McLaughlin, 315–39. Oxford: Oxford University Press.

INDEX

Italicized page numbers indicate illustrations.

Barak Kalir is Assistant Professor of Anthropology at the University of Amsterdam and coordinator of the research program Illegal but Licit: Transnational Flows and Permissive Polities in Asia.